HAUNTING CRIES

Stories of Child Abuse from Industrial Schools

HAUNTING CRIES

Stories of Child Abuse from Industrial Schools

KAREN COLEMAN ∾

Gill & Macmillan

Gill & Macmillan Ltd
Hume Avenue, Park West, Dublin 12
with associated companies throughout the world
www.gillmacmillan.ie

© Karen Coleman 2010
978 07171 4792 2

Typography design by Make Communication
Print origination by O'K Graphic Design, Dublin
Printed by Scandbook, Sweden

This book is typeset in 12/14/5 pt Minion.

The paper used in this book comes from the wood pulp
of managed forests. For every tree felled, at least one
tree is planted, thereby renewing natural resources.

A CIP catalogue record for this book is available from the
British Library.

5 4 3 2 1

This book is dedicated to all those children who were abused in Irish religious institutions.

CONTENTS

ACKNOWLEDGMENTS

This book would not have been possible without the consent and courage of the people featured in it to open up to me about their pasts and to endure hours of questioning from me. At times that required painful recall of their childhood experiences in the religious institutions in which they were incarcerated. I am truly grateful to them for putting up with my questions and allowing me to feature their stories in *Haunting Cries*.

I also want to thank some of the people who continue to campaign for survivors of institutional abuse, who gave me their time to help me with research information for the book. These include John Kelly and Patrick Walsh of Irish SOCA (Survivors of Child Abuse), Michael O'Brien of Right to Peace, Christine Buckley of the Aislinn Education and Support Centre and Paddy Doyle, author of *The God Squad*. Film-maker Stephen O'Riordan also gave me invaluable help with information about the Magdalene laundries.

There are other people I met during my research for this book whose stories of institutional abuse have not been included here due to space and time constraints. These include Mrs Kathleen Byrne and Maria and James Byrne. I am grateful to them for the time they gave me in meeting to prepare my research for *Haunting Cries*.

As usual a book like this requires a team of people to help put it together. I am very grateful to Tess Tattersall who edited the book, Fergal Tobin of Gill & Macmillan and his editorial team, my literary agent Jonathan Williams and to researcher Ultan Monahan who diligently sourced pictures for the book.

Writing a book like this requires support and encouragement from family and friends all along the way. I am truly grateful to all of those people who were there for me during that time and especially to Professor Frank Sullivan whose generosity and support were invaluable.

AUTHOR'S NOTE

Many pseudonyms have been used in this book to disguise the names of those accused of being abusers by the people who feature here. Pseudonyms were also used in the Ryan Report and some of them have been referred to in this book.

Chapter 1 ∾

EXPOSING THE ABUSE: THE RYAN REPORT, MAY 2009

There is a lane in the heart of Connemara, Co. Galway that leads from the village of Letterfrack up into a wooded area, where a small graveyard is tucked behind the trees and hidden from the main road. A narrow gateway opens onto a patch of ground where small headstones in the shape of black marble hearts nestle in the grass. Each headstone carries the name of a boy and the year he died. Seventy-nine boys are buried there in total; all were inmates of the notorious Letterfrack Industrial School that was run by the Christian Brothers. The first boy buried there died in 1891; the last in 1956. Their ages range from four to 16.

This graveyard is not a place of rest. It is instead a burial ground of abuse where the ghosts of the boys interred there seem to hover in silence as the visitor sheds tears for their stifled cries for help. It is a place laden with such profound sadness it provokes a speechless mix of disbelief and guilt; disbelief that religious orders could have been capable of such gross inhumanity against children in their care, and guilt at being part of a State that participated in that abuse through ignorance, poverty and negligence.

Letterfrack Industrial School graveyard is a spine-chilling illustration of religious child institutional abuse and an example of how Ireland allowed vulnerable children to be destroyed by tormentors masquerading as guardians. A walk along the lines of black hearts reveals a journey of suffering. Young lives struck down year after year. In 1918 alone 10 boys died in Letterfrack Industrial School; seven died within 20 days of each other in that year.

Those seven boys included Michael Bergin, who died on 13 November 1918. He was 15. Michael Sullivan died seven days later. He was 14. Joseph Boxan shut his eyes for the last time on 26th of that month. He was nine. And Thomas Hickey was only 10 when he died on that same day. Two days later Michael Walsh took his last gasp at just 11 years of age. He wasn't the only one to die that day. Anthony Edward, who was the same age as Michael, also passed away. Four days later William Fagan's life was also cut short when he was only 13. Today they all lie together in Letterfrack.

The Christian Brothers put these boys' deaths down to influenza-pneumonia. That explanation may be plausible; after all the Spanish flu of that era claimed millions of lives worldwide. But the boys' premature deaths occurred against a backdrop of unremitting hardship at Letterfrack, where a climate of fear propagated tyrannical and sadistic behaviour among the Christian Brothers running the place. One hundred boys are estimated to have died in Letterfrack from the time it first opened its doors for business in 1887 to its closure in 1974.

For decades stories of abuse told by former inmates of industrial schools such as Letterfrack were dismissed by many in Ireland as the false rants of people embittered by their circumstances. But on 20 May 2009 their accounts were finally vindicated when the report of the Commission to Inquire into Child Abuse[1] was published. The five-volume tome is a shocking account of child abuse that took place in religious industrial and reformatory schools and other institutions from the 1930s up to the time of their closure.

The brutality of Letterfrack cited in the Ryan Report exposed Ireland's dreadful history of child neglect. Physical, emotional and sexual abuse were systematic there. Punishments were meted out for minor misdemeanours. Boys were battered by Brothers who abused their positions of power and vented their anger on children too poor and vulnerable to complain. Inmates who absconded in winter were hauled back, stripped of their clothes, hosed down in the yard and left to stand in the freezing cold in their underpants for hours; other absconders had their heads shaved and were subjected to perverse forms of solitary confinement, which meant their fellow inmates couldn't talk to them until their hair had grown back. Bed-wetters were ordered to drag their wet mattresses out into the open yard where they were humiliated by their fellow inmates. Boys were lashed with leather straps, tyres, fists, legs and whatever other instruments of torture the Brothers could get their hands on. They were made to work as child slaves on the bogs and in the workshops and they were never paid for any of their hard labour. The Christian Brothers who didn't participate in this sadistic type of cruelty colluded in it by remaining silent. Few spoke out against their superiors and even when they did their pleas were largely dismissed. The reputation of the Church and the Congregation took precedence over any form of justice for the children in their care.

One former resident of Letterfrack told the Ryan team about the reign of terror that pervaded the school when he was there in the 1950s and early 1960s.

> From the time you went into that you lived in fear, you were just constantly terrified. You lived in fear all the time in that school, you didn't know when you were going to get it, what Brother was going to give it to you, you just lived in fear in that school.[2]

Another former resident described how 'it was awful, it was very very cold, it was very very lonely, but the worst thing about it all, it was so scary'.[3] Letterfrack's endemic violence cultivated a culture of bullying among the boys themselves with peer sexual abuse at the extreme end of the spectrum.

> . . . you had to fight for survival because there was a lot of bullying and a lot of stuff going on. You had to be on your guard all the time because there was bigger kids and stronger kids, different kids and different types. Rough kids and bad kids; there was all different types.
>
> Yes, it was dog eat dog. It was survival, you had to do everything to survive, you know. You had to fight, scratch, you had to do everything for survival. There was no love or affection or caring from anyone, you know. And there was no one to talk to, you just had to form your own way of survival.[4]

Letterfrack was one of 21 religious institutions extensively documented in the Ryan Report. Its publication shocked the Irish nation; people reeled with disbelief as they read about the staggering levels of physical, sexual and emotional cruelty children endured in these ghastly places since the 1930s. The Report shook the already battered reputation of the Catholic Church and it highlighted the negligent role the Irish State played in the incarceration and abuse of children. In the weeks following the Report's publication, people tried to comprehend how vulnerable children could have been treated in such an appalling way. Ireland was swamped by a tsunami of shock and grief.

The Commission to Inquire into Child Abuse marked a watershed in contemporary Irish history. It validated the stories of religious brutality that former residents of these institutions had been describing for years and it raised numerous questions about the Catholic Church, the Irish State and Irish society. People wondered what kind of a country they were living in and even the most committed Irish Catholics questioned their faith. The Report was the result of a nine-year investigation into the treatment of children in institutions run by religious orders from the 1930s to the present day. The nuns and Brothers who abused their power in these hellholes were exposed as sadists and rapists, bullies and misfits. The Ryan Report showed how the lives of thousands of people had been destroyed in these pious prisons, supposed to be institutions of care. The Report blew apart the smokescreen of moral perfection that the religious orders had hidden behind for decades and it illuminated the hypocrisy of their self-righteous preachings.

The Report's executive summary confirmed a legacy of reprehensible neglect and brutality in the institutions investigated. Ryan concluded that the incarceration of children in these miserable places was 'an outdated response to a nineteenth century social problem'.[5] They were like Dickensian prisons where children went to bed hungry because the food was inadequate, inedible and badly prepared. Ryan declared that schools depended on 'rigid control by means of corporal punishment'[6] and that the harshness of the regime was 'inculcated into the culture of the schools by successive generations of Brothers, priests and nuns. It was systemic and not the result of individual breaches by persons who operated outside lawful and acceptable boundaries.'[7] Fear was the instrument of control in these institutions where, in many schools, 'staff considered themselves to be custodians rather than carers'.[8]

Witnesses to the Ryan investigation team spoke of scavenging for food from waste bins and animal feed.[9] Bullying was widespread in boys' schools, where the younger inmates were frequently deprived of food as the older boys grabbed their rations. Children were badly clothed and they were left in soiled and wet work clothes throughout the day. Accommodation was cold, spartan and bleak and the children slept in large unheated dormitories with inadequate bedding.[10] Sanitary conditions were abysmal and little provision was made for menstruating girls. The children received completely inadequate education in these tyrannical institutions. The Ryan Report found that in the girls' schools, children were removed from their classes in order to perform domestic chores or work in the institution during the day.[11] Instead of providing basic industrial training, the institutions cynically profited from the children by using them as child labour on farms and in workshops.

The Report showed how a climate of fear pervaded these industrial and reformatory schools where physical abuse was systematic. The Brothers and nuns engaged in excessive beatings, sometimes with implements designed to deliver maximum pain. Children lived with the daily terror of not knowing where the next beating was coming from.[12] Girls were frequently left shaking with fear for hours in cold corridors as they waited for their veiled executioners to deliver their frenzied lashings. Absconders were treated with particular ferocity. Their heads were shaved and they were flogged savagely for daring to escape from their sadistic custodians. The Report exposed how the Department of Education failed abysmally to investigate why children were absconding from the schools. Had they bothered to do so, they could have revealed decades of abuse and prevented thousands more children from enduring lasting damage.

Ryan concluded that sexual abuse was endemic in the boys' institutions and that the Congregations protected sexual predators and covered up their crimes to safeguard their own reputations. A culture of silence meant paedophiles were able to abuse with impunity and their behaviour was rarely brought to the attention of the Department of Education or the Gardaí. And even on the rare occasions when the Department found out about the sexual abuse, Ryan stated that it colluded in the silence:[13] 'There was a lack of transparency in how the matter of sexual abuse was dealt with between the Congregations, dioceses and the Department.'[14] Paedophiles were shunted on to other institutions where they continued to prey on vulnerable children. When faced with accounts of abuse by former residents, Ryan declared that some religious orders remained defensive and disbelieving even in cases where men and women had been convicted in court and admitted to such behaviour: 'Congregational loyalty enjoyed priority over other considerations including safety and protection of children.'[15]

The shameful cover-up went further. In some cases former Brothers with histories of sexual abuse continued their teaching careers as lay teachers in State schools after leaving the religious orders.

Emotional abuse was widespread in these despotic establishments. Children were belittled and humiliated on a daily basis. Bed-wetters were forced to parade their soiled sheets in public. Ryan found that private matters such as bodily functions and personal hygiene were used as opportunities for degradation and humiliation.[16] Children were told they were worthless and their families were denigrated. The psychological fall-out was enormous. Young girls and boys lived in constant fear of being beaten. Witnesses told the Ryan team how they were still haunted by the cries of other children being flogged excessively. Sibling bonds were smashed to smithereens as brothers and sisters were separated from one another. The remote locations of some of these austere institutions made it almost impossible for family visits and the unfortunate children unlucky enough to end up in these places felt abandoned by their parents and family members.

Particularly vulnerable children, such as those with disabilities, were also abused in institutions like St Joseph's School for Deaf Boys in Cabra in Dublin. Ryan described St Joseph's as a 'very frightening place for children who were learning to overcome hearing difficulties'.[17] The Report found that corporal punishment was 'excessive and capricious' there and that the boys incarcerated in St Joseph's suffered from sexual abuse from staff and older boys.[18]

The Ryan Report dominated the headlines over the days and weeks following its publication as journalists waded through the massive document and extracted stories of staggering cruelty. We read about the notorious Ferryhouse Industrial School in Clonmel where one boy recalled a sexual assault there by a Rosminian Brother: 'He was just like, I do not know, the eyes of him, he was like a man who was possessed, you know. He got me . . . down and he beat my face off the ground. He done his best to penetrate me.'[19]

The Goldenbridge Industrial School, which was run by the Sisters of Mercy, was castigated for its cruelty. Witnesses spoke about the terror of waiting for the head nun to administer a walloping to girls on the cold landing outside the nuns' private rooms. The older girls used to push the young children to the front of the queue so that they would receive the brunt of the nun's vicious temper. One woman told the Ryan Commission how 'The screaming of children will stay with me for the rest of my life about Goldenbridge. I still hear it, I still haven't recovered from that. Children crying and screaming, it was just endless, it never never stopped for years in that place.'[20]

We heard about the young boy in Artane who was knocked unconscious by a Christian Brother who punished the young fellow for missing sports training:

> When you seen this man when he lost his temper he was like a wolf. His jaws literally went out and he bared his teeth and he just lashed at me. I was running trying to get away from him. He hit me, it didn't matter where, legs, back, head, anywhere. During that I must have passed out because when I came around there was water running on my head.[21]

The case of Mickey Flanagan was highlighted in the chapter on Artane. Mickey's arm was broken in three places by a Christian Brother who smashed the handle of a brush over him. The injured lad was hidden away in an outhouse for a couple of days while his broken arm was left untreated. His distraught mother was refused permission by the Brothers to visit her son when she found out about the beating he had received. Mickey's family believe he was permanently damaged from that day's assault and that he never recovered from the psychological fall-out of the attack. Mickey Flanagan's story is told in this book.

The catalogue of brutality was astounding. People's emotions were in turmoil as they read and heard the harrowing accounts of abuse. Some Irish people refused to discuss the Ryan Report: its chilling details were too much to absorb. Others shook their head in disbelief, unable to comprehend the magnitude of the abuse. And running beneath the surface of this nationwide shock was the unpalatable reality that the entire country had, in one way or another, played a role in the abuse of the children. It was as if a mirror had been held up to us and we were forced to scrutinise our collective responsibility in the unimaginably cruel treatment of children in the religious institutions.

Uncomfortable questions were asked. Were our parents or grandparents the ones who used the inmates of industrial schools as child slaves on their farms? Did we buy the turf that had been back-breakingly dug up in the cold wet bogs of Western Ireland by boys from Daingean and Letterfrack? Were those rosary beads we had as children made in places such as Goldenbridge, by little girls who spent hours stringing the beads together under the vigilant supervision of a nun? Did Irish people from the villages near the institutions turn a blind eye to the black and blue marks of the young fellow who escaped from one of these diabolic institutions and did they take him by the ear and march him back into the black abyss that was supposed to be his home? And what were the doctors, who were supposed to be treating children in these places, doing? How did they manage to overlook the obvious signs of maltreatment? Why did hospital staff not properly investigate cases of children who turned up in their emergency wards with inexplicable injuries? Did their deferential attitude to the Church influence their ready acceptance of the lies given by the Brothers and nuns?

The Report spoke volumes about the prevailing attitude of Irish society for most of the twentieth century when these institutions were thriving. Back then, children from industrial schools were seen as miscreants and troublemakers who needed the strong disciplinary hands of the Brothers and Sisters to put manners on them. Irish people believed they owed a debt of gratitude to the holy guardians of these miserable institutions for sorting out these 'deviant' children. Much of this attitude was shaped by ignorance, poverty, insularity and an unwavering deference to the Catholic Church, a deference that really began to wane only in the 1990s. That unswerving submission blinded our national capacity to see beyond the collars and the veils and to question the behaviour of the religious orders who were abusing with impunity behind their high institutional walls. Irish people elevated the priests, nuns and Brothers onto pedestals where they were beyond reproach. Inevitably, some of them abused their privileged positions and that had a devastating impact on tens of thousands of children who were incarcerated in their care.

The abusive treatment of children in these places also raised disturbing questions about the Irish justice system, which gave judges the power to hand down draconian sentences on children who were too poor to have any legal representation during their trials. These judges committed children to religious institutions for having 'improper guardians' or being illegitimate or having a widowed father who was struggling to take care of his children on his own. Tiny babies were dispatched by judges to spend the next 16 years of their lives in religious institutions. Judges handed down criminal sentences to juvenile offenders for crimes as minor as taking pigeons from the attic of a derelict house, mitching from school or being found with a bar of chocolate that someone else had stolen. These court orders gave officials the authority to remove children from their homes and subject them to years of institutional abuse. The Irish Society for the Prevention of Cruelty to Children (ISPCC), formerly known as the National Society for Prevention of Cruelty to Children, was also culpable in breaking up families and taking children from their homes.

The Irish Department of Education contributed significantly to prolonging institutional abuse. Under the Children Act 1908, the Department had legal responsibility for all children committed to industrial and reformatory schools. The Ryan Report found that the Department failed to properly inspect and supervise the institutions to which it had subcontracted the care of children. Ryan stated that 'Officials were aware that abuse occurred in the Schools and they knew the education was inadequate and the industrial training was outdated.'[22] The Department's deferential and submissive attitude to the Congregations compromised its statutory duties to protect children. Ryan declared that 'It made no attempt to impose changes that would have improved the lot of the detained children. Indeed, it never thought about changing the system.'[23]

The system of funding the institutions through capitation grants was also flawed. In fact, the Congregations had a vested interest in ensuring large numbers of children were committed by the State to their institutions. To put it crudely, the more children they received, the more money they got from the State.

Not all survivors of institutional abuse were happy with the Ryan Report. Some were bitterly disappointed that it did not result in the prosecution of individuals and religious orders who were exposed as abusers during the Ryan investigations. The use of pseudonyms was widely condemned. The majority of the religious people cited by witnesses were given anonymity in the Report. Critics said the abusers should have been named and shamed in the Report. People were also unhappy with the cherry-picking process that led to only a sample of witnesses giving evidence. Not all survivors of institutional abuse who had volunteered to speak to the Ryan Commission were able to do so. Those who were not invited to give evidence felt they had been denied the opportunity and right to ensure their stories of abuse were heard and documented. The official explanation for choosing a sample of witnesses was that it would have taken far too long for everyone's story to be heard.

The Ryan Commission was also criticised for its failure to properly investigate the role the Irish courts and judges played in incarcerating children in the industrial and reformatory schools. It did not conduct a thorough investigation of the Irish justice system that enabled judges to hand down excessive sentences on children for minor offences. It also did not explain why judges seemingly so readily incarcerated children for many years when they had at least one living parent and extended families who may have been able to take care of them. In many cases, these children had no legal representation in court, a situation that should never have been allowed.

However, despite the reservations and shortcomings of the Ryan Report, there is no denying it served a significant purpose in exposing the magnitude of the physical, emotional and sexual abuse that had taken place in Irish religious institutions. Irish people were left in no doubt about the pitiful lives thousands of children had been forced to endure in these vile prisons.

The reputation of the Church was in tatters after the Ryan Report. The religious orders were subjected to a ferocious lambasting as the media gave blanket coverage to the Report. Commentators and survivors of institutional abuse jammed the airwaves with blistering attacks on the Congregations who had run abusive schools. Calls were made for the removal of all Church involvement in the running of schools and hospitals. Some Irish people even recoiled in horror when they saw priests, Brothers or nuns near them.

The Church took a further hammering when the report by the Commission of Investigation into the Dublin Archdiocese[24] was published six months later. It showed the extent of the cover-up of clerical child sexual abuse. The Catholic hierarchy was exposed for its cynical movement of paedophiles from one place to another in order to safeguard the reputation of the Church. That was of paramount importance and above all other considerations, including the protection of children who were in danger of being abused by priests in their communities. Murphy reported on how bishops in Ireland knowingly protected abusive priests and covered up their criminal sexual activities to avoid any damage being done to the Church.

The Ryan Report's shocking exposure of religious institutional abuse set the people of Ireland on a painful journey of national self-analysis. Tough questions were asked: How could such a God-fearing Catholic State so badly neglect and abuse its own children? To what extent were the Irish State and Irish society complicit in the destruction of these people's lives and in what way was everyone culpable for the abuse? Why was the Church allowed to have so much power for so long? And, perhaps most importantly of all, what stark lessons must be learnt from Ryan's searing record of cruelty?

Ireland in the immediate post-Ryan weeks was like a country suffering from a collective hangover that was paying a high price for the excesses of its past. Its publication dovetailed with the implosion of the Irish economy — a crash that generated an equally powerful avalanche of emotions. The Catholic Church and the Celtic Tiger were like badly wounded animals limping towards an uncertain future. Both the Ryan Report and the crash highlighted the perils of unfettered greed and religious control and they symbolised the hazardous consequences of allowing powerful players to stray too far into unbridled terrain.

On the Sunday morning following the publication of the Ryan Report I presented a three-hour special programme on it for my show 'The Wide Angle' on Newstalk. I was joined in studio by three survivors of institutional abuse. One of them was Michael O'Brien, who had spent eight years of his childhood in Ferryhouse Industrial School in Clonmel. I will never forget the spine-chilling moments when Michael described how he was sexually and physically abused in Ferryhouse. He spoke movingly about how thorns became embedded in his nails when he was forced to reap hay on local farms with his bare hands. His raw emotional recollections left us all reeling. When I left the studio that day I was in a kind of stunned stupor, unable to fully comprehend the stories of cruelty we had discussed that morning. By the time I arrived home I decided I needed to play my own role in further documenting the accounts of religious institutional abuse during this appalling chapter in Irish history.

This book is based upon stories of people who were in industrial and reformatory schools as children. It explains how they ended up in the schools in the first place, what happened to them during their incarcerations and how their lives were affected by their childhoods in these despicable prisons. Their experiences are an example of what happened to thousands of children who ended up in religious institutions. Their stories also illustrate the power of the human spirit and the extraordinary survival instincts of human beings. The people I interviewed for this book had to dig deep within themselves to find enormous wells of strength to survive their horrific childhoods.

The plight of women who were put in Magdalene laundries is also covered in the book through Maureen Sullivan's story. The Magdalene women were not allowed to seek compensation from the Residential Institutions Redress Board because the Irish State said it had no responsibility for the laundries. The Magdalene women remain outraged that they were ostracised from the redress process and the Commission to Inquire into Child Abuse.

The book also offers brief insights into why Ireland cultivated a crop of religious sadists who were able to abuse with impunity for decades. It examines the role the Irish State played in abdicating its responsibility for the care of the children. The failures of the Redress Board are also investigated. The redress scheme was supposed to provide adequate compensation to survivors of institutional abuse. But many people who applied to the Board for redress were deeply traumatised by the whole process. In some cases they were subjected to aggressive cross-examinations during redress hearings. Claimants felt they were effectively put on trial and unfairly made to justify their stories of abuse as children. Their anger was exacerbated by the gagging order they had to sign when accepting redress, which prevented them from revealing any details of their experiences of the redress process. They also had to sign a waiver to agree not to pursue any legal actions against any of the people or organisations they had named in their redress applications as being implicated in their childhood abuse.

Haunting Cries follows a series of courageous works produced over the last 20 years that have exposed religious institutional abuse. Autobiographical accounts of institutional abuse told in books such as Peter Tyrrell's *Founded on Fear* and Paddy Doyle's *The God Squad* gave us searing insights into how these horrendous places operated. The 'Dear Daughter' documentary about Christine Buckley exposed the atrocious treatment of girls in the notorious Goldenbridge Industrial School in Inchicore, Dublin, which was run by the Sisters of Mercy. The groundbreaking investigations done by Dr Eoin O'Sullivan and the journalist Mary Raftery lifted the lid on Ireland's legacy of institutional abuse. Their book *Suffer the Little Children* and the RTÉ series 'States of Fear', which was produced by Mary Raftery, influenced Bertie Ahern's 1999 apology to survivors of institutional abuse and led to the establishment of both the Commission to Inquire into Child Abuse and the Redress Board. Their stories are essential reminders of Ireland's legacy of abuse and they epitomise the courage it took to highlight what was going on in these places and to ensure their voices would not be silenced by their former oppressors.

Chapter 2 ~

NOEL KELLY AND DAINGEAN

Noel Kelly can never escape the ghosts of his childhood tormentors who sexually, physically and psychologically assaulted him in St Conleth's Reformatory School in Daingean, Co. Offaly. They plague his thoughts every day and they puncture his sleep at night with paralysing dreams that plunge him into a state of petrified consciousness. His 17 months' incarceration in Daingean destroyed his life permanently.

> I think I never got over Daingean. Sometimes I walk the floor at night and I think I never got over Daingean. I left something buried in Daingean that can't be replaced; that can't be fixed or mended.[1]

Daingean was a notorious gulag that was run by the Oblates of Mary Immaculate. Witnesses who gave evidence to the Ryan Commission recalled how they were beaten, sexually assaulted and emotionally scarred in this bleak, desolate purgatory. Daingean was different from the other religious institutions investigated by the Commission because it was a reformatory for boys aged between 12 and 17 who had been convicted by the courts of criminal offences.[2]

In 1870 the Oblates established their reformatory in Daingean in a remote part of Co. Offaly. The buildings were originally used as a military barracks in the middle of the eighteenth century. After the barracks closed, the Irish Constabulary used Daingean as a training ground before it became a prison for adult criminals and later St Conleth's. In the 1940s a new building was erected that housed two large dormitories for senior and junior boys and woodwork and metalwork classrooms. The complex also had a large recreation hall, washrooms, other classrooms, a piggery and a poultry house, a scullery and storerooms.[3] Daingean also had a significant farm, which meant it was virtually self-sufficient. Its isolated location made it extremely difficult to get to and there were no direct bus routes to Daingean village. Such an inhospitable location meant that it was practically impossible for Noel Kelly's mother to visit her son.

> They were taking us away as far as possible. Going to Daingean was like going to bloody Australia.

Juvenile offenders ended up there for crimes ranging from larceny to common assault. The majority of them came from Ireland's main cities of Dublin, Cork and Limerick. The Ryan Commission found that many of the complainants who gave evidence ended up in Daingean for trivial offences that owed more to poverty than criminality.[4] Severely psychiatrically disturbed children were also sent there.[5]

Noel Kelly was one of the young offenders from Limerick who served time in Daingean. Born in 1952, he was reared in Limerick City with his large family of 10 brothers and five sisters. His father worked as a seaman and he was frequently away from home and Noel's mother had to raise her children with little resources. Noel was the black sheep of the family. He never got on well in school and he abandoned his education when he was 13. His problems began when he started mixing with gangs of troublesome youths in Limerick.

> What I wanted to do was pal around with the bigger boys rather than the smaller boys. I thought they had a better time than the smaller boys.

Noel began to spend nights outside his home sleeping rough. He became involved in petty crime that then escalated into breaking and entering. In 1968, when he was 15, he broke into a house in Limerick and stole some money.

> I was caught stealing a couple of bob from the gas meter and things like that.

The guards caught him stealing and arrested him. On 10 May 1968 Noel
Kelly was brought to the Children's Court in Limerick and given a two-
year sentence that he was to spend in Daingean. His detention there tore
his life apart.

> Fear was the byword of this institution. Fear was the tool most
> brutally used. Fear was the weapon used from morning to night,
> seven days a week, fifty-two weeks a year.

When Noel arrived in Daingean he was stripped of his name. The
Brothers told him he wasn't entitled to one and that he would be known
as number 6398 for the rest of his incarceration there. He will never
forget his first night in that miserable institution.

> It was evening time. I didn't get much of a view going in because it
> was dark. I was brought in by a couple of guards and introduced to
> a Brother. The guards signed their documentation and off they
> went. That's when I first came into contact with Brother Smith.[6]

When he first met Br Smith, Noel Kelly had no idea what kind of a brute
he was but he would soon find out. During his sentence in Daingean,
Smith kicked, whipped and punched him and left him writhing on the
ground with pain. But on that first night he left the youngster alone
when he took him to the washroom.

> I was told to take off my clothes — everything. I had to stand into
> the cubicle and I was told to strip off. And that's what I did. And he
> [Br Smith] walked around me and looked at me. Then he gave me a
> nightshirt and he put that on me and I was marched up to the
> dormitory. I walked up the stairs up into the dormitory where I met
> Br Liam.[7] He said a couple of words to Br Smith who then went
> away. Then he led me down the row of beds and said, 'There's your
> bed.' I got into the bed. He told me where I was and how long I was
> going to be there for. I cried my eyes out that night. I was in no way
> prepared for what was to follow then. No way.

Noel was bewildered by the dormitory's enormous size and the long
rows of beds. He had never slept with so many boys in one room. Br

Liam warned him to keep his hands outside the blankets and not to make a sound. He spent his first night fighting back the tears as he struggled to comprehend what was happening to him. The loneliness was unbearable. The next day Br Liam ordered him to wash and polish the dormitory floors and organise the boys' laundry. The brutality began within a short time of his arrival in Daingean and lasted throughout his time there. Noel was punched, slapped and caned by the Brothers for the slightest breaches of the rules. He was so terrified he began to wet the bed. It was an unfortunate condition that was met with savage retaliation.

> This was considered to be a major crime within the Reformatory. Let me take you through a night in the life of a bed-wetter in Daingean. When it is first discovered that you are a bed-wetter, you are moved from the bed in which you are sleeping to a bed at the back of the dormitory nearer the toilet. It is then the responsibility of the night watchman, who was a lay person, to wake you up at regular intervals. Unfortunately for me I still wet the bed.
>
> When Br Liam came on duty in the morning, the night watchman would inform him that six-three-nine-eight (being me) had wet the bed. Then when everybody was called to go to the washroom, I was to remain in the dormitory. Brother Liam would tell me to remove all the clothing from my bed, turn my bed up on its side, put the mattress and the blankets over the upended bed and while all of this was going on he would be shouting and roaring at me as to why I had wet the bed. He would also be hitting me around the face and the head. I then had to take the wet sheets down into the washroom.

Noel would be forced to walk down the middle of the washroom and hold up his wet sheets in his hands in front of the other boys who mocked him and called him 'Pissey Limerick' — a nickname they frequently used for him. The embarrassed young lad was extremely upset by this humiliating punishment, which he had to endure regularly as he continued to wet his bed throughout his time in Daingean. The abuse gradually worsened. Around four months after his arrival there, Noel's life changed irrevocably when he was sent to the bakery to work with Br Marc.[8]

That's where I was sexually abused for the first time . . . he sexually abused me from all angles. I had to perform all kinds of [sexual] acts for this fella. He was a sadist. He'd bite me in the neck and the head. He'd bite my nipples.

Noel remembers Br Marc as an older man whom he reckons may have been in his sixties. The bakery was located at the back of the main building in Daingean and Br Marc had complete control over who could enter and leave it.

The bakery was a small place, more of a shed than anything else. There were large oven trays for the bread. And that's what I did. I had to make the bread. I had to grease and wash all the trays. The door was always closed from the inside. He would always have the key with him. He could do what he liked, when he liked, as often as he liked. Nobody would walk in on top of anything. People who'd come along and want to get into the bakery they'd have to knock on the window. Half the window was blacked out. And there was a small kind of timber windowsill on the inside where you could sit out and that's where most of the abuse went on.

Noel's first week in the bakery passed off without incident and he thought he had landed on his feet. Initially Br Marc was nice to him and he used to give him buns and sweets that he kept in a biscuit tin in a corner of the bakery. It was as if he was sweetening his prey before he pounced.

I remember the sweets well. They were Roses with all the different coloured papers . . . I was a good boy. I'd be told to do something and I'd do it.

On his second week in the bakery Br Marc began to make sexual advances towards Noel.

While we were waiting for the bread to bake we'd sit on the windowsill and he came over to me and told me to stand up which I did. And he told me to turn around which I did. And he put his arms around me from the back and he started telling me I was a good boy and he started biting me on the neck and on the head. Then he turned around and he started kissing me. And that's as far as it went that day.

When he had finished fondling the traumatised youngster, Br Marc gave him sweets and a bun. Noel stumbled out of the bakery in shock.

I think my mind just blanked out. I couldn't say anything. How many times have I said this to myself, 'Why didn't I push him away?' He wasn't that big. I've seen that man so many times in my mind. I was frightened.

The abuse got progressively more violent after that day.

The fondling went on for a while and all that kissing and biting. I would have to pinch him in the nipples and all of that. He was into the pain kind of thing. At the time, I didn't know that. He started taking off my clothes then. He'd take off my jumper and shirt and he'd take off his shirt. The biting got worse then. And the kissing and turning around and all of that.

He didn't seem to be afraid of leaving marks. I was very sore in the nipples, they'd be black and blue . . . he got a thrill out of that. He got a thrill out of the pain, out of seeing me in pain . . . I was just numb. He could have hit me with an iron bar and I wouldn't have felt it. I was just out of it.

Noel was desperate to get out of the bakery but he was like a prisoner who had been stripped of all rights. There was nobody he could to turn to as complaints of abuse weren't tolerated in Daingean. The sexual assaults gradually worsened over Noel's eight months of horror in the bakery and Br Marc began to violently rape him.

He used to turn me around and I used to have to put my hands on the windowsill and that's when he raped me. I did roar then but no one came . . . I couldn't really say what was going through my mind. I think at that stage I just kind of gave up. I didn't give a shit after that.

Br Marc went on to abuse Noel on a daily basis. Some days he would rape him; other days he would fondle him or bite him or force the young boy to masturbate him.

> He would do something every day but he wouldn't rape me every day because I was very sore. And I was passing blood as well. He had this small clothesline and he had all these cloths hanging on it and he'd rub me down with them and he'd rub himself down . . . He was enjoying it. He never said anything only 'Just do this, do that, take that off, take this off' and that was it.

The sexual abuse was so bad Noel was desperate to get out of the bakery. One day he decided to approach Br Smith to tell him about Br Marc. It was a decision that would have dire consequences for the teenager, who would experience first-hand the cunning cover-up the religious orders engaged in to hide paedophiles within their ranks.

> I was carrying bread over to the boys' kitchen and that was about the only time you'd be left out of the bakery, when you'd be carrying it to the kitchen. There was no other way out. And I seen Br Smith in the hallway so I put down my tray of bread and I went up to him and I said, 'Could I speak to you?' And he said, 'About what?' and I said, 'I want to speak to you about Br Marc.' And he said, 'Get in there!' [to his office]. And I said, 'He's doing things to me and I don't want him to be doing it to me any more.' I started to pull up my jumper and I started to show him what he was doing. And he just lashed into me with his fist. The first dig he gave me was into the chest and I kind of went down and then he started digging me. And then I went down on the ground and he started kicking me. And then Br Marc turned up. The whole place had heard me screaming. Br Smith said, 'Take that thing out of here.' And I was brought back down to the bakery and he [Br Marc] closed the door. He took off his habit and he started beating me then. He hit me with one of the bread trays. He gave me a good beating.

Noel was writhing in pain on the ground. He screamed for help but Daingean's merciless law of the jungle meant the scared youngster was on his own.

He was calling me all kinds of things like 'You filthy thing, you, I'll kick the fear of God into you.'

That evening Noel limped out of the bakery and went over to the washroom to clean himself. Despite the extensive bruising to his body, none of the other boys or staff enquired about his injuries.

At this stage I'm walking around like I felt I had plaster of Paris on both legs I was so sore. I'm black and blue. My nose is split open. There's a big scab on my nose. My eyes are black and blue. And I started to wet the bed which wasn't a help either. I got a beating for every time I wet the bed. I tried everything not to wet the bed. I stopped drinking. I'd put a string around my stomach at night-time. I made a nappy out of a canvas bag.

Noel believes the other boys knew exactly what Br Marc was doing to him and that he was not the only inmate in Daingean who was being sexually abused.

You could pick them out because of their zombie kind of appearance. You could tell.

The stigma of the abuse silenced the boys who were sexually assaulted in Daingean. That self-censorship enabled the Brothers to abuse with impunity. Noel decided an escape from this hellish prison was the only way to avoid the unremitting maltreatment he was being subjected to. One evening he just walked out of Daingean's gates and into the local village. He had no idea where he was or what to do next. Within a short time a local man spotted him and knew, by his ragged clothes and appearance, that he was a Daingean lad. He grabbed the runaway and warned him he was taking him back to the school. Noel pleaded with him and told him about the beatings but the man dismissed his pleas despite the obvious bruises on his face and body. He hauled the distressed lad back in through Daingean's gates, where the Brothers were already waiting for him.

Four or five Brothers came running down the pathway. When I saw the posse turning up I said, 'Here we go again.' They marched me back down in the door and I got a whack from behind, a slap in the face from behind that blinded my eye. I just braced myself to take what's coming . . . they called me anything and everything: you dirty this and dirty that, filthy this and filthy that.

I was taken down into the washhouse and they practically ripped the clothes off of me. And I got a couple of slaps and digs and kicks. I was taken up into the dormitory; I got no supper, nothing. I never seen anything like it. Daingean was just unreal and how in the name of God them boys could be put into the care of these people at all is still a mystery to me. I can't answer that after all these years. And to say that there was some good ones and some bad ones and the good ones didn't see anything or didn't hear anything that's a big white lie . . . I think these people were exiled to Daingean for probably something else they done somewhere else. I think they were the worst of the worst. Whatever they did somewhere else Daingean was their punishment. They had nothing more to gain from their career so they took it out on us. That's what I think about the people that were in Daingean. That was their exile, that was their punishment and they took their frustrations out on us.

Noel attempted a second escape from Daingean with another inmate. The two lads ran as fast as they could when they got outside the school's premises. But their freedom was short-lived. As soon as they escaped, they could hear the roars and shouts of the Brothers running towards them.

We went through the village of Daingean like two wild animals. We were running through the fields, we stopped for a rest. Five or six Brothers suddenly surrounded us. We took off again but the boy with me was caught. I could hear him screaming because of the beating he was getting from these animals. I kept running towards a distant hedge and with the sound of the Brothers getting close and my pal screaming I fought my way through the hedge with my bare hands.

It was a mixture of hedge and thorn bushes. Despite the pain I kept on running but I don't know how long until I eventually collapsed. It was only at this stage that I realised I was torn to pieces. What I thought was sweat pouring down my face was in fact blood.

The skin was hanging from my hands and I must have passed out for a while because when I awoke it was getting dark. I saw someone approach me on a bike and in desperation tried to get up and run, but I fell to the ground again. I can still see the expression of horror on the face of the man. He told me to stay still and that he was not going to hurt me. He kept saying 'Oh Jesus', and he was blessing himself.

He got on his bike and cycled away. He told me he was going for help. Not long afterwards the reformatory lorry came along with two Brothers in it. They put me into the lorry in between both of them. As we were going back towards Daingean I saw the man who had tried to help me earlier. He was standing at the side of the road holding his bike with one hand and shaking his fist with the other. To this day I don't know if he was shaking his fist at me or them.

That night Noel was called out of his bed and ordered to go to the top of the room by one of the Brothers, who demanded to know why the youngster had escaped. Before Noel could reply, the Brother knocked him to the floor and dragged him to the landing outside the dormitory where another Brother was waiting. The two men kicked and punched Noel until they were breathless. They warned him never to try to escape from Daingean again.

Shortly after one of these escapes, Noel was told he was being moved from the bakery to the farm where he was to work with Br Pat,[9] who was in charge of Daingean's substantial agricultural industry. The boys rarely got to enjoy the farm's produce as the Brothers sold whatever food they did not consume themselves. Noel's daily tasks included cleaning the milking parlour and feeding the pigs. He had to wear the same clothes every day for a week despite the filth and dirt of his tasks. Initially he was relieved at the move because it meant an end to the sexual abuse by Br Marc. But several weeks into his new job he got a ferocious beating from Br Pat, who was a 'giant of a man'.

I was cleaning out one of the sheds with the pigs in it. And I had the shed cleaned out. I had just got out the door when one of the beasts stuck out his head and I had the yard brush and I tried to push him back in with the yard brush. The next thing I heard these footsteps coming up behind me. You could hear him coming for a while because he wore steel caps on his boots and he grabbed the brush out of my hand. He closed the door and got the pig in and he beat the brush off me and knocked me onto the ground and I fell on all the pig shit and all that. He gave me a good thumping as well. He broke the handle of the brush off me.

Br Pat roared at Noel and demanded to know why he was hitting the pig with the brush.

I tried to explain to him that I was only pushing him in with the brush. I wasn't hitting the pig with the brush.

The stunned lad picked himself up from the ground. He tried to catch his breath and recover from the vicious pounding. His ribs were extremely sore and his nose was bleeding. Noel endured many frenzied attacks from Br Pat, who ran the farm with domineering brutality. On another occasion he flogged Noel in the potato shed.

We were stacking a load of potatoes onto straw. We were just acting the fool and he walked in and he caught me eating a potato. He punched me in the face and I don't remember much about that because I think he knocked me out. I woke up in the cow-shed. The boys were cleaning me up. I was bleeding from inside my gums. I had two big swollen lips and he never said nothing to me.

Noel's gums were so badly cut and his lips so swollen he was unable to eat that evening. That night a terrifying reality hit him: he had swapped the sexual abuse in the bakery for violent physical abuse on the farm. Life in Daingean was so unbearable for Noel that he decided to make yet another attempt to abscond when the boys were taken to Drogheda for a rare day out. When they arrived in the town, Noel and another inmate slipped away from the group.

We didn't know where we were. We didn't even think about what's going to happen if we were caught and brought back.

The two runaways got a lift to Dublin where they remained on the loose for 10 days. They had no money and were desperately hungry so they decided to break into a butcher shop to get meat, but they were caught red-handed.

> We could see all the puddings hanging up. We weren't that good at robbing. That's what we were caught for. We were held in some barracks; I think it was the Bridewell . . . I remember it well, we got a burger wrapped up in paper and tea and we were quite content.

The two runaways were brought back to Daingean by two Brothers who had travelled to Dublin to collect them. It was late when they reached the school and they went straight to bed. Later that night Noel was shaken from his sleep when he got a thump across his legs. He was ordered out of the bed and dragged down to the washhouse.

> The door opened and Br Pat was there and he said, 'Come on, you're coming with me.' I had a good idea what was coming . . . I just got down to the end of the stairs and I got a belt to the back of the head and I went straight through the doors [of the washhouse]. I don't know how many of them [Brothers] was there. Then I got kicked all over the place . . . I only got a couple of digs when I passed out. I woke up in the washhouse. I had blood all over me and I was black and blue again. I'll never forget Br Smith was pushing my head into the sink. I remember banging my teeth off of the tap and splitting my teeth. I remember walking up the stairs shaking. I didn't think I was going to make it. I was praying I'd die.

Noel Kelly never attempted another escape after that ordeal. His remaining detention in Daingean was characterised by constant physical and psychological abuse. There was nobody to talk to about the abuse and he felt terribly alone. He couldn't bring himself to tell his mother on the rare visits she made to check up on him as he was too ashamed to admit that he had been raped by the Brothers. He also felt she wouldn't believe him. In 1960s Ireland the notion of a boy being sexually abused by a Brother would have been met with disbelief. He dismissed his mother's queries about the bruises on his face and body by saying he had sustained them on the farm or from fights with the other boys.

Noel Kelly says several paedophiles operated in Daingean during his incarceration there. One of them was Br Ramon,[10] who was one of the younger recruits in the school.

> He was into lifting the weights and he was in the shed where all the weights used to be. He never abused me but he did fondle me [genitals]. I used to do the weights for him for a couple of times but then he started touching me up and all that so I stayed far away from him. He'd show you how to lift the weights and he'd be touching you and saying this is where the muscles are and down here and all that kind of craic and I knew straight away to get out of there.

Br Ramon was later convicted of sexually assaulting boys in a residential institution in Wales. The Ryan Report has a segment on Ramon. It states that Ramon had been on the staff of Daingean for 17 years from the mid-1950s.[11] He was removed from Daingean in the early 1970s, apparently against his wishes as he protested against the move.[12] The reasons for his removal are unclear. The Report raises suspicions that the Oblates shifted him out of Daingean because of reports of abuse. Ramon went on to work in a hostel for homeless immigrants in London where he stayed for 10 years before moving to a college in Wales where he was appointed as a Housemaster.[13] His sexually abusive behaviour in this college led to his conviction for indecently assaulting 10 boys.[14]

The Ryan Commission heard from witnesses who gave evidence that Br Ramon had sexually abused them. One man described an assault.

> Br Ramon he used to work in the bakery. There was one morning I was sent over to get the bread to put it out for the breakfast. I went over and he was there and he started tickling me and messing about, that kind of thing. Then he opened my trousers and put his hand in . . . and he touched me. I was pushing him away, trying to get away from him and he grabbed me by the hand and he tried to force my hand onto his private part. I managed to struggle and then he just let it go at that. I got the bread and brought it back over to the recreation room . . . He would give me Brylcreme, sweets, toothpaste, toothbrushes and things like that . . . when I was working in the kitchen. He started groping me again and then I gave in, I masturbated him about probably four to six times.[15]

Compelling evidence in the Ryan Report illustrates how the Oblate order ignored allegations that Br Ramon was abusing boys. In 1967 a firm of solicitors, acting on behalf of a young boy, wrote to the Secretary of the Department of Justice about the alleged abuse of a 15-year-old whom they described as being 'mentally retarded'.[16]

They said he was 'sexually assaulted and perverted while an in-mate of the Reformatory'.[17] The Ryan Report stated that, although he was not named, the alleged abuser was Br Ramon. Ryan states that the letter was seemingly passed on to the Department of Education, which then received a letter from solicitors acting on behalf of the Resident Manager in Daingean. They said the allegations had been investigated with the full co-operation of the Resident Manager and found to be untrue.[18]

> Following their enquiries the Garda Authorities were satisfied that there was no evidence of any improper conduct by any member of the Staff . . . In view of the serious allegation made in the letter to your Department based on the story of this unfortunate boy our client wishes this unequivocable [sic] denial of the allegations placed on your file.[19]

In another correspondence Daingean's Resident Manager described the allegations as a 'malicious concoction'.[20] The Ryan Report is highly critical of the Oblates' failure to investigate Br Ramon's behaviour in Daingean after he had been charged with indecent assault against boys in Wales. The Report found that the Oblates did not record or follow up on allegations of abuse and they developed a culture of fear that prevented any reporting of abusive behaviour.

The sordid behaviour of the Oblate Brothers cultivated a macabre subculture of abuse among the boys themselves. The Ryan Report concluded that sexual behaviour between boys in Daingean was systemic and widespread.[21] Bigger inmates preyed on smaller boys. One man described how he was raped by the leader of an established gang within Daingean who picked on him.[22]

> He was an aggressive guy with a horrible sort of personality. He had a group of guys and he was the sort of leader of these group of guys . . . On a weekly basis whenever the opportunity would — I would be dragged off into a pig shed, hay shed, wherever, and buggered

. . . he was leader of a group of guys, they could make your life hell
. . . You are living with these people, you can't get away from them,
you are there.[23]

Daingean's peer abuse spawned a weird vocabulary. A 'hag' was a young
boy who was befriended by an older boy. He was treated like a girlfriend
and expected, in some cases, to perform sexual acts for the older boy.

> Most of the older boys had a hag . . . It was more or less a status
> thing. When you were there twelve months you knew all the ropes
> and it was kind of like a girlfriend more or less but there was
> nothing sexual about it. It was like you were kind of protected. You
> see it was in the small sections and when all the fellows in the small
> sections knew that he was your hag they wouldn't go near him.[24]

Another witness used a different term for the same lurid phenomenon.

> We called them wan dolls, it's like a pal . . . I am not saying you
> wouldn't have sexual abuse with them or something like that, I am
> sure you would . . . you would masturbate them and they would
> masturbate you . . .[25]

Once an older boy formed a relationship with his 'wan doll' it was
common for the boys to stay together as a kind of a couple until the end
of their stay in Daingean. An impenetrable veil of silence was then
drawn over their sexually charged association once their sentence was
up. One witness described in the Ryan Report the reaction of a former
Daingean inmate whom he met years later. When he asked him who was
his 'wan doll' in Daingean, the man 'never said another word, he got up
and walked away . . . Nobody talks about it.'[26]

Boys who performed oral sex were bullied and ostracised, especially
at meal times.

> They had to mark their teacups with a knife. There wasn't delft
> down there . . . The saucers, the cups, the plates were Bakelite, that
> was kind of plastic, I remember. If a young fellow was sexually
> abused . . . after gobbling [oral masturbation] somebody, they had
> to mark their cup [indicating] with a knife and they could only

drink out of that cup . . . No one else could drink out of them.[27]

In their submission to the Ryan Commission, the Oblates denied that such abuse was systemic or widespread in Daingean or that such behaviour was in any way tolerated.[28]

Noel Kelly left Daingean on 3 October 1969 when he was nearly 17. In less than two years, the place had broken him and destroyed his life. He has never been able to get over the abuse he suffered there. Years later, psychiatrists diagnosed him as suffering from post-traumatic stress disorder as a result of his experiences in Daingean.

> It still affects me today. I can't forget about it. You can't just block it out of your mind. Night-time is my biggest enemy. Some nights I might get away with it and some nights I just don't. The tablets I'm getting from my doctors help me but there're only so many tablets you can take. I get nightmares, cold sweats, flashbacks. I try not to but it just comes on you and that's it. The smell of him. I can smell him Br Marc. I hear people say now, 'Oh, this is an historical thing.' It's not historical for me. I can reach out my hand and touch it.

When he first left Daingean, Noel tried to live with his family in Limerick but that didn't work out. Within a short time he ended up in trouble again after breaking into a house in the city. He struggled to lead a normal life but the ghosts of Daingean kept shadow-boxing around him every day. He moved to London where he ended up sleeping rough in derelict houses. During this time he met other young Irishmen also sleeping on London's streets who were former inmates of industrial schools like Daingean. They too were broken people. None of them ever spoke about their horrendous experiences in the institutions; instead they buried their pasts in deep psychological vaults. Noel survived in London by making a bit of money selling hotdogs, washing windows and unloading produce from the fruit lorries in Covent Garden.

> We'd get our veg for our home made stew in the squat . . . It was a lot better than being raped.

After a while he returned to Ireland, where he drifted into a cycle of crime and anti-social behaviour and he spent several spells in various prisons, including Mountjoy and Limerick. The fall-out from Daingean had made Noel vulnerable to mood swings, he was plagued by frequent bouts of depression and he had a tendency to self-harm. Noel's outbursts of anger and recurring violence towards others led to his admittance to psychiatric units in various institutions when he was in his twenties. These included the Central Mental Hospital in Dundrum where, at one stage, he was declared insane. He also attempted bizarre suicidal acts. Once he injected himself with a syringe full of urine. On another occasion, while in Mountjoy prison, he set fire to himself in his cell and suffered serious burns. He had to spend over 10 weeks in hospital as a result.

> I was drinking raw bottles of brandy. I tried to see how long it would take me to have a heart attack. [I was] staying in an old scruffy flat falling down on top of me.
>
> I'm lucky to be here today I've tried so many stupid things in my time. Some of them [victims of religious institutional abuse] live with it and cope with it. Some of them do it better than others.

Noel had significant problems controlling his anger when he was younger and he found it almost impossible to trust anyone or have a lasting intimate relationship with a woman. When he was 19, he got married and had three children but that relationship broke up. He went on to form a relationship with another woman and they had six children together. At the time of writing, they were not living together because of his psycho-emotional difficulties.

> I can't even live with myself so how on earth can I live with anybody else.

When Noel left Daingean, he was unable to distinguish positive sexual activity from negative sexual patterns. On one occasion, when his partner kissed him on the nipple, he broke her jaw after her physical affections catapulted him back to the bakery when Br Marc used to maul and rape him. A series of personal tragedies marred Noel Kelly's ability to establish long-term stability. In 1994 he went into a deep depression after being involved in a serious road accident. He became very disturbed and ended up smashing his own pottery shop in Limerick.

When the Commission to Inquire into Child Abuse was originally established in 2000, Noel got intensely involved in highlighting the abuse of children in the religious institutions and in May 2001 he protested outside Dáil Éireann. At one point during his very intensive campaign, he doused his body all over with petrol and set fire to himself and sustained serious burns to his feet, legs and buttocks. More family tragedy rocked Noel's psychological wellbeing. In 2003 he was re-admitted to the psychiatric unit attached to Limerick Regional Hospital for treatment when he had once again tried to hang himself after one of his sons committed suicide.

> He took his life when he was twenty-five on the day of his birthday. He got involved in drugs and taking drugs. He was into that scene . . . I had seen him two nights before he done it . . . he hung himself off a railway bridge.

Noel Kelly had kept Daingean's dark secrets locked away for over three decades. But in 2003, after his son's death, he started attending a clinical psychologist and for the first time in his life he began to discuss the sexual and emotional abuse he had suffered at Daingean. The secure and sympathetic environment provided by the psychologist enabled him to release the demons that had shackled him for so long.

> At first it took me a while. But after two sessions I had my mind made up to go all the way with him . . . We kept it too long to ourselves but what could we do? Every day we kept it to ourselves, we were making the situation worse. We were getting more bitter and more frustrated. Some of us were getting more dangerous. And then we started to inflict it on other people; not the abuse but the hurt. We had no respect for nothing or anybody.

Noel's therapy work has been beneficial but, as for so many other survivors of institutional abuse, it will not reverse the permanent damage that was done to him in Daingean.

> I still wake up every morning of my life with Daingean and I go to sleep every night with Daingean.

Today Noel Kelly lives on his own in a flat in Limerick City.

Chapter 3 ∾

MICHAEL O'BRIEN AND FERRYHOUSE

On Sunday, 24 May 2009, four days after the publication of the Ryan Report, Michael O'Brien was a guest on my radio show, 'The Wide Angle' on Newstalk. We were broadcasting a special three-hour programme on the Report and Michael had travelled up from Clonmel to talk about his experiences in St Joseph's Industrial School, Ferryhouse, Clonmel. This miserable institution, which was run by the Rosminian Brothers, was described in the Ryan Report as a place where the use of corporal punishment was 'pervasive, excessive, unpredictable and without regulation'.[1] Ryan stated that sexual abuse was systemic in Ferryhouse and 'that it was not seen as a crime but as a moral lapse and weakness'.[2] The Ferryhouse buildings were 'poor, unhygienic, inadequate and often overcrowded'[3] and the boys were 'hungry and poorly clothed'.[4]

The atmosphere in the studio was electric when Michael described how he had been raped by a Rosminian priest shortly after his arrival in Ferryhouse.

> I'm going [to] call him a bastard because that's what he was. I'm sorry to have to say this in public, to call a human being a bastard, but he wasn't a human being. We were destroyed for life.[5]

Michael broke down in tears during the interview. It was one of the most compelling pieces of radio I had ever heard. After his appearance on my show he was contacted by the RTÉ 'Questions and Answers' programme, and was asked to go on the show the following night. Michael agreed to do so. During the show, he confronted the Fianna Fáil

Minister Noel Dempsey, who was one of the panellists. He criticised Mr Dempsey for the adversarial way survivors of abuse had been treated by the Commission to Inquire into Child Abuse and he accused him of not understanding the suffering endured by children in industrial schools. His riveting outburst prompted a review of the financial compensation paid by the Congregations to the Redress Board and they were pressured to contribute more funds.

In August 2009 I met up with Michael O'Brien to hear the harrowing details of his childhood. He told me his life began to unravel in 1942 when a man and a woman arrived at his home in Clonmel and dragged him and seven of his siblings out of their house. Michael was eight at the time. Up until then, his childhood had been a happy one even though times were tough in Ireland during the Emergency years and the O'Briens struggled to survive as most other Irish families did in that era. But Mary O'Brien always ensured there was enough food on the table for her children.

'I never remember being hungry,'[6] said Michael as he fondly recalled a typical Sunday dinner when the 15-strong O'Brien family would sit around the large kitchen table in front of a glowing fire.

> There'd be a dish of cabbage, a pig's head and a big pot of spuds in the middle of the table. That was our Sunday dinner and boy was it gorgeous.

There were 13 children in the O'Brien family. They all lived together in a modest two-storey cottage in the small rural village of Newtownadam outside Clonmel. Michael's father John worked for the local council as a labourer. Young Michael got on well with his siblings and his childhood memories of the family home are happy ones.

> We were always looking after one another and we'd be out playing houses or hopscotch . . . Sometimes we'd have to go out and turn the cow patches and bring them in when they were dry and we used to burn them. They were as good as any turf that you'd get in any bog to burn. And I remember going off for sticks for the fire . . . We used to thin beet for farmers and the mother would be thinning them and the pram would be on the head with the youngest child. And half ways through we'd have the sandwiches and the brown cake and

the country butter and the tea out of the billie can. It was brilliant.

Michael remembered his mother as a gentle woman with long red hair that used to spook superstitious farmers in the neighbourhood.

> One of the farmers would be coming down the boreen with his cattle and he'd ask her to stay inside in the house because it was bad luck to see a red-haired woman first thing in the morning.

Mary O'Brien was an accomplished cook who would bake up to 10 cakes of bread a week to feed her large family.

> They'd be all out on the window and I'd sneak up and grab one and run off with it and put some butter on it when it was hot. It was gorgeous. I can still smell the bread when I talk about it. I can actually smell the bread baking in a round kind of pot and you'd put cinders on top as well as underneath. It was beautiful bread.

In February 1942 Michael's halcyon childhood was shattered to pieces when a telegram arrived announcing the death of his beloved mother in Clonmel Hospital. She had contracted pneumonia after giving birth to her thirteenth child. After Mary O'Brien's death all hell broke loose in the O'Brien household. Shortly after her funeral, a man and a woman from the National Society for the Prevention of Cruelty to Children arrived at the O'Brien home.

> I still can see them coming in with the two big black cars outside … This man and woman came in and he started taking us out one by one. I remember the woman taking the baby from my sister's arms. And I remember her taking the other children. The other two girls were screaming at being taken out. We were all screaming. We were just put into a car and taken away and that's the last time I seen the inside of my house.

John O'Brien was out working at the time and wasn't there to stop the irreversible disintegration of his family. It was a terrifying experience for the traumatised children who had no idea why they were being taken away from their home. Michael's older sister screamed and pleaded with the 'cruelty' woman not to take the newborn baby to whom she desperately clung. Michael was grabbed and shoved into the car before he could say goodbye to his older sisters. The horrified children were then driven to Clonmel where they were hauled before a judge in the town's District Court. The drab grey building was an intimidating place for the O'Brien children, who huddled together in petrified bewilderment. They were still missing their mother and they wished their father would come to take them home.

> I remember there were big black flags on the floor. And I'll always remember a woman coming in and giving us a packet of broken biscuits. At that time you'd get broken biscuits in Woolworths for tuppence or a penny. That's all the food we got for the whole day. This man that took us didn't care if we had food or not.

The judge declared that the O'Brien children were destitute and that they should be sent to industrial schools. Michael and three of his brothers were to be held at Ferryhouse until they were 16 years old. The youngest boy was sent to Cappoquin and the three girls were sentenced to a convent in Cashel. Michael O'Brien is still indignant that the judge declared them destitute.

> I don't believe we were destitute. Destitution means you are lying there with nothing whatsoever. We were being fed. We were being looked after. We were being sent to school. So what was wrong?

He believes that money was the motivating factor for their incarceration.

> I believe that Ferryhouse [the Rosminians] or somebody went to him [the cruelty man] and said that they were short of people in institutions and they wanted extra people to keep up the capitation grant. And I maintain to this day that that was how we were sent in there because there was no reason whatsoever to send us in there. And the judge that done it was completely wrong. These people didn't care about any human beings at all. They were feathering their own nests all along the way and I'm talking about the government as well as everybody else. They were as much

responsible as if they perpetrated the crime themselves. It was a crime to send us to Ferryhouse. As far as I'm concerned the government committed a crime as much as the judge did.

The O'Brien children were wrenched apart. After the judge handed down the sentences, Michael and his three brothers were ordered into a car. They didn't even get the chance to say goodbye to their sisters and younger brother. As they drove away, they watched the little girls crying outside the courthouse.

It was done in an inhumane fashion. There was no pity, no nothing there for us. We were treated like animals.

The four boys were driven a few miles down the road to Ferryhouse. For Michael O'Brien, that journey marked the beginning of an eight-year stint of hell and a childhood destroyed by sexual, physical and psychological abuse. When Michael and his brothers arrived at Ferryhouse, they trembled at the sight of the high walls that surrounded the institution. It was a formidable, unwelcoming place. The boys were taken into a yard that was packed with around 200 boys who stared at them.

I remember arriving in Ferryhouse yard and all these boys looking at you . . . I remember one fella tried to take the biscuits off Eamon [brother] but we all gathered around and he didn't get away with it.

A Rosminian Brother told the boys to follow him to the washroom where they had to wash in cold water. Their hair was cut and their own clothes were taken off them.

We were given these old baggy short pants and very old pairs of shoes. We weren't even given socks. There was no underwear.

Within hours of his arrival at Ferryhouse, Michael got his first taste of the Rosminians' cruelty. After the boys put on the old shabby clothes they were sent out into the yard where the Brothers barked at them to get into lines and march to the church for benediction. It was the first time Michael had been to a benediction and he had no idea what to do.

His confusion caught the attention of one of the Brothers, who belted him ferociously on the back of his head when he failed to join his hands to pray. The thump was so hard the stunned little boy hit his forehead against the pew in front of him and he was knocked unconscious.

> Some time after I woke up outside. I was lying down outside in the cloisters with a couple of people around me. That was the first time I ever got a clap in my life.

That night Michael and his brother Eamon were taken to a huge dormitory that was lined with rows of beds packed together. Thin bedclothes covered old grey mattresses that were shabby and uncomfortable. Michael shared his bed with Eamon, who was a fragile, vulnerable youngster. From that night on, he would always look out for Eamon during their harsh years in Ferryhouse. The lonely young lads were absolutely terrified. They grieved for their late mother and ached for their father and siblings. The two boys clung to one another as they longed to be back in the warm loving atmosphere of their family home. They slept fitfully that night and when dawn broke the next day they were roughly ordered out of bed and given tasks to complete.

Within days of his arrival at Ferryhouse, Michael O'Brien's childhood was irrevocably destroyed when he was sexually abused by one of the Brothers. He still has nightmares of that terrifying incident and he wakes up in a sweat after his dreams are visited by a towering dark figure looming over his bed. On that unforgettable night, when he was first sexually assaulted, the Brother in charge of Michael's dormitory walked into the large room and came up to Michael's bed.

> I was lying in bed. And shortly after lights out this Brother instead came down to me and he said, 'Come with me.' I followed him.

Br Mick[7] yanked the young boy out of his bed and he took him to his own bedroom outside the dormitory.

> He started messing around with me then.

The Brother pulled down his own pants and forced the young boy to lick and fondle his penis so that he could masturbate in front of him.

That was the first time anyone ever done anything like that to me. And to this day I would say I honestly didn't know what he was doing. I didn't even know if it was wrong or right. But this bastard done that to me . . . It was the most frightening thing that ever happened me in my eight years up to then . . .

This so and so comes along and changes the rest of my life for good. He changed the rest of my life at eight years of age.

After the Brother masturbated, he sent Michael back to the dormitory.

I came out and went into the bed with Eamon. And I said to him, 'Are you all right?' He said he was and I kind of went into a sleep that I was awake. The least thing would make me jump up in the bed again.

Michael was sexually assaulted by that particular Brother on several occasions. The following night he returned to the young lad's dormitory and once again yanked him out of his bed and forced him to engage in oral sex with him in his pokey bedroom. At the time a lay supervisor was in a room adjoining the dormitory and he was supposed to be looking after the boys.

I maintain that the man who was in the room watching the boys knew what was going on. To this day I believe he knew what was going on.

This second assault was much more violent. Michael doesn't understand what happened that night but Br Mick lost his temper and lashed out at the young boy when he was assaulting him.

Whatever went wrong that night while he was doing it he either kicked me or hit me a belt of the fist. And to this day I think he was trying to penetrate me but it didn't work and he lost it. I fell on the floor and he either hit me or kicked me but I ended up with a big black eye the following morning. The eye was actually cut.

The next day when Michael was walking in the yard, the Rector of Ferryhouse, who was riddled with arthritis, came up to him and asked him how he had got a black eye.

> He was a dirty so and so. He was full of arthritis and I hope he
> suffered all his life from it.

When Michael told him about the Brother's assault, the Rector went
into a rage and shouted at him to get out of his sight. He warned him
never to say anything about the abuse to anyone. That night Br Mick
returned to his bedside. This time he carried a long leather strap in his
hand. He was seething with anger and the veins in his forehead were
throbbing beneath his thin skin. He roared at the two boys to get out of
the bed and he ordered Michael to remove his clothes. Eamon, who was
petrified with fear, curled himself up in a ball by the bed.

> He made me lie across the bed without a stitch of clothes on me and
> he gave me the most vicious hiding I have ever got in my life that
> night. I had never got slapped or hit even in the school . . . It was
> unbelievable what he done to me with the strap . . . That landed on
> my body everywhere and anywhere.

Michael suspects that the Rector had told Br Mick what Michael had
said to him in the yard earlier that day and the paedophile was
determined to seek revenge. The lights were on in the dormitory and
the other boys witnessed Br Mick's frenzied attack on the helpless young
fellow.

> They are monsters. They were monsters. And they are monsters
> forever. When you look up at someone with a big strap what do you
> think but that he is only a monster?

By the time Br Mick finally stopped flaying his victim he had expended
all of his energy and he left the dormitory without saying anything else.
Michael was in agony from the pain of the lashings and he curled up in
the bed next to Eamon, who was shaking and weeping. The two boys
began to absorb the awful fact that they were facing years of
unremitting misery in that heinous place.

> I cried myself to sleep in agony. Nobody bothered. Nobody cared in

the world. What was wrong? What in the name of Jesus was wrong that somebody didn't care? What was wrong with this country? Why did they treat children like that? And they ask us today to forgive them.

After that night, Br Mick left Michael alone for a while. But several months later he started to force him again into giving him oral sex in his bedroom. One day out of the blue the abuse stopped and Br Mick left him alone for the rest of his time in Ferryhouse. Michael suspects that he had sourced other boys to abuse and that he got a sexual thrill from hunting down new prey. But that was not the end of the sexual abuse. A couple of years later, when Michael was around 13, he was targeted again by another sexual predator, this time a Rosminian priest, Fr Joe.[8]

I hadn't been sexually abused for a number of years. I thought it was over and done with. But then this man arrived. Now he had been a Brother but he never touched me when he was a Brother.

The first time it happened was a Saturday. I was coming in from the playing fields that were around Ferryhouse. And he called me and he said, 'O'Brien, come here.' He brought me into the laundry which was a big room for doing the sheets. It had big tumblers and washing machines and all of that sort of thing.

The priest pulled down Michael's pants and forced him to lie over a table while he unzipped his own trousers. Then he raped him. He was frothing at the mouth as he came all over the boy. But sexual satisfaction was not enough for this sadist. After he raped Michael, he beat him to a pulp and told him to get out of the laundry room. It was as if he blamed Michael for the abuse.

He was a vicious human being. He was a complete animal. This man wasn't satisfied with abusing me, he gave me a hiding afterwards as well. And the following morning he put Holy Communion in my mouth. That man should have died a horrible death on the altar that morning if there was any justice or any God at that time. And I would have been delighted . . . It was a sacrilege that he was saying Mass the following morning.

I remember it as if it only happened today. I could hardly walk after it. And to this day, only I can't prove it, I know he done the same thing to my younger brother.

I seen Eamon doing something the way I'd do and crunch up after it [rape] happened. He had the same antics as I'd have but he took it worse than I did. He used to come into the corner and fold up his body knowing that something very bad was happening and I'd go over and he'd just tell me to go away.

Several years after leaving Ferryhouse, Eamon phoned Michael and told him he wanted to meet him in Cashel because he had something very important to tell him that would shock him. Michael believes Eamon was going to reveal that he had been sexually abused in Ferryhouse. The two men arranged to meet in a pub in the town but Eamon clammed up and he never discussed his secrets with Michael. Shortly after their meeting, Eamon left for England and the next time Michael saw him was when he was in a coma in hospital after being knocked down by a car in a hit and run accident. He died shortly afterwards.

Sexual abuse was a harrowing part of life in Ferryhouse for Michael O'Brien. He was raped in the laundry room over and over again by Fr Joe, sometimes up to two or three times a week. The rapes were sometimes followed by a beating, depending on the priest's mood at the time. The abuse lasted for around five months but the psychological damage was permanent.

[He raped me] when he felt like it or when he wasn't with anybody else. This fella was a genuine paedophile that couldn't do without it.

Michael O'Brien suspects Fr Joe raped other boys in Ferryhouse when he was there. After his appearance on RTÉ's 'Questions and Answers', he was inundated with queries and visits from former inmates of Ferryhouse. Men came to his office and, in confidence, discussed their experiences of sexual abuse at the hands of Fr Joe.

After Michael was raped by Fr Joe in Ferryhouse, he vowed to himself that some day he would seek revenge against the man who had ruined his life. When he left Ferryhouse he was too ashamed to tell anyone about the sexual abuse and he never went to the Gardaí to press charges because he felt he would not be believed.

If I had said this about sexual abuse I would have been ostracised. I would have been made out to be a liar and I still wasn't believed until the [Ryan] Commission report came out and then they believed us. No one believed us up to that.

Michael was determined to apply his own justice to Fr Joe and, in 1993, when he was Mayor of Clonmel, he travelled with his wife Mary to Upton, where Fr Joe was living in a retirement home run by the Rosminians. His intention was to kill the ageing paedophile. He brought a bottle of whiskey with him to give to the priest. His plan was to follow him up to his room with the whiskey where he would then choke him. But when he met Fr Joe, who was by then riddled with arthritis, he realised the ailing man was nearly dying and there was no point in killing him.

I was delighted when I seen him so bad. He was decrepit and dribbling and his flap was open in his pants and he had white cigarette ashes all over his clothes.

Michael demanded to know why the old man had ruined his life by sexually abusing him in Ferryhouse.

I turned on him and I said, 'Why?' And he said, 'Oh Michael, they were the times and I'm sorry.' And I said, 'Who the fuck did you think you were? Do you know you ruined my life forever?' I said to him that 'Due to the fact that you've one foot in the grave, I'll leave you die out.' But if he was in any way physically able I'd have killed him.

Michael's hatred for the feeble paedophile was so deep he gave little thought to the consequences of murdering him even though they would have been detrimental.

I didn't care about the consequences. I needed revenge against him in particular ... This man was with more than me and he knew what he had done. But as far as I'm concerned he didn't care ... for the religious orders the most important thing for them was the protection of the order and they would protect the order no matter what they were doing and that's what they were doing, they were protecting the order.

After Michael left Fr Joe that day, he got a certain satisfaction from the knowledge that the ailing priest was in poor health, but it was not enough to eradicate the deep hatred and anger he felt towards him.

I hate this man. I really hate the man. I always will . . . I can't forgive. Why forgive for something that they done? Why should we forgive? . . . I will never forgive the sexual abuse because it should never ever have happened.

When Michael rejoined his wife that day he never told her about his plan to kill Fr Joe. Instead he kept his mercurial intentions a secret from her for years and it would take him decades to open up about the sexual abuse he had endured at Ferryhouse.

Ferryhouse to me was a hellhole and always will be. Ferryhouse was a place that you were sent to be looked after. You were supposed to be properly fed and properly clothed and educated and prepared for afterwards. None of them were done properly. We were badly fed and badly clothed. We were made to do slave work out on farms around the place. We got no education. I have no certification of education anywhere. I haven't even a primary cert.

Life at Ferryhouse was an insufferable combination of abuse, deprivation and hard work. The boys' days began with a shrill awakening when they were routed out of their beds at 7am. They would then go to the washrooms where they washed themselves in cold water in rows of wash-hand basins. In winter they would shiver on the cold slabs as they doused themselves with freezing cold water. The boys were always on their guard in case they caught the ire of one of the Brothers or lay workers who would walk up and down the washrooms inspecting the proceedings.

I'll always remember a man there and he had a piss pot and he'd come along and he'd dip that down in the ice cold water and throw it down on top of you. And it would go down on your back and your pants. That's how you'd have to stay for the day in your wet pants in the freezing cold in the middle of winter.

Michael shivered as he recalled how he could still feel the icy cold water being thrown down his back by one particular lay worker.

The people in jails for serious crimes were better treated than we were and better fed and better looked after than we were. And why I do not know. We were the children of the State who were supposed to be protected by the State. But we weren't. We were abused by the State and by the religious orders and the Catholic Church.

What they done down there was unbelievable. Beating us for nothing at all. Walking us around the yard and you don't know when you'd get a belt for nothing on the back of the head or the side of the face.

After their wash, the boys were marched off to the large refectory for a paltry breakfast of bread dipped in jam with a half cup of cocoa or tea in enamel mugs. Paint fell from the damp ceilings of the grim hall, which was lined with long tables of ravenous boys. Hunger was a permanent feature in Ferryhouse as it was in many other industrial schools at the time, but while the half-starved youngsters fought over crumbs, the Brothers enjoyed substantial breakfasts of bacon, egg and sausages in their own dining hall. After breakfast, the boys were supposed to go to school but they received little education in Ferryhouse. Michael was almost illiterate when he left at 16 as he had spent most of his time there working.

While you were in school someone would come in and say, 'You, you, and you out!' And you were put into a truck or a farmer's tractor and trailer or maybe a horse and cart and you were taken away to these farms and you would work there for the day picking stones or beet or potatoes or saving hay. I remember on several occasions raking the hay with my hands. We were all put in a line along the field and you'd get thistles and that night you couldn't even bend your fingers with the pain in them and in your bare feet. The horse that was bringing in the hay was better looked after than we were. He got fed. He got oats in the evening and he was put into a stable with straw. The animal that was working in the field was better looked after than we were.

Up to 10 boys could end up working on any one of the local farms. They frequently slaved away until 7 or 8 at night, especially in the summer when hay or beet had to be reaped. Sometimes they worked all day without any food depending on the farmers in charge, but they never got paid a penny for their work.

> Some farmers were nice, others were not ... The farmers were poor at that time too and for a farmer to feed ten children would cost him a nice penny.

By using the boys as child labourers, the farmers colluded in the Brothers' exploitation of the children and turned a blind eye to their willing acceptance of the boys' hard work during school hours.

> They wouldn't have known about the sexual abuse or the beatings but they would have known that we were being sent out. They probably thought at that time that we were being fed.

When the boys at Ferryhouse were not out on neighbouring farms, they were frequently used to work on the land attached to the industrial school. St Joseph's was self-sufficient and produced its own vegetables and eggs and reared its own chickens and cattle. But the boys rarely got to taste the produce they toiled so hard on. While the Rosminian Brothers and priests enjoyed fresh produce from their own farms, the boys in their care were half-starved.

> When school was over you went to your workshops. We had a shoe shop, a tailor shop, a knitting shop. Why they were teaching boys knitting I will never know and that's where I got stuck.

Sunday was the boys' only day of rest from the interminable work. Sometimes they went for walks in the neighbouring fields where they would scavenge for crab apples, plums and sloes to relieve the hunger. There was no let up in the abuse and beatings that were a daily part of life at Ferryhouse.

You were in fear of getting a clattering or getting a hiding for no reason at all . . . I always maintain that these beatings that we got were sexually orientated. They were getting their kick by doing this and seeing bare kids being dragged across them and being beaten. Some of them were frothing out of the mouth when they were doing it. They were bastards. They're all in hell now anyway.

Michael will never forget one ferocious flogging he received shortly before he left St Joseph's in 1950. He was nearly 16 at the time and he had been put in charge of cleaning and washing one of the elderly Brothers.

I'd have to go up to him in the morning to bring him up bottles of water to wash him and take him out of bed and then put him back into bed which was wrong. I shouldn't have been doing it. Boys shouldn't have been allowed to mix on their own with people like that although he never done anything to me. He was a decrepit old so and so.

One Sunday morning Michael went into the kitchen to collect hot water for Br Gus.[9] He bumped into the Rector in the kitchen. The two talked for a while and the Rector told Michael he was going off to Knock to say Mass. At that time it was a spiritual requirement to fast for 12 hours before attending Mass. When Michael went up to Br Gus he told him he had met the Rector just before he left for Mass, but he never mentioned anything about breakfast. But when Br Gus relayed the story later he twisted the facts and said Michael had squealed on the Rector and told him he had broken his fast.

At three o'clock that day this big Brother called me in [to his room]. 'Strip off and get over that chair,' he said. And I said, 'For what?' and he said, 'You told Br Gus the Rector went to Knock after having his breakfast.' 'Oh no I didn't,' I said. 'You did!' he said and he started to beat me with a leather strap. And with that another one of them came in and he started beating me as well.

Michael managed to run out of the room and he fell into the arms of a priest, who shouted at the two Brothers to leave him alone. He ordered Michael to get dressed and to get out of the room. Michael met that same priest in 2003 when he gave evidence to the Ryan Commission. He had been brought back from Rome by the Rosminians to deny allegations of abuse. When he met Michael he denied all knowledge of that day and he claimed he had never met Michael O'Brien in his life.

And that same priest who saved me that day told me he never knew me, he never heard of me or he never saw me in his life.

The isolation from loved ones in Ferryhouse was paralysing. Michael can remember his father visiting him only once during his incarceration. That sole visit was on the day the children were originally taken away from their family home.

I remember he came to Ferryhouse that evening. I seen him in the distance. I knew 'twas him. He was trying to take us out but seemingly he was hunted away by the Brothers and priests that was there.

It seems that John O'Brien abandoned his children once they entered the high walls of the industrial schools they had been sent to. His absence from their lives angered Michael when he was in Ferryhouse, especially on the days when the parents of other boys came to visit their children.

My father should have kept the family together. If he went away himself he should have kept in touch with us all. My mother would never have left us. Nothing would ever have happened [to us]. And even if he was gone, and my mother was there, nothing would ever have happened. No way would Mary O'Brien have ever let any one of us be taken away.

Michael believes his father may have appealed to the courts to reverse the decision to incarcerate his children but his efforts were futile.

Yet the law stated that if a parent was opposed to his children being put in they shouldn't have been put in. Everything was done under cover. Everything was done to demonise the children, to treat the children like animals. No way were we ever to be treated like human beings again.

It seems that John O'Brien left Ireland shortly after his children were taken from him. He first travelled to Liverpool where he stayed with his sister and later moved to Scotland and married a woman who had one child from a previous relationship. He did not keep in contact with his own children, who were left to fend for themselves amid the brutality of their childhood prisons.

> I half blame my father for what happened. I maintain he shouldn't have got married again. He should have made sure we were all right. I would do that today. That's my nature.

John O'Brien's departure from Ireland meant the end of the family home.

> I remember for some reason [at one stage] in Ferryhouse they sent everybody home. And we had to go home as well, the three of us, Seannie [Michael's younger brother, who was later sent to Ferryhouse], Eamon and myself. But when we went to the homestead there was no one there. They told us we had a sister in Clonmel and she was the same sister I went to afterwards. So I went into her and she got us put up by a neighbour. So we had to stay with the neighbour for the holidays and we actually slept on the floor of the kitchen, the three of us together. But we didn't want to go home [after that] because we knew there was no one at home.

Michael did not see his father again until many years later, when he returned home for a visit from the UK. By then Michael was working as a chef in the Army barracks in Templemore. It was a tense reunion.

> I arranged for a bed and breakfast for him. That's all I could afford at the time. And my mother-in-law fed him and looked after him . . . I remember him at the station [when he was returning to England] looking for a pound that I owed him. I had borrowed a pound off him during the trip when we were going around. I was short of money for something and he paid for it and he looked for it back at the station and I gave it to him.

John O'Brien didn't express any remorse for virtually abandoning his children in the industrial schools. During a second trip home Michael confronted his father about his desertion of all of them.

> At the meeting the second time I wasn't too happy at all. I was beginning to say, 'Look, let's call a spade a spade here. You didn't do anything.' So I was up in my sister's house one day and he gave out to my younger sister who was also living up there. And I said, 'Stop! Stop! You gave up that job long ago. That's my job now. Any controlling that has to be done with the family in Ireland I'll do it even though I'm not the oldest. Stay clear of it and leave it.' And that was the last time I spoke to my father.

Michael never saw his father alive again. He did not even know he had died until a family member informed him. He still struggles to forgive his father for abandoning his children to the religious tyrants.

> It still makes me angry. But you see do I blame him or do I blame the State for breaking up the family? I blame the State. The State gave money to an institution to look after me. Why didn't they give that to my father? It would have made him a very rich man.

The religious orders were adept at creating chasms between family members. Siblings who entered institutions at very young ages grew up sometimes oblivious to the fact that they had other brothers and sisters in the same institution. In some cases a child would be given special treatment to make other siblings jealous. When the O'Brien children were originally separated in 1942, Michael's younger brother, Seannie, was sent to Cappoquin, where he soon lost all contact with his older brothers. They never knew what had happened to him. It later transpired that Seannie was taken to Ferryhouse when he was about five or six. But the young boy was never told he had older brothers also resident there. The Rosminians kept Seannie's identity a secret from Michael and his brothers for two and a half years. They only discovered the truth about him when their older sister began to make enquiries. She became concerned when she discovered that Seannie had left Cappoquin and she went to the courthouse in Clonmel to report the young boy missing. It was only then that the courts revealed to her that Seannie had been sent to Ferryhouse. She was stunned at the news and she went to tell the rest of the O'Brien boys. They were all then summoned by the Rector to meet their younger brother.

> We were called into the office and there were two civilians there. And the Rector was there and he said, 'This is your brother, Seannie. This is the boy who was sent to Cappoquin. Out you go.' And that was it.

It was nearly impossible for the O'Brien boys to rebuild the family bonds with their younger brother. The brutality of Ferryhouse had shattered the close-knit ties they had enjoyed before their mother died.

> They tore families asunder. They wreaked complete families ... once we were taken away the family bond broke. If a great friend of mine died, I'd be very upset about it. If my brother died I mightn't be that upset about it because I haven't lived with him and I haven't been with him.
>
> The family tie is not there. There's no use in saying it is. I keep saying this. There's no point in saying it's there because it's not. That was part of the system — to break the family.

Michael O'Brien finally left Ferryhouse when he was just about to turn 16. It was his first taste of freedom in eight years. Initially he worked as a messenger boy in a fish shop in Clonmel delivering fish to people in the town.

> I had to learn how to ride a bicycle. I didn't tell them I didn't know how to. I used to walk it initially. They used to ask me why I was always late because I wasn't cycling at the time.

In 1952, when he was 18, Michael joined the Army and began a new life working as a chef for the Defence Forces.

> The Army was a great place for comradeship. You'd make great friends in the Army. My Army career was brilliant. I didn't get very far but I had a great life in the Army. It was a good clean life and I served overseas.

He first met his future wife Mary at ballroom dancing classes in Dublin.

The couple married in 1955 and had four children together. Michael was lucky. His marriage has been strong and lasting but the psychological fall-out from Ferryhouse left him initially confused about his own sexuality and awkward with women.

It took me an awful long time to take up with women or even to be in their company. That was probably bred into us that women were bad, that they were demons.

It took Michael many years to pluck up the courage to tell Mary about the sexual abuse he had suffered in Ferryhouse as he was terrified she would leave him if she discovered the truth.

To hide that from her was a massive thing for me, to make sure I never mentioned it . . . It's the shame of it. There's a wicked shame attached to this.

In 1999 Michael attended a public meeting in Dublin on the Commission to Inquire into Child Abuse in religious institutions. During the meeting, Michael made a reference to the sexual abuse he had experienced at Ferryhouse. It was the first time he had mentioned it in public. That night he told Mary the full truth about his harrowing childhood in Ferryhouse.

It was out and things were rough for a while between us. It had nothing to do with sexual abuse. It was the idea that I didn't confide in her or my children. That was the problem. They would have wanted to help me in every way as they still do today.

Michael O'Brien went on to become involved in local Irish politics. He was a Fianna Fáil councillor in Co. Tipperary and was elected Mayor of Clonmel in 1993. He continues to campaign for survivors of institutional abuse through his organisation, Right to Peace.

Chapter 4

THE GIRL WITH THE BROKEN HEART: TERESA GORMLEY AND THE SISTERS OF MERCY

Teresa Gormley's story epitomises the infinite void that can never be filled when a childhood is snatched away and a warm loving home replaced by a cold and cruel institution. Her 14-year incarceration in two industrial schools robbed her of a future happiness and left her emotionally paralysed from utter loneliness.

I first met Teresa at the March of Solidarity for survivors of institutional abuse in Dublin in June 2009. She was standing close to the makeshift stage where representatives of survivor groups addressed the packed streets. She held a home-made placard in her hands that had the words 'love', 'mother', 'father', 'presents', 'Christmas', 'joy', 'birthdays' and other references to the essential ingredients of a happy childhood that she had missed out on. Teresa was different from the majority of the survivors who shifted uneasily around her. Her calm demeanour contrasted sharply with their anguished faces. She seemed more like a sympathetic bystander than a survivor herself. I later discovered that she had developed a tranquil exterior to disguise a gnawing loneliness that constantly hovers around her. She's never succeeded in shaking off the emptiness inside her ever since she was forced from her home and put into the care of the Sisters of Mercy.

When Teresa Gormley received psychological counselling many years after suffering abuse in industrial schools, she confronted the harrowing memories of her stolen childhood. During intense relaxation sessions, she saw a little girl sitting all alone on the floor of a large room that was entirely empty except for two chairs. The child was bawling crying and Teresa longed to pick her up and hug her. Her therapist explained to her that she was actually seeing herself as an abandoned little girl in the first religious institution she was put into and that she was trying to rescue her own damaged childhood like a ghost fighting to come back from the dead.

Teresa has deep emotional scars from her traumatic experiences in both industrial schools. While she certainly sustained physical abuse, the overriding damage was caused by the psychological persecution that was inflicted with rigorous application by the Sisters of Mercy who ran both institutions. The constant degradation of her confidence, the erosion of her self-esteem and the denial of any love left her permanently yearning to fill the loveless void of her childhood.

> I don't remember one day of love in my life growing up. Not one. I don't ever remember anyone picking me up when I fell or when I was sick. The biggest loss in my life is love.

Teresa Gormley was only a toddler when she was wrenched from her home and brought to Ennis District Court where a judge declared her the victim of improper guardianship. Up until then, she had lived with her parents, two sisters and three brothers in the Turnpike in Ennis, Co. Clare. Times were hard for the Gormleys. Her father was a builder's labourer who didn't make much money and Mary Gormley struggled to keep her children fed and clothed.

In October 1956, when Teresa was two and a half, her mother died of blood poisoning after giving birth to twins. Several days before her death, the 32-year-old had fallen near her house and cut her knee. She became ill and went into an early labour and gave birth at home. The young mother's problems were exacerbated when she developed complications after the births and she refused to go into hospital. She was dead within days. The twins also passed away.

> She had a doctor in attendance all right. They had the pints of blood hanging over the door going into her so she probably lost a lot of blood.

Within a fortnight of Mary Gormley's death, the family was torn apart.

Although she has no direct memories of those harrowing days, Teresa
has tried to piece together the events that led to her incarceration in
religious institutions for the next 14 years. It seems her father was
incapable of looking after his children. Teresa believes State officials got
wind of their dire circumstances and, 14 days after her mother's death,
they organised a visit to the Gormley home by the ISPCC[1] who came to
take some of the children into care.

> My father couldn't take care of six of us. We were very poor anyway
> I know that but sure who wasn't poor in those times?

That day, four of the Gormley children were removed from their home
and brought to Ennis District Court. The decisions taken that day
severed the children's close sibling bonds and they were never able to re-
establish them as adults. The court declared that Teresa and her older
sister should be committed to Our Lady's Industrial School in Ennis,
which was run by the Sisters of Mercy. Several years later she was
transferred to Mount St Vincent's Industrial School in Limerick. Her
younger brother, John,[2] who was only one year old at the time, was sent
to an institution for babies and young children in Killarney. He later
ended up in the wretched St Joseph's Industrial School in Glin, Co.
Limerick, which was run by the Christian Brothers.

John's experiences there were so horrific he went to England as a
young man and he cut all ties with his family. Over the years, Teresa
made numerous attempts to trace her younger brother but she got
nowhere. Today she doesn't even know if he is alive or dead. Her two
older brothers were left at home with their father while her eldest sister
was also committed to an industrial school.

> I know she was in one [industrial school] but where she was I don't
> know. She won't ever talk about it. She ran away from it apparently
> ... She wants to forget about that part of her life. She won't speak
> about that. I've never asked her because I know she doesn't want it
> to be known.

Teresa's life changed dramatically after her committal to Our Lady's.
The nuns ran the industrial school with a military-like precision where
rules and regulations replaced compassion and love. This austere

bastion of piety illustrated the inability of the Sisters to care for vulnerable children. They were miserable substitutes for the parents and families of the children in their care. Throughout her 14 years in the two industrial schools, Teresa never remembers a single demonstration of kindness by any of the nuns looking after her. She was a very shy and sensitive child who was overwhelmed by the death of her mother and the separation from her family.

> I'm sure I was very traumatised at the time because my mother had only died and then to be taken out of a home environment and brought to this massive place and the door opened by nuns. For a child at that age it must have been very traumatic.

Teresa has sporadic flashbacks of her time at Our Lady's. She remembers crying herself to sleep in the large dormitory and desperately missing her mother and siblings. She also recalls the rare occasions when the Red Cross visited the children at Christmas to give them fleeting moments of joy.

> They used to have presents for us. I don't ever remember owning anything or having any toys or anything. I don't remember any of that.

When the Red Cross left the building, the nuns took the presents from the children. It was as if they wanted them to believe they did not deserve any gifts in life, that they were inferior, second-class citizens in a God-fearing country where good boys and girls didn't end up in industrial schools. This kind of cruelty was repeated in many religious institutions across the country. Birthdays were rarely acknowledged and Christmases were endured and not celebrated. Many former residents of institutions have spoken about the invisible birthdays that arrived without a greeting and departed in silence; the only marker left behind was a deeper cut through the heart of the birthday boy and girl.

Teresa felt she was all alone in the world throughout her time in Our Lady's. Although her sister Frances[3] went in there with her, the two girls were separated immediately and not encouraged to grow up together as sisters. Within a short time, they had grown apart. In fact, Teresa did not discover that Frances was her sister until she was several years older.

She [Frances] was probably as traumatised as I was and she was that bit older than me so she would have known my mother more than I knew her . . . It's something we didn't talk about in school that you're my sister and I'll play with you because you're my sister. That never came about. Our main thing in that school was just to survive and everyone for themselves. For you to survive in that you were totally alone no matter if you had family with you. It didn't matter because you were on your own and you had to survive in that.

When Teresa was seven, Our Lady's Industrial School in Ennis closed down and the children were moved to different institutions. It was another distressing episode in the little girl's life.

We came home from school one day and we were given a little brown suitcase. I remember the small little brown suitcase. God knows what was ever in it because I never opened it. And all of us were put on buses. Different buses came because the children went to different places. We didn't all go to the one industrial school. We had a tag stuck on us with our name and where we were going to. That was very traumatising because I was leaving the only place I ever knew. To me in a way it was home because I knew no other home. We were all separated. I had grown up with these children no matter whether we were friends or not we were still one large family.

Teresa and Frances were brought to Mount St Vincent's Industrial School in Limerick City, which was also run by the Sisters of Mercy.

I can remember going in [through the big convent door] and seeing how clean everything was and the floors all shiny and being brought into this parlour with the nuns. And I suppose we were handed over. I do remember being taken down these steps. It was so big. For me it looked massive because there seemed to be a lot more children in that one.

Teresa spent a miserable seven years in St Vincent's. Like so many of the religious institutions run by the Sisters of Mercy, it was a cold brutal place characterised by emotional and physical abuse.

I never got one bit of love, affection, hugs, praise for all the years I spent in industrial schools. Not one kind word. I can't say all nuns were the same but I never remember any love. The biggest loss in my life is affection and love.

Teresa remembers every dreary day beginning with an early morning call for Mass. After Mass they would make the beds, have breakfast and clean the institution before going to school.

Our whole life was like being in the Army. Every day was the same except Sundays. We still went to Mass but we didn't do as much work on a Sunday.

Teresa never went out at weekends because she never received visits from relatives to take her on trips. Instead she would spend her Saturdays scrubbing the long corridors and working hard to make the school spotless.

All day Saturday was spent cleaning. You'd have to take the whole bed apart, clean the whole bed and put it back together. They'd go around and check for all the dust. We'd have to change the sheets.

One of the Sisters in St Vincent's used to frighten the life out of Teresa. She was a small, heavy-set woman with a vicious temper who would lash out at the children for the slightest reasons. The timid little girl was scared stiff of this powerful, cruel woman.

I remember getting a fair few slaps myself being there and screaming and terrified. I remember seeing other children getting beaten. They used to beat you with anything . . . I do remember one time being beaten by this nun and I was screaming and she put her fist in my mouth to stop me from screaming. I can still nearly get the taste of her fist in my mouth to this day. Her fist always reminded me of mince meat. And to this day I still can get that smell. That taste remains in my mouth to this day.

She was just cold. I know I was terrified of her. So were a lot of children afraid. When I think back how much power one person had over so many children, that we didn't rebel against it, that we didn't fight back. Why we didn't I can only imagine that we were too traumatised. There was nowhere to go. There was nowhere to run to. Like any prison camp or Nazi camp we had to conform. We had no one to tell. We had no choice. We had to obey.

The emotional abuse Teresa endured at St Vincent's left profound psychological scars. Whilst her fragile little body recovered from the physical punishments, her human spirit was all but destroyed by the constant erosion of her self-esteem. The nuns' incessant belittling of the youngster peeled away her dignity like a toxic chemical corroding her spirit.

> I was deprived of any kind of love, any kind of affection, any kind of recognition that I was a human being. I was just like an onion. I was just stripped of all my identity — layer after layer. Every bit of my identity went. I was left only as a number.

The nuns degraded the girls in St Vincent's with their disparaging remarks and criticisms that fostered inferiority complexes. They told them they were stupid and useless and they called the girls orphans even though many of them, like Teresa, had at least one living parent. This constant derision lumbered the girls with low self-esteem and impaired their ability as adults to shake off the inferiority complexes they had developed at St Vincent's. The Sisters' psychological cruelty extended to a humiliating name-calling system. The Ryan Report outlines how the Sisters of Mercy, who also ran the Goldenbridge Industrial School, called the girls by the number they had been given when they first entered the institution. In other places, like St Vincent's, the girls were referred to by their surnames.

> I found that very hard when I came out when people used to call my first name. I found it very hard to actually hear it because I suppose I'm so used to being called by my last name. But anything that was to be about us was all by our number. Our clothes were numbered. Everything was numbered.

During her incarceration in St Vincent's, Teresa attended the secondary day school for girls located on the same grounds as the industrial school. It was another distressing experience, this time set against a backdrop of educational apartheid. The nuns ignored girls like Teresa who came from the industrial school. For starters they were made to sit at the back of the class where they were expected to remain in silence during the day without raising their hands or voices. They were the ghost-girls discriminated from receiving a proper education; their muted presence in the classrooms reinforced a second-class complex.

> Nobody had any interest in us because we were only orphans . . . In my mind now I think they felt we weren't going to amount to anything so what's the point of teaching them anything. We're never going to be anything anyway in life. I educated myself in school.
>
> No attention was paid to us. We just sat and got on with what was going on. And if you were able to pick up on what was going on well fair enough. But you soon lost interest because if no one shows you any interest, you'll soon lose interest. And you'll soon begin to believe you are stupid, that you can't learn. I wanted to learn. I loved learning. Anything I absorbed, I absorbed by listening not by what they taught me.

The 'orphan' girls like Teresa were not permitted to fraternise with the day pupils. They just stuck together at the back of the room where they dared not try to outwit the other girls by showing their intelligence. Teresa was so terrified of the nuns teaching in the school, she never attempted to ask questions or display a knowledge of the subjects for fear of a retaliation. The ever-present threat of a beating or verbal abuse silenced the timid little girl at the back of the room.

> The fear never left you. Where the nuns were concerned, the fear never left you. You were fearful all the time.
>
> I do firmly believe they thought we were all really stupid or that we were mentally slow. And I was left-handed and I remember being absolutely murdered for being left-handed. I used to get the two rulers together and the size of them put down on your knuckles. I remember the terror of that. And then when you were made to write with your right hand and your writing wasn't good enough you'd get more beatings for that because I couldn't write with my right hand. I firmly believed they thought that because we were left-

handed we were in some way possessed by the devil.

Teresa tried to learn as much as possible at school despite the discrimination. Although she completed Christmas and summer exams she never passed any of her subjects. She believes the nuns deliberately failed her as part of a cynical ploy to deny her the chance of succeeding in life. Like so many children in Irish industrial schools, Teresa deeply regrets not receiving a proper education.

> I wasn't stupid. If I had been given the chance I could have been anything I wanted to be but I wasn't given that opportunity. I suppose the way they looked at it was, how could an industrial school child be more clever than a day pupil coming in here. It wouldn't look good if an industrial school girl was excelling over a day pupil.

Teresa was slight for her age and she remembers feeling frequent hunger pangs in St Vincent's because she couldn't eat the meagre rations of food that were slopped up to them every day from large containers. She was very thin because of the lack of nourishing food. Breakfast consisted of lumps of porridge and supper was a stomach-churning mix of bread in milk and sugar known as goody.

> I never remember a thin nun but I remember an awful lot of thin children. I couldn't eat the food. I just couldn't. I always felt sick. I don't remember any butter. Some might say there was butter but I never saw the butter. It was probably grabbed because it was all for whoever got to the food on the table — the slices of bread or whatever. If you weren't quick enough you got none. We were starving.
>
> We used to steal the porridge oats because everything was under lock and key. The nuns had thousands of keys and everything was under lock and key, every bit of food. She'd forget to lock it and we'd go in and steal the bag of raw porridge and we'd put the sugar in and mix it with the porridge and we'd eat all that. We'd have terrible diarrhoea.

St Vincent's was not unique in the severity of its nuns. The Ryan

Commission investigated five industrial schools that were run by the Sisters of Mercy. They were all criticised for the unacceptable levels of abuse that took place behind their forbidding walls. One example cited in the Ryan Report was St Michael's Industrial School in Cappoquin, Co. Waterford, which looked after very young boys up until 1969. One man, who was admitted to Cappoquin in the 1950s when he was four years old, told the Commission about a severe beating he got one day from a nun because he didn't hear a bell ringing.[4] The poor boy had just come out of hospital after an operation on his ears and his bandages affected his hearing.[5]

> I couldn't hear nothing and all I could see was everybody running. So I didn't run. Next thing Sr Mariella[6] started belting me with the cane, all over and she hit me in the ear and I ended up back in there again, back in the hospital.[7]

Another man, who was put into Cappoquin in the 1950s when he was a baby, described a frenzied assault by one of the Sisters. At the time he was naked in bed because he had been treated with ointment.[8] One of the lay staff had given him a painting set, which he used to colour two religious statues in the room.[9] The Sister went ballistic when she walked in and saw what he was doing.

> She kind of lost reasoning and, I suppose, from her point of view I was desecrating something very religious but from my point of view I was just painting, you know. She just kept hitting and hitting and wouldn't stop. So I ran for the door . . . I was running in the dark, I just wanted to get away, I was just running in panic. She just kept hitting, and coming after me down the stairs . . . and I kept banging on the door and banging and banging until somebody actually came out and stopped her.[10]

Lay workers in Cappoquin also abused the children. A former resident who was prone to bed-wetting was terrified of one woman who picked on him for soiling his sheets.[11]

> Ms Lambert[12] would come up in the mornings and if we wet our bed we had to lie in our own bed. Often the case I ended up lying in my

own urine and excretion at times and she would hit us over the legs, the buttocks and on the back. She was quite cruel.[13]

One man who was in Cappoquin in the 1940s and 1950s used to hate bath-times, when lay staff would be in charge of washing the children.

> They would hit me and hit my hands if I am holding the bath on the side, you know when you are very small and you are trying to hold the bath and I was fearfully afraid of water, and they would hit your hands away and catch your head like that and push you down underneath and try to get the soap off you. Sometimes they would be laughing while they are doing this and they would take a great bit of fun in doing — ducking you under the water and making you feel like you are going to drown.[14]

The Sisters of Mercy were not the only nuns capable of abusing children in their care. The Sisters of Charity, who ran St Patrick's Industrial School in Kilkenny, could be equally cruel. Bed-wetters were punished severely in St Patrick's.

> The punishment I received for wetting the bed was I was put into a galvanised bath down near the toilets, this was full of Jeyes Fluid, and a bucket was put into the bath and the water poured over my head and I was made sit there for five minutes. As I got out of the bath I was beaten on the behind.[15]

Another bed-wetter was tied up with a towel by one of the Sisters because he was wetting his bed so much.

> I went out to the toilet after the one gave me a belt on the back of the neck to get me out of the bed. She followed me out to the toilet, I was lying on the floor and she pulled my legs up on the rails and tied my legs to the rails, I was upside down. She went out and closed the door. I thought I was going to be left there all night. That was it. It could have been five minutes or five hours, I don't know. She came back in then and put me back in the bed.[16]

The cruelty that was systematic in industrial schools such as St Vincent's was worsened by the lack of parental visits. Teresa Gormley cannot recall any visits by her father during her incarceration in either institution. She believes he made no effort to see his daughters and neither, it seems, did her aunts or her grandmother on her mother's side. Over the years Teresa has grappled with her relatives' apparent indifference to herself and her sister who were like helpless children abandoned to the mercy of the nuns. It was as if they had never existed.

> My brother said my father visited me. I don't ever remember my father coming to visit me. I think it would be something that if he did come to visit me, it would have stayed in my mind. I never remember any visitors coming ever to see me while I was in industrial schools.

When Teresa later tackled her aunts about their failure to visit her in the institutions, they became extremely uncomfortable and quickly changed the subject. Her father was equally reluctant to offer an explanation for his absence during his daughters' incarcerated childhoods. When Teresa met him again after leaving St Vincent's, he was like a stranger to her. She never really liked him and never formed a bond with him and she decided not to ask him why he had so easily acquiesced to their committal to institutional life.

She later discovered that one explanation for his absence could have been attributable to his drink problems. When Teresa met her older brother after leaving St Vincent's, he told her about the life he and his other brother had endured when the rest of the family were taken away. It transpired that their father was a raving alcoholic who made life almost unbearable for the two boys who stayed with him. Ironically, they believed their sisters were the lucky ones because they were taken into industrial schools but the boys had no idea of the cruelty their siblings had endured at the hands of the Sisters of Mercy.

> He said you were better off going into an institution because our life at home was a living hell . . . He said that they were hungry all the time. The father was drinking all the time. He drank everything, I think. It was amazing they were allowed to stay with my father if he was drinking.

Teresa's father died when she was just 20.

> I never spoke to my father about anything about the institutions. He
> never spoke to me about it. He never asked us how we got on. It was
> like they just did not want the subject to be brought up. Maybe he
> felt guilty. I don't know if the man was capable of feeling guilty.

When Teresa was 16, she was told she was to leave St Vincent's. At the
time she was studying for her Intermediate Certificate and she had
several months left to finish the year and to take her exams but she was
denied the opportunity to do so. The nuns explained that as she was
now 16 she was no longer their responsibility. She initially went to stay
with her older sister, who was married and living in Ennis, but despite
being reunited with her sibling, Teresa could not form any bonds with
her. In fact, she hated the experience and she was entirely unprepared
for the world outside St Vincent's.

> I was completely institutionalised. I didn't know anything else but
> an institution. I didn't know anything else but when to be told to get
> up in the morning and do this, do that, go here, go there. I didn't
> know how to handle money. I didn't know anything. I was just
> thrown out of this school with no preparation for the world at all
> like we were just dirt. 'Out you go now, that's all we can do. Out you
> go. Live or die.'
> I was put on a train to Ennis all alone. Imagine sending a
> vulnerable child like that out on her own? I had hardly been outside
> [the convent walls]. As it was coming near my time to come out my
> sister used to come and take me out on a Sunday. I couldn't wait to
> get back to the industrial school. She was a stranger to me. I didn't
> want to be out with her because it was another form of trauma for
> me going out with someone who was a stranger even though she
> was my sister. And they were pawning me off on some other stranger
> again. I was being abandoned again. My father abandoned me to
> industrial schools. I'd been abandoned when I was moved from one
> industrial school to another industrial school and there again I was
> being abandoned out again. All my life, all I was being was being
> abandoned by everybody. And then I ended up with my sister I
> didn't even know. That was another form of abandonment, pushing

me onto someone I didn't even want to go to. I didn't even like her and she was my sister. I didn't have any feelings for her because she was a stranger.

Teresa ended up living with her sister for two years.

I hated living there. I absolute hated it. I felt so lonely. Maybe it was leaving all the girls in the school. I was so used to so many people and then I had to come to dealing with two adults. I never had to deal with adults in my life.

To begin with she worked in the mental hospital in Ennis as a domestic cleaner. She later moved to laundries attached to an old people's home that were also run by the Sisters of Mercy. The work there was tedious and extremely hard.

I hated that too. God almighty I felt I was just going backwards. There was no escape from them. The only thing about the laundries was that I got some money out of it for working there. It was the Eastern Health Board that was employing me and not the nuns. The work was very hard. You were washing for many patients. It was absolute slave labour. I might as well have been in the Magdalene Laundries it was just as bad working in those laundries emptying out big machines. I was only a sixteen-year-old child having to do all that heavy work. It was endless that work. The nun over there was awful cranky. Everything had to be immaculate to the crease. Imagine ironing nuns' habits when they had all the pleats and having to do all them with perfection.

When Teresa was 18, she married a plumber from Dublin. They originally met when he was doing an apprenticeship in Clare in an old folks' home. He was the first man who demonstrated genuine affection towards her and she was so starved of attention she was instantly drawn to his kindness.

God help the poor man. I do feel sorry for him because really in my mind I wasn't really prepared for marriage but I'd say I'd have married anyone that would have shown me any affection. If a man of ninety had shown me affection I would probably have married him for the safety and comfort of that love.

Although her husband knew that she had grown up in institutions, Teresa never spoke to him about her past. The couple had two sons together but throughout their marriage Teresa was shackled by a nagging belief that she did not deserve to be loved. While giving came easily to her, receiving love and affection was an insurmountable challenge.

I'd say all my life I fought against it — that love because I didn't know what love was. And my whole life I didn't trust people's love because I never had the trust of anybody growing up so I didn't trust that love. I probably thought that one day that love is going to all go and I don't deserve that love.

For many years Teresa buried her past and devoted her life to looking after her two sons, whom she adored. She ensured they got all the love they needed.

I swore when my sons were born straightaway it was like something in my head clicked in with the love for those that I was going to protect both of them. They were mine and no one was going to take them away.

Teresa was determined that her sons would get all the love she was denied as a child. Throughout their upbringing she never sought counselling to try to heal the wounds that festered away because of her childhood incarceration. In the end she couldn't keep the demons locked away and eventually her past caught up with her. When she was in her early forties, she became increasingly depressed by an overwhelming feeling of loneliness. Although outwardly she came across as a confident and loving person, inside, she was imploding. The pressure to maintain a façade of normality pushed her to the brink and one night she contemplated suicide.

I went very very low. I phoned the Samaritans and they were very good. I told them I didn't want to live anymore. Now when you're in such a black hole, you see nothing else. It's horrendous. I can see how people commit suicide because I've been in that black hole. Nothing else matters outside of that black hole. There's no one else exists only you in that black hole. When I think back, I feel guilty because I didn't think of my children. I didn't think of what my suicide would have done to my children. Because you go so bad you see nothing else. Nothing matters. It's just you. You're in this black hole and you cannot get out of it.

The Samaritans saved Teresa Gormley from ending her life that night. The woman she spoke with pleaded with her to hang on until the morning and to go to her doctor for help. Somehow she got through the night and the next day she released a cascade of emotions when she finally revealed to her doctor the cause of her deep depression. It was to be the beginning of Teresa's long and painful process confronting her past. Within days she went to see a professional counsellor and she began a journey through psychotherapy. Today she is on permanent medication for depression as she is likely to fall into an abyss of desperation if she dispenses with her daily doses of anti-depressants.

Despite the years of psychotherapy, Teresa continues to be weighed down by a deep well of loneliness. Her psychiatrist once told her she was one of the loneliest people she had ever met.

She said, 'I can understand; it's a loneliness that's from your childhood and it will never leave you. You'll always have it because your heart was broken as a child and no matter what comes into your life it will always be broken.'

Sometimes it's very hard even though it's many years later it just never leaves you. Certain feelings never leave you. How people can treat children like that it's nothing short of the Nazi camps. It's the same thing. It's just as bad. We were starved of everything.

Even though I'm surrounded by love it's very hard to trust love when you've never had it because love can be snapped away. For me it's very hard when someone says to me 'I love you.' If my children say it to me, that's fine I can totally take it. But if someone else comes along and says to me, 'I love you,' I say, 'Why do you love me?' The question that would always come is 'Why? Why do you love me? What is it you love about me?' I have to question the whole thing of love. Is it true or are they just being false?

People can go on and live happy and healthy lives after industrial schools and get good jobs and many have done it. But for me it will never leave me . . . it never leaves you because your childhood is your future. There was no childhood so therefore there is no future.

Chapter 5 ∾

THE BOY WITH THE BROKEN ARM: MICKEY FLANAGAN AND ARTANE

Mickey Flanagan's tragic story was encapsulated in the white words emblazoned on the black T-shirt his brother Kevin wore in June 2009 during the march for survivors of institutional abuse. Kevin Flanagan milled around the large crowds gathered by Dublin's Garden of Remembrance on Parnell Square as they prepared to walk in silence through the city centre. The stark phrase on his T-shirt summarised Mickey's pitiful life: 'Artane 1954 The Boy with the Broken Arm'.

Mickey Flanagan's arm was broken in three places in 1954 by a raging Christian Brother in St Joseph's Industrial School in Artane, Dublin. Mickey was not around to take part in the march himself as he had died in London in 1998 following a life marred by alcoholism, epilepsy and mental torment that stemmed from his time in Artane. His brother Kevin has been campaigning for years to prosecute the Christian Brothers for battering his defenceless brother to a pulp and leaving him with suspected brain damage.

> I'll never get justice for Mickey 'til they're brought into a court of law. I hold them responsible for the death of my brother . . . My brother was sent in there [Artane] for doing something wrong but he certainly wasn't sent in there to get his arm broke or his head fucking busted open. He was sent in there to be educated and he came out a broken man.[1]

Artane Industrial School was a dreadful abyss where boys were neglected and physically, psychologically and sexually abused. The Ryan Report's chapter on Artane is a damning indictment of the Christian Brothers' violation of power that left generations of boys permanently scarred. The school was located in a north-eastern suburb of Dublin some 5 km from the city centre. It began operating as an industrial school in July 1870 and it closed in 1969. Artane was nationally famous for its Artane Boys' Band, which used to perform in public concerts and at GAA matches in Croke Park. The Irish public thought the band of boys from the industrial school was a charming example of institutional care. But behind the Band's brassy façade lay a legacy of obscene brutality. Former members of the Band say they were frequently beaten and their pristine performance clothes taken off them as soon as they returned to Artane.

Mickey Flanagan was committed to Artane in October 1952 after being charged by the Dublin District Court with a housebreaking offence. He was 13 at the time and he was to stay there until September 1955. He'd been caught by the Gardaí stealing lead from the roofs of houses in Killester. He used to climb up on the roofs with his younger brother James (known as Jack as a boy) and the two of them would take the lead into Dublin's city centre and sell it on the quays.

> They were empty houses. They were mostly these big mansions that were empty on the Killester Road but they had loads of lead on the roofs. All Mickey ever took was the lead off the roofs.[2]

Mickey stole the lead to earn some cash as his mother struggled to provide for her 11 children. His dad, Joseph Flanagan, had gone to England to work as a labourer on building sites but work was sporadic and he didn't always have money to send home. Kathleen Flanagan did her best to keep her children fed and clothed but it was difficult controlling all the boys in the family, according to Kevin Flanagan.

> We were wild. All the kids around that time were wild. And every time you done something wrong you were threatened with Artane or Daingean but it didn't quieten us down.

The Flanagans lived in a two-bedroomed corporation house in

Donnycarney, north Dublin. Kevin recalled how they squeezed into the modest house like sardines in a tin.

> The boys used to sleep in the back bedroom and the girls slept in the front bedroom and me ma and da slept in the parlour downstairs … nobody had anything so everybody just helped each other out.
>
> I remember we used to have to go into the pawn shop to bring me dad's suit into the pawn of a Monday to get the money so that we could get food and then me ma would get it out for him to go to Mass on Sunday.

Kevin Flanagan was just a year old when Mickey was sent to Artane. James Flanagan, who was a year younger than Mickey, was already in Artane having received an eight-year sentence for mitching from school. James remembered how Mickey was picked on by the Christian Brothers because he was more rebellious than the other boys.

> He was treated worse than me because all I ever see was bruises on his hands from getting the strap and marks up to his elbow and there would be a big red mark down his arm. He'd say, 'I'm getting peed off with this.'
>
> They [Christian Brothers] were complete animals. And we as kids, who didn't know what was going on at the time, were taking it sitting down. But in the end people started rebelling. Mickey rebelled because he wouldn't take the slaps on the hand no more. He'd had enough.

On 14 April 1954 Mickey was involved in an altercation with another boy in one of the classrooms where Br Michel[3] was teaching. The Brother went berserk and he tried to hit Mickey but the young fellow resisted as he was becoming increasingly intolerant of the Brothers' brutality. He ran into a corner and picked up a brush to defend himself against Br Michel, who was hurtling towards him in a rage. Br Michel then told one of the boys in the class to run up and get Br Cyrano[4] who was teaching nearby. Br Cyrano rushed into the room in a mad fury. He grabbed the brush from Mickey and smashed its handle on the boy's head, face and arm. He broke Mickey's arm in three places and hit his head with such force it bled badly. Both Kevin and James Flanagan believe those blows to Mickey's head triggered the epilepsy that plagued him after that day. James Flanagan was in one of the other classrooms when he heard about Mickey's beatings.

> I heard a big commotion and nobody knew what was going on and then somebody shouted, 'Your brother is getting beaten up in the class.' But we couldn't get out of the class because the doors were locked. So what happened was all of a sudden we saw three or four Brothers dragging my brother out of the class further down and dragging him up towards the punishment hall.

The next day James went looking for Mickey as he was extremely concerned for his welfare. He discovered the shocked youngster shaking with terror in the large open shed by the punishment block where boys would be sent for lashings. Mickey was hardly able to speak.

> There was blood coming down the side of his head and his left arm was dangling. He hadn't been treated. I asked him if he had been to see the doctor and he said, 'No.' He said they just stuck the plaster on his head and left him as he was. He said he was in agony. He could hardly stand up. They made him stand up in the shed on his own but he had to lean against the post.

James pleaded with one of the Christian Brothers to help Mickey but his pleas were met with a violent response. The Brother dragged James out of the shed, lashed him with a leather strap and warned him not to approach Mickey again. The Flanagans believe Mickey was left untreated for a couple of days and not brought to the doctor. James suspected he was hidden away so that the other boys wouldn't see the extent of his injuries.

> All the Brothers closed ranks. Nobody knew where he went, where he slept and where he'd been. As far as I know he was in the punishment block. That was the closed-in area. I think he spent the time in there.

During this time, the Christian Brothers didn't tell Mickey's mother what had happened to her son. She only discovered the truth a few days later when one of the boys in Artane was out visiting his family for the weekend. John Byrne, who was a neighbour, went up to Kathleen Flanagan's house to tell her about Mickey's beatings. Mrs Flanagan was shocked at the news and she visited Artane and demanded to see Mickey but she was denied access. She then asked to speak to the school Superior but she was once again fobbed off until the following Tuesday when the Superior met her and admitted that one of the Brothers had beaten Mickey and broken his arm. By now Mrs Flanagan was beside herself with worry and she begged to see her son but the Superior refused her request.

Mrs Flanagan then decided to contact her local political representative. After writing a letter of complaint to Captain Peadar Cowan, TD she was finally allowed to see Mickey eight days after he had been barbarically assaulted. She was shocked at the state he was in. His body was badly bruised and his personality had changed dramatically. Mickey was in a catatonic stupor and all the joie de vivre seemed to have drained out of him. By then his broken arm was in plaster as he had been taken to the Mater Hospital in Dublin for treatment. When James Flanagan finally saw him again he was aghast at his appearance and demeanour. The young boy was solemn and sad and wouldn't speak.

> He just wasn't the same person. He was completely different . . . It completely changed him. It turned him into a zombie-type of person. He wasn't interested in anybody and he ended up a recluse in the end and he stayed like that until he died. Before that he used to mix with people. He had many friends. John Byrne was a friend. Lots of people were friends of his before he got the beating but after that he didn't want to know anybody.
>
> He just went into himself. He used to walk around on his own and never say anything to anybody.

Mickey began to have epileptic fits after that assault and he continued to suffer from epilepsy for the rest of his life. The Flanagans attribute his epileptic condition to the beating he got in Artane as he had never suffered from it before then. His decision to defend himself that day left him physically and mentally damaged, said James.

I think myself what done Mickey was the bang on the back of the head. That's what done him because when I seen him the next day with the blood coming down the back of his neck I said to him, 'Didn't you get any treatment?' and he said, 'No.' And I said to the Christian Brother, 'Can you do something for him?' and he just said, 'We're doing all we can.' But they never did anything for him because they left him there for days.

Captain Peadar Cowan raised the assault of Mickey Flanagan in Dáil Éireann on 23 April 1954. He called on the Minister for Education to explain the beating and he reminded the Minister that children who were sent to industrial schools such as Artane were the responsibility of his ministry. He told the House he was profoundly shocked when he heard about Mickey's beating and he asked for the Minister's reassurance that such an incident wouldn't happen again.

> I think the House and the country will want to have from the Minister an assurance that an incident such as has occurred in this case will not be permitted to occur again. I am informed that the Brother who injured the boy was barely past 21 years of age, not much older than the little boy who was injured in the fashion I have described. I think the House will want an assurance from the Minister, and the country will want an assurance from him, that punishment, if it is to be inflicted on those sent to industrial schools, will be inflicted by some person of experience and responsibility. If punishment were to be imposed in a fit of hot temper, it would be exceptionally bad and, in fact, as in this case, it would be dangerous.
>
> I regret very much that I have had to mention or raise this matter in this House. I have lived for many years convenient to Artane Schools. For many years, whenever I was asked, I have been a subscriber to the funds of the schools. I have seen their boys week after week passing my house, looking exceptionally fit, well clothed and happy. All of us have seen their magnificent band playing on big occasions in Croke Park and it would be regrettable that an incident, such as I have mentioned in this case, should be permitted under any circumstances to occur in a school of that kind. I myself personally am satisfied that it is an isolated instance. I am satisfied that the superiors will take appropriate action against the Brother concerned. The very fact that the incident did occur shows how

necessary it is that this House, through the machinery of the Department of Education and through the Minister charged with that responsibility, should have the closest supervision of schools such as this, where children, many of them without parents at all, are sent to be brought up.

This incident, when I heard it yesterday morning and heard the details subsequently, profoundly shocked me. I am perfectly certain that the fact that it has been raised in this House, that the Minister has investigated it, will ensure that no similar incident will occur in the future. It will be a guarantee to the parents and relatives of children who are in these industrial schools that this House and the Minister and the staff of the Department will jealously guard and protect those children while they are under the care of the State in these institutions.[5]

The response to Captain Cowan's concerns by the then Minister for Education, Sean Boylan, speaks volumes about the State's relationship with the religious orders and its abject failure to properly supervise those institutions under the care of the State, even when faced with stark evidence of brutality behind their doors.

I think Deputy Cowan has been quite reasonable in admitting that this is an isolated incident and that in general his appreciation of the work of the Artane School and of the condition of the children there has not lessened. The boy was hit and his arm was broken. I would be as much concerned as the Deputy is if I thought it was anything other than a very isolated incident and in one sense what might be called an accident. I would not tolerate cruelty to any boy or misuse of any boy in any institution. I visited Artane and found the boys were healthy and well cared for. I visited the schools there and it struck me that there was great evidence of very earnest endeavour, even of notable achievement, in the schools. It would be very difficult to improve the conditions under which the schools operate, certainly without a very substantial subvention from this House for the upkeep of the schools and for the development of what may be essential and necessary there. I would like to remind the House that the community provided the lands in Artane, the building and the equipment from their own resources; and they did this in a

Christian endeavour to ameliorate certain conditions the development of which had not been provided for in any way by anyone. I cannot conceive any deliberate ill-treatment of boys by a community motivated by the ideals of its founder. I cannot conceive any sadism emanating from men who were trained to a life of sacrifice and of austerity. They are also trained to have great devotion to a very high purpose.

The point is that accidents will happen in the best regulated families and in this family there are about 800 boys. Many of them were sent to Artane because of the difficulties of their character and because of a good deal of unruliness of conduct. These boys are difficult to control at times. Maybe it is essential now and again that children should be punished. I am not all at one with the people who claim that children should never be punished, but I think the punishment should be administered, as Deputy Cowan says, by a responsible person in conditions of calm judgment.

I do not know how the edge of the strap is used, but I will make an inquiry into that. I think it would be an evil thing for the school, for the character of the children, for the future of the children, that any misuse should arise in any school like Artane. Because of the unfortunate background of many of these boys, possibly due to evil social conditions, Deputies must realise how careful the handling of them as a group must be and how far from easy it is to ensure the working of such an institution.

I deeply regret that there should be such a happening and I appreciate the anxiety of the boy's mother. Apart from my high regard for the Brothers concerned, the community concerned, there is also a very constant system of inspection for all such institutions. I personally have visited practically all of them and I make personal and constant inquiry as to what is happening in them. I know in that particular school how deep is the anxiety for the children's spiritual and physical welfare. This is an isolated incident; it can only happen again as an accident.[6]

Minister Boylan's response was a staggering endorsement of Artane Industrial School and an illustration of how the Department of Education abdicated its responsibility to properly investigate the conduct of the Christian Brothers. Boylan's approach epitomised the

State's culpability in propping up the Congregations and in ignoring the abuse that was a systematic part of Irish industrial schools. The Minister appeared to be describing a parallel universe when he spoke glowingly about the Brothers' devotion to the ideals of their founder, Edmund Rice. His pompous approval of Artane, following his visits to the school, raises numerous questions about the Irish Ministry of Education and its supposed supervision of these religious institutions. On what basis did he conclude that the boys in Artane were healthy and well cared for? Had the Minister bothered to properly investigate Mickey Flanagan's appalling treatment he may have exposed the very sadism he declared the Brothers were surely incapable of and he could have stopped the cruelty that continued in Artane until its closure in 1969.

The Ryan Report's chapter on Artane depicts a dystopian society where violence straddled sadism and where the Christian Brothers behaved like despots, striking terror into the children they were supposed to be nurturing and educating. One former Artane resident told the Ryan Investigation Committee about the day Br Beaufort[7] lashed out at him because he thought he was laughing at him.

> He jumped straight at me, picked me up, threw me like a dog around the place. I hit desks, hit the floor. I landed after some time on the floor. The commotion of boys screaming had brought Br Quintrell[8] who was in Eleven school, which was the next school, he flew in and pulled him off. I know I was unconscious, and I know to God that if it hadn't been for him coming in, I do not think I would be here today, in all honesty. The attack was vicious. Moments later, he was apologising, crying.[9]

Injuries the boy had previously sustained in the carpenter's shop re-opened when Br Beaufort hit him. His left eye and neck were bruised and some of his teeth were broken. The poor lad lost one tooth on one side of his mouth and two on the other.[10] Br Beaufort was on the staff of Artane throughout the 1940s and early 1950s.

Another eyewitness told the Ryan Commission about one incident that happened after another Brother attacked him for apparently trying to avoid playing hurling. At the time the boy had a blister on his finger and he tried to lance it with a needle. When Br Olivier[11] caught him doing that, he accused him of deliberately trying to harm himself in order to avoid going training.

> He said he would cure it for me. That evening in the dormitory, him and Br Boyce[12] called me into the boot room . . . they had a kidney shaped utensil and boiling water. They got hold of me and I realised what they were going to do and I tried to make a run for it. The pair of them got hold of me and Br Olivier got my finger and shoved it in. I screamed and roared and tried to pull it back and they held it. After 10 or 15 seconds the pain went. It just went numb and it was bearable. They held it in for a while and out it come. That's when he told me to walk the passageway, gangway which was linoleum in the centre of the dormitory. As time went on it swelled, it swelled. He obviously went to bed.

The night watchman found the boy, who had not gone to bed because of the instruction from the Brothers to 'walk the passageway, gangway', and told him to go to bed.

> The next morning I got up, my finger was a white ball of flesh, waterlogged. I reported sick, I reported to Br Cretien,[13] which you had to do to get to see the nurse. I told the nurse what happened. I was treated at least a month or six weeks until eventually all the skin peeled off. Sometimes the nurse would cut it. After some weeks I was like a plucked chicken, bare skin. In time the skin grew back on the nail. To this day that finger, especially in cold weather, is numb, there is no feeling in it. I swear they must have burned the nerve ends.[14]

Some considerable period later the same boy encountered Br Olivier's vicious temper again when he failed to turn up for training.

> He brought me into the washroom. He told me to kneel down on the floor and he stood over me with his arms folded. He was quite cool and calm and he said, 'I have told you now more than once to come out and I am going to give you the hiding of your life' real calm. He was enjoying it. He said, 'Hold your hand out. Hold your left hand out and don't drop it until I tell you.' He took this leather strap out and he gave me four or five straps. I couldn't hold it out

any longer because the strap was starting to go up my arm. I had welts on it. I dropped it. He said, 'I have warned you not to drop your hand. Now, put your other hand out' and I did. He started to beat me again. Again I dropped it. He said, 'I did tell you' and he went berserk.

When you seen this man when he lost his temper he was like a wolf. His jaws literally went out and he bared his teeth and he just lashed at me. I was running trying to get away from him. He hit me, it didn't matter where, legs, back, head, anywhere. During that I must have passed out because when I came around there was water running on my head and the taps from these baths were about that wide . . . real old fashioned taps. I must have thought I was dreaming it. Then I thought I was drowning. I drew back and I cracked my head on the nozzle of the tap so I had blood coming down, I had tears, I was soaking wet. He wasn't finished then. He threw me on the ground and he said, 'You'll walk that floor for the rest of the night.' Of all nights I thought the watchman would come but the watchman didn't come that night. Nobody came and I walked that passage until six-thirty the next morning. I was so terrified of going to bed that he might come back and beat me again. I walked the whole night without sleep, I swear to God . . . The injuries, you just put up with them. I was black and blue but I just had to put up with them . . . I never missed a session after that, I can assure you.[15]

Br Olivier, who gave evidence to the Ryan Investigation Committee, said he couldn't remember that incident and he queried the man's recollection of the beating. However, he did admit with shame that he was capable of such brutality. Olivier was also involved in another stomach-churning act of depravity against another boy in Artane, who accidentally defecated on the floor in the sports dressing room. When Br Olivier came into the room, some of the excrement ended up on his shoes. Astonishingly, he ordered the boy to lick the faeces from his shoes. In the 1990s he wrote an apology to the former resident and he supplied a written response to the Ryan Investigation Committee in which he gave his account of what happened.

On the day in question I was playing football with another Brother in a field far away from the dressing room. When we finished playing we returned to the dressing room to change and I noticed [the complainant] coming out of the dressing room. I asked him what he was doing there and he said he had to go to the toilet. I brought him back in and noticed the floor and my shoes were covered in faeces. I told him to clean up the mess and he replied he had nothing to clean it with. I spontaneously told him to lick it, meaning my shoes. To my horror he proceeded to do so and I immediately told him to stop and to go back to the class or he would be late. I did not give him any beating or bath and I proceeded to clean my shoes and the floor myself.[16]

The Artane chapter in the Ryan Report is riddled with accounts of sadistic cruelty. The Report also concluded that sexual abuse was a chronic problem in Artane and that Brothers who served there included those who had previously been guilty of sexual abuse of boys. Ryan found that during one year alone in the 1940s there were seven Brothers in Artane who were sexual abusers. The Ryan Investigation Committee also discovered that sexual activity between boys was common and there was a significant amount of predatory sexual behaviour by bigger boys on small, vulnerable ones.

Ryan concluded that the Christian Brothers failed to properly investigate cases and allegations of sexual abuse. They were neither reported to the Department of Education nor to the Gardaí. In a damning indictment of the cover-up of clerical paedophilia, Ryan found that 'Sexual abuse by Brothers posed a serious risk of damaging the reputations of the Institution and the Congregation if it became public, and cases were managed primarily with a view to protecting them against that danger. The offender was an incidental beneficiary of this policy.'[17]

Abusive Brothers were moved to other institutions including other industrial schools without any regard for the safety of the boys there and with no evidence that the Superior was alerted to any abusive background. And even when repeat offenders were pressurised to leave the Congregation, they were invited to seek dispensation from their vows. That meant they could leave the Order with a clean bill of health and without any suspicion attached to their character. These ex-Brothers could then continue teaching in a lay capacity. The failure of the Christian Brothers to take action against paedophiles in their ranks meant offenders were able to continue abusing children for many years.

The unfortunate Mickey Flanagan never lived to see the Ryan Report's condemnation of the hell he had been sent to in the 1950s. Shortly after leaving Artane in 1955 he headed to England, leaving behind his distraught younger brother Kevin.

> I remember him going to England and he had a paper bag with two pairs of stockings and a shirt. That's what he went to England with. I remember them [my brothers] all going away and I remember when they used to go away I used to be roaring and crying.

Mickey first lived in Birmingham, where he worked in a bicycle shop. Later on he moved to London to work as a porter on the platforms of the railways. He spent his last working years in Young's Brewery in London where he used to load and unload the barrels. Kevin Flanagan believes Mickey never recovered from his appalling beating in Artane. He became a chronic alcoholic and lived in squalor in dingy flats in London. He wasn't able to look after himself and he never learnt to cook properly, said Kevin.

> Even when you'd go over for a week's holidays everything would be just out of the chippers. He couldn't cook. He couldn't boil an egg. He learnt no skill coming out of Artane.

Kevin remembers visiting him in London in the late 1960s where Mickey was living in appalling conditions in a dirty flat and was tormented by nightmares.

> There was a bed in the corner and there was only two legs on the bed. Everything was just thrown around the place. Clothes were just thrown around the place and beer cans were all over the place.
> I used to listen to him screaming and roaring at night-time when he'd wake up screaming in the middle of the night. He'd wake up roaring and crying and he'd be screaming, 'Get away from me.'

Mickey never got married and by all accounts was awkward with women although Kevin and James believe he fathered two children from a woman he had a relationship with when he was a young man.

She eventually left Mickey and took the children with her. The Flanagans have no idea where she went but James believes his brother wasn't able to cope with the intimacy of the relationship.

> He just couldn't settle with anybody. He kept having fits and that. And if she was out shopping all of a sudden he'd have a fit. She used to get very nervous and very upset about it and she used to wonder what was wrong with him and we used to say, 'Well, he got that in Artane when he was beaten up.'

For most of his life Mickey was a loner who sought solace in drink and betting. He was a sad soul and he suffered from poor health in his later years, according to Kevin.

> He had everything. He had gout. His lungs were in bits. He smoked. All he lived for and all he loved was horses, dogs and drink. That's all he ever done. And the other thing about it was he couldn't read or write . . . when I was over in London with him it was always the pub, the bookies, the pub, the bookies especially Saturdays.

The impact of Mickey's incarceration in Artane was brought home vividly to Kevin during the funeral of their sister, who died in the 1990s. That day they drove by her house and travelled past the old grounds of Artane's industrial school. All of a sudden Mickey became agitated and Kevin was taken aback by his reaction.

> Mickey looked around the back and he looked at Artane school and he turned around and he said to Mark [his nephew], 'Mark, see there? That's where I went to school.' And the tears were in his eyes and he said, 'Fucking bastards, I'd love to burn that school down.'

Mickey Flanagan died alone in his flat in London in January 1998. His niece discovered his body on his kitchen floor. He had been dead for several days.

Chapter 6 ∾

'JOHN BROWN' AND UPTON AND LETTERFRACK

John Brown[1] is a tall thin man with greying hair and bright blue eyes that light up with a vivid anger when he recalls his childhood experiences in St Patrick's Industrial School in Upton in Co. Cork and in Letterfrack Industrial School in Connemara, Co. Galway. He describes Ireland as a dirty, filthy, despicable state that was complicit in the abuse of children like him in religious institutions. He is vitriolic in his condemnation of the State's judicial system, which enabled judges to hand down severe sentences on young offenders for minor misdemeanours.

When you talk to John about his past, his anger is so palpable his eyes well up as he recalls the abuse he endured during his four-year incarceration in the two institutions. He has never given up his fight to put his childhood abusers on trial, including the Irish State, for giving him a life sentence of trauma. John believes he will never rest until he receives justice in the courts for the crimes committed against him as a child. He is one of the few survivors of institutional abuse who refused to participate in the redress scheme because it would have meant waiving all rights to pursue legal action against those responsible for his childhood abuse.

He admits his dogged pursuit of justice is eating him like a cancer that has consumed him for years. John chain-smoked throughout my extensive interview with him in his house in Tallaght, Co. Dublin. Through a waft of cigarette smoke, he described how his childhood experiences have tainted his views on Ireland.

Had we been still under British rule while this was going on, I would find some way more easily to be able to accept it because I'd say at

least it was a foreign power but it was our bleedin' own that done it
to me, me own nation that done it to me and that part is the really
sickening filthy part.

John has good reason to be angry at the Irish State. It failed miserably
to supervise his care while he was being physically and psychologically
abused in the industrial schools and it actively participated in his
incarceration through its court system.

John Brown was born in Dublin in 1953. He first lived in Arbour Hill
and then moved to Prussia Street with his two brothers and three sisters.
His father worked in the Guinness brewery as a lorry driver delivering
the kegs of beer from the boats to the Guinness headquarters on the
quays. Tragedy came early for John when his mother died at 38 of
tuberculosis when he was just nine years old. Her devotion to her
children left John and his brother unprepared for the unremitting
cruelty they would later endure in the industrial schools.

> She was overprotective and then going into these places we didn't
> have a clue and wouldn't have been street-wise . . . she was a very
> caring person and her priority was the six of us.

It was tough on John's father coping with six children on his own but
he'd overcome significant challenges in the past. Before his marriage, he
had fought with the Irish Guards in the trenches of Europe during
World War II. John Brown gets very emotional when he recalls his
father's war-time bravery, which he says the Irish State rewarded with
the incarceration of his two sons in brutal institutions.

> The best thanks at this stage was to take two of his children and fuck
> them into the hands of them dirty bastards . . . he got various medals
> . . . My father was highly decorated and commended for his actions
> in the Second World War. When his wife died the greatest credit that
> this State could show him was to take two of his children and fuck
> them into them bastards.

John's dad did his best to keep his children clothed, fed and educated.
John's Confirmation photograph is a testament to his father's care. He
seems smart and happy in his pristine coat and shiny shoes and he

certainly doesn't look like a neglected child. But on 19 November 1964, when he was 11, his life changed irrevocably. That day he and his older brother Jim visited a derelict house on Prussia Street in Dublin. The place was an old haunt of the boys, who were fond of climbing its rickety stairs to access the attic where pigeons sheltered. The two young fellows used to grab a few of the birds and take them back home where they'd put them into a hut out in the back garden.

> It was a condemned derelict house. All the windows had galvanised sheets on them. We used to access it from the back. We'd be able to get into a paddock over our back wall and walk down to the back of this house. It was like a jungle, it was. It was a child's delight for playing. We used to be able to pull a bit of the galvanised from the back window and we'd get in. There was floor boards torn up. The plaster was falling off the ceilings. And we used to go up the stairs and get up into the attic. The roof was in tatters. We'd wait for the pigeons to come in and we'd corner the pigeons and put them up our jumpers and bring them to a makeshift loft over in our back garden.
>
> One particular day we happened to be up there and heard voices down underneath the attic door and a torch came up and it was the police who took us down.

John and his brother were caught red-handed when the guards entered the abandoned house and arrested the two boys for trespassing. Their apprehension had devastating consequences. They were brought to the Bridewell Garda Station for questioning and then taken to a holding institution for young offenders.

> I heard my father outside in the police station and I thought I was going to be brought back home but I was put in a car and brought up to Marlborough House.

Marlborough House was a stopover for young offenders in Dublin. John and Jim stayed there for a few weeks while their cases were being processed in the courts. In documents he obtained years later, he discovered that a variety of charges had been brought against him including causing malicious damage worth £52.10 to the roof, housebreaking and being found in an enclosed yard. When John was brought to court, he had no legal representative to defend him. The youngster was completely bewildered by the court system and he had no idea what was going on.

> I was eleven and a half. I didn't have a clue. I had nobody defending me. There was no adult there to speak on my behalf. It was like a twilight zone. I didn't have a clue.

Ironically, John Brown would go on to get more justice as an adult from the Central Criminal Court when he later got involved in terrorist activities. On 10 December 1964 he was given a four and a half year sentence to be spent in Upton Industrial School. At that young age, he hadn't a clue what an industrial school was and he was totally oblivious to the abuse that went on in these institutions. John believes his sentence was completely unjustified and that the Irish State owes him an explanation for the decision the judge took that day to give him such an exorbitant sentence for a minor offence. Poverty no doubt played its role in the judge's attitude. In the 1960s Irish courts took an unsympathetic view of juvenile offenders from poor backgrounds.

John's childhood was destroyed the day he received that sentence. He says the punishment in no way related to the crime as the derelict house already looked like a bombsite.

> It was as if you were after throwing a grenade into each room. The whole place was in tatters. If anything it was probably more of a danger [to us]. Even going up the stairs, the first three steps there was hardly any banister. The place was just totally annihilated.

After their conviction, John and his brother were taken by a guard on a train to Upton Industrial School, which was run by the Rosminian Brothers. They were also in charge of the notorious Ferryhouse Industrial School in Clonmel. The boys were met at the station by a Rosminian Brother who drove them to Upton. Initially everything seemed OK. He was friendly to them in the car and the first night was spent without any incident. They were given their tea and allocated beds in separate dormitories. But John was desperately lonely. He missed his father and siblings and he was still reeling from all the events that had brought him to Upton. He spent his first night crying in the massive dormitory, bewildered by the sheer physical isolation of the school, which was situated on a 114-acre farm 14 miles from Cork.

> It would have been frightening looking at the various other young fellas. I used to think Upton was a thousand miles from the city of Cork. I used to have the idea that Jesus you were in a different country, an entirely different planet.

Over the next 18 months John would experience Upton's sinister, sadistic side. Like so many other industrial schools at the time, violence was an endemic feature there. Sexual abuse also took place at Upton. Although John was fondled inappropriately by the Brothers, he was lucky enough to avoid being raped because he was tall and able to fend off their approaches. He had some schooling while he was in Upton but his days were mostly spent working. He was assigned to the shoe shop and during the summer worked on the lands thinning beet, weeding the potatoes or gathering the hay. The threat of physical violence was always present.

> When one of them would come out at meal times they'd either blow a whistle or give one clap of their hand and if you didn't stop and go statue wise, when you were done you were on report and you'd get a belt of the leather afterwards.

John was regularly beaten in Upton. He'd get a lash of the leather strap on his hands or be given what he called the 'benders', which meant he'd have to drop his trousers and get a thrashing on his bare bottom. The young lad was always terrified of being targeted by the Brothers and he was scared stiff of doing something wrong that would warrant a punishment. It didn't take much to enrage the Brothers.

> In the refectory when you'd be doing grace before meals if you turned your head you'd have to report after the meal. You'd be held back and he'd give you a leathering. Or it could be while you were out thinning the beet or weeding the potatoes if you messed with one another you'd be reported for the most trivial kind of things. You went and stood outside the office for him and you'd be there

rattling and waiting and it was done on purpose. Another act they'd do again in the same way as Letterfrack, is that they'd put you on report and they'd let it go for a day or two and you'd be saying, 'Oh lovely, he's after forgetting about it' and they'd let it go for three or four days and then they'd pull you in and give you a beating. That was another kind of tortuous thing to let you think that they'd forgotten about it.

The most trivial and minor of offences were punished with vicious retaliations. One of John's tormentors at Upton was Br James,[2] who took a sadistic pleasure out of abusing the boys both physically and sexually. John vividly recalled one frightening assault by James that happened by the swimming pool in one of the fields. When the burly Brother ordered John into the pool, the youngster explained that he couldn't swim. His resistance intensified James's temper as he couldn't abide any boy challenging his orders.

> He manoeuvred a couple of young fellas to grab me and shag me in the pool which they did do and when I was thrown into the pool I just went down into the bottom.

When John sank to the bottom he flayed around on the floor of the pool gulping in large mouthfuls of water as he gasped for air. He wasn't able to swim to the surface and he was nearly drowning when suddenly he was hauled to the surface by another boy who had jumped in to rescue him. Br James sneered at John as he coughed and spewed out water by the edge of the pool. The poor lad was completely traumatised from his near drowning but he got no sympathy from the Brother.

> Had I drowned in the pool, it would have been just looked upon as a prank with kids messing and that. And when I was taken out of the pool James was looking down on me as I was gasping as if he was saying 'I'll get my way with you.' To me it was clearly deliberately done. It was orchestrated. James done it to put the fear in me.

John suspects James wanted to frighten him into sexual submission and that his sadistic behaviour amounted to a power game to get the boy to acquiesce to his sexual advances.

They used to have pantomimes where there was a room off one of the dormitories where they'd have all the costumes. And he'd take you up there for one of the rehearsals and when you'd be trying on a costume he'd be pulling you into it . . . he'd try to mug me he would . . . you'd pull away from him and I was making excuses and angling out of it . . . there was definitely something evil with him.

The dormitories were hunting grounds for the sexual predators in Upton. Once the lights went out, the Brothers in charge of the dormitories would walk around the beds checking on the boys. They would come to John's bed and sit down in a friendly way and slip their hands under his bedclothes and try to grope his genitals. He tried hard to avoid their advances by turning away from them in the hope they'd move on. John learnt that reporting any of the Brothers' abusive behaviour was futile and downright dangerous.

If you went to confession and you said it to the priest, the priest back-loaded it to the collars.

A beating would be an inevitable result for any confessional victims. Fear pervaded Upton's atmosphere. If John didn't get lashed one day he'd almost certainly get a thrashing the following day. Upton's physical harshness was complemented by extreme austerity. When it came to mealtimes, it was no different from the rest of the industrial schools where the food was woefully inadequate.

You were starving all the time. In Upton, for the breakfast there was two pieces of bread that was dipped in dripping that was stuck together. And they used to come in with large deep trays and they used to give you two of these slices with the dripping in between and a fella used to go round with a kettle and give you a ponnie [tin mug], with tea and milk.

Dinner was equally unpalatable, with meat served only on rare occasions while tea was a meagre serving of bread and jam. Upton's poor food left John, who was a tall strapping lad, badly malnourished. The law of the jungle operated in Upton as it did in so many other industrial schools and other boys, who were bullies, would grab the food from the younger boys who were too scared to fight back.

John Brown shifted uncomfortably on his sitting room sofa as he recalled his childhood incarceration at Upton. Sometimes the memories were so strong they triggered painful emotions, causing him to leave the room for a break. This occurred when he explained what happened one day in June 1966 when he discovered his father had died in Dublin. He was out working in the fields that day, doing some weeding, when suddenly he saw a Brother walking quickly towards him. He told John the head Brother wanted to see him. The young boy was scared stiff as he thought he must have done something very bad and that he was going to be beaten. He was surprised when he met his own brother Jim outside the office. By then the two brothers had grown apart as they had been separated for a while and had become slightly estranged. They both looked at one another perplexed as they entered the Brother's office.

> We walked in and he said, 'I've a bit of news for you' and I think he actually went to a drawer and gave us two sweets each and he said, 'It's bad news: your father has died and gone to heaven.'

The shocked boys didn't know how to react and they were unable to absorb the magnitude of the news. Now they were orphans and they hadn't even seen their poor father since they went to Upton. The Brother didn't even tell them how he had died and, instead of a sympathetic hug, dismissed them with a cold shrug and told them to get back to their work.

At this stage of our interview, John's mug of tea shook in his hand. Tears welled up in his eyes and he couldn't take any more. He broke down and left the room, unable to continue his conversation with me. When he came back, John's face was contorted with anguish as he recalled that dreadful day's events with startling clarity. He later discovered that his father had died following a fall from the second-floor window of his own home. He had put his head out the window for air after catching something in his throat but he missed his footing and fell to the ground.

Two days after hearing the devastating news of their father's death, John and his brother were put on a train to Dublin to attend his funeral. Another older brother warned him not to go up to the coffin because he would be shocked at the state of his father's battered corpse. John was distraught at losing his second parent and his emotions were a mix of melancholy and anger. He blamed his father for not doing more to prevent the incarceration of his two sons in Upton but later in life he came to appreciate that his father was too poor to secure proper legal representation for the boys during their trial. Impoverishment also prevented him from visiting his sons in Upton.

John stayed at Upton until 1966 when a decision was taken to shut down the industrial school. The Ryan Report states that 'falling numbers, lack of trained staff, and the reorganisation and rationalisation of the schools run by the Order ultimately led to its closure as an industrial school'.[3] A fire in July of that year, which gutted some of Upton's buildings, accelerated its closure. When it shut down, there were 83 boys in Upton: 16 were transferred to Letterfrack, 10 to Artane, 10 to Tralee and 28 to Ferryhouse. The rest were released.[4]

In August 1966 John and some other boys at Upton were put on a bus and sent to Letterfrack Industrial School in Connemara, Co. Galway. As John trundled through the countryside, he had no idea what horrors awaited him in the bleak isolated institution that was run by the Christian Brothers. Only the sheep on the hills provided some form of life as he stared out the grease-stained windows of the bus and wondered where on earth he was heading to. Letterfrack was situated in the middle of the barren Connemara landscape, miles away from anywhere. The tiny village was more than 84 km from Galway and parents and relatives of boys incarcerated there found it almost impossible to travel there to see their children. This industrial school should never have been granted a licence to operate.

Letterfrack had a chequered history. In 1849 a wealthy Quaker couple moved there from England and bought a large tract of land, which they then developed. A large residence and a school for children in the locality were built on the land. In 1884 the property was sold to the Archbishop of Tuam, Dr John McEvilly. He then applied to the Lord Lieutenant of Ireland, Earl Spencer, suggesting that the property was 'admirably suited for a boys' industrial school'.[5] His application was received with universal scepticism and advisors to Lord Spencer stated there was no need for an institution in such a remote part of the country. But the Archbishop would not be deterred. He vigorously pursued his determination to establish an industrial school at

Letterfrack and on 14 November 1885 sanction was given to McEvilly to go ahead with his school.[6]

Letterfrack opened as an industrial school on 12 October 1887 after the Christian Brothers applied for the reception of 75 boys to their care. Within a few years they had expanded their intake of boys. The Ryan Report states that from the outset 'there was pressure to increase the certified numbers of boys in Letterfrack in order to make it a financially viable project'.[7] When John arrived in 1966, more than 100 boys were being detained there. It was a miserable pit of despair and an ideal breeding ground for paedophiles and sadists.

> The isolated environment in Letterfrack nurtured an institutionalised culture separate from society and other institutions. It also led to another unforeseen problem: those people who chose to abuse boys physically and sexually were able to do so for longer periods of time, because they could escape detection and punishment by reason of the isolated environment in which they operated.[8]

The violence of Letterfrack is well documented in *Founded on Fear*[9] — a memoir by Peter Tyrrell that included his account of his incarceration in Letterfrack from 1925 to 1932. Tyrrell committed suicide in London in 1967. He had deliberately set fire to himself. He had tried for many years to draw attention to the abuse he had endured in Letterfrack but the Catholic Church closed ranks, the Christian Brothers dismissed his accounts of abuse and Irish politicians refused to believe him. Tyrrell's memoirs were discovered years later among the papers of the former Senator and lecturer Dr Owen Sheehy Skeffington. He had encouraged Peter Tyrrell to write his memories as he shared his goal of abolishing corporal punishment in Irish schools.

Letterfrack received boys who had been committed by the courts as juvenile offenders or who had been declared homeless, without proper guardianship, destitute, or found guilty of missing school. It also received boys who were voluntarily admitted by parents or guardians.[10] The majority of the children incarcerated there were from Dublin and Leinster like John Brown.

> It was another place of torture. It would have been more severe [than Upton]. One of the things I detested in the summer was the

bog. The work on the bog was pure savage. In them times you did get good summers so they'd take a load of us up onto the bog and you'd be either stacking the turf or bagging it.

Former inmates of Letterfrack say the Christian Brothers used them to work as child slaves on their farm and bogs, workshops, bakery, kitchen and in other places. The boys were also made to work on local farms during the harvest season. They never got a penny for this unacceptable exploitation. That abuse of the boys' basic human rights characterised John's incarceration in Letterfrack, which amounted to an unbearable and constant ordeal of cruelty.

In the wintertime it was pure bitter cold. And the clothing that you had certainly wouldn't be anything near anything warm and you'd be standing there in the yard in the bitter cold in the winter. And the same thing would happen when you'd go up to Mass every morning, the only heating that they had in the church was coming from the candles that was lighting on the Altar.

John remembers how he'd have to drag the heavy bags of turf along the bogs and lift them up onto a trailer attached to the tractor. The Brothers or lay supervisors would run behind the boys and lash them on the legs if they were loitering with their load. As soon as they reached the tractor they would have to grab another bag and run back down onto the bogs and fill it with another load of turf. Sometimes the lads stayed on the bogs all day long in the summer heat with little breaks in between the gruelling work.

You'd have the heat and you'd take off the shirt with the dust and with the sunburn then it was more than uncomfortable and you'd have one of these trying to take the legs off you and then the midges used to be in the clouds and they'd be eating you.

On one particular day, John and some of the other boys revolted on the bog. They were sick and tired of the cruelty and hard labour. The boys downed their tools and refused to do any more work. When they returned to Letterfrack, the Brothers were out in force to punish the young rebels.

I knew there was something going to go down here. They blew their whistle and clapped their hands and told us to get into lines.

The boys were ordered to take their socks off and put their wellingtons back on. They were then forced to run around the yard in the sweaty wellingtons and engage in punishing training. By then, they were already exhausted from their day on the bogs, and some of the boys began collapsing from the heat and dehydration. The Brothers took up different positions around the yard so that they could thrash the boys with their leather straps when they passed them.

Each time you passed the Brothers, you were getting lashed across the legs and told to hurry up. And that went on for hours.

The Ryan Report concluded that corporal punishment in Letterfrack was severe, excessive and pervasive, and created a climate of fear. It said it was impossible to avoid punishment because it was frequently capricious, unfair and inconsistent. Ryan found that formal public punishments, and punishments within sight or hearing of others at Letterfrack, left a deep and lasting impression on those present. Witnesses told the Ryan team how they were still troubled by memories of seeing and hearing other boys being beaten.[11]

Ryan declared that:

The lack of supervision and control allowed Brothers to devise unusual punishments and there were sadistic elements to some of them . . . The rules on corporal punishment were disregarded and no punishment book was kept, which meant that Brothers were not made accountable for the punishments they administered . . . The Congregation did not carry out proper investigations of cases of physical abuse. It did not impose sanctions on Brothers who were guilty of brutal assaults. It did not seek to enforce either the Department's or its own rules that governed corporal punishment . . . The Department of Education was at fault in failing to ensure that the statutory punishment book was properly maintained and reviewed at every inspection . . . In dealing with cases of excessive punishment, protection of the boys was not a priority for the Congregation and, because the Department left supervision and control entirely to local management the children were left without protection.[12]

Letterfrack's isolation fostered the sadistic conduct of several Christian Brothers. It was a feeding ground for bullies and sexual predators. One witness told the Ryan Commission about Br Percival's[13] disposition for violence. Percival was a sports fanatic who lashed boys with his hurley if they didn't play properly. If his team lost a hurling game, the boys could expect a tirade of beatings over the following week. Percival also brought his maniacal tendencies into the classroom. The witness described how one day this overpowering brute unleashed his temper on one poor young lad who was in callipers.

> This day he took this lad who was talking in the class, and he said, 'Get out there.' [The boy] had callipers on his legs, he could hardly walk. When he got out he just gave him a dig with his fist, knocked him to the floor and jumped on him like he was a bag of potatoes. That lad was in callipers.[14]

The Ryan Report on Letterfrack is a breathtaking record of brutality. One Christian Brother acknowledged his shame to the Ryan team for making a boy eat his own excrement while he was resident in Letterfrack. Another witness described watching one boy being beaten to a pulp on a stage in front of all the other boys.

> ... [he] was called up for his punishment on the stage, and he was battered and beaten by Br Iven[15] in front of — we all had to sit in these chairs as if you were watching a play on the stage and Br Iven battered him, beat him, lashed him, punched him and kicked him and because he wasn't getting any satisfaction, he couldn't make him cry, he started to take off his collar and take his habit down or whatever you call them, and he started to lash him, you know with his fists and stuff. It seemed like it went on for a long, long time and we had to sit there and watch this.[16]

Another boy was beaten badly for attempting to abscond from Letterfrack. He was punished in the washroom next to the dormitories.

The Manager turned off the radio that was playing in the dormitory and invited the rest of the boys who were in their beds to 'now listen to some music' as he brought the boy out to be beaten. His screams were heard throughout the dormitory.[17]

John Brown vividly remembers the haunting cries of boys being beaten by Brothers who worked themselves into an uncontrollable frenzy. He tried to block out the screams by pulling his blankets over his head and his hands over his ears but it was impossible to silence the terror.

> When you were listening to somebody else it was nearly worse than you getting the beating yourself, watching or listening to the screams of somebody getting it.

Aside from the physical and sexual abuse, the boys were shamefully neglected in general in Letterfrack. They were not properly educated and they were frequently cold and hungry. John Brown will never forget the gnawing hunger pangs in his stomach every day. He was a large boy with a big appetite but the food in Letterfrack was woefully inadequate despite its substantial farm. He used to scavenge for food whenever he could. One day those scavenging exploits resulted in a ferocious beating by two Brothers. That day he had been sent up to the vegetable garden in front of the church to do some weeding.

> I was up doing the weeding and there was nobody around so I went over to the Sacristy door of the Church and opened it. I went into the Sacristy and opened the wee press and there was bags of communion. I opened them and started eating them. As such it wasn't Holy Communion because it hadn't gone through the process. You'd want to eat a sack full of it to quench the hunger. Then I got heaps of it and stuck it in my pocket and went back up doing the weeding. But my clean up job mustn't have been the best because that night in the dormitory there was something going down.

Two Brothers strutted into the dormitory that night in a furious state, their faces red hot with anger. They marched down the dormitory like bloodthirsty wolves hunting for prey. John suspected they had discovered that someone had taken the Holy Communion and he tucked himself under the bedclothes hoping they wouldn't pounce on him. But he was their prime suspect. The two Brothers hauled him out of his bed and dragged him down to the washrooms.

> The two of them tore into me between kicking me and beating me with leathers. I was actually lying on the corner in a foetus position and the two of them were shouting, 'You heathen, you desecrated the body of God, you're nothing but a devil' and all this fucking screaming and roaring. I think they were nearly hitting one another in trying to get me.
>
> I walked up to bed that night and Jesus Christ I was in some tatters after the two of them. These people obviously didn't even know their own religion, shouting and screaming at me about desecrating the body of God. The thing has to go onto the Altar and go through the process of Mass. It was just ordinary bread that I ate like did these people even know their own religion?

The Christian Brothers frequently used the washrooms to terrorise the boys. John dreaded Saturday nights when they would have to line up to take a shower.

> The showers had about eight to ten on each side of the shower room. And there was a wee trough that you'd stand in. And various ones [Brothers] used to do the showers. I'd jockey to get into the showers first because if you got into the showers first you'd go to the furthest one away down in the end because your man would be standing there with a lever to turn the water on. And he'd turn the water on to absolute pure scalding that would take the scalp off you. You'd have your back against the wall with the scalding water coming down and he'd turn the lever again to absolutely freezing cold. It was like a drowning situation. And if you jumped out, they'd come along and they'd beat you back in they would. So if you were the furthest away you'd have that bit more manoeuvrability to dodge and duck.

The boy unfortunate enough to take a shower beside the Brother in charge of the lever had little chance of escaping the alternate cascades of scalding hot or freezing cold water.

The Ryan Report concluded that sexual abuse by the Christian Brothers was a chronic problem in Letterfrack. Ryan stated that two Brothers committed long-term abuse of boys over separate periods of 14 years each. The Report is a damning indictment of the Christian Brothers' appalling negligence in failing to act on knowledge of sexual abuse in Letterfrack.

> The Congregation knew that Brothers who sexually abused boys were a continuing danger. It was therefore an act of reckless disregard to send known abusers to any industrial school and, in particular, one as remote and isolated as Letterfrack.
>
> The manner in which sexually abusing Brothers were dealt with is indicative of a policy of protecting the Brothers, the Community and the Congregation at the expense of the victims.[18]

Two Brothers were eventually convicted of the sexual abuse of boys during their residency in Letterfrack. One of them was the notorious paedophile Maurice Tobin, who was given the pseudonym Br Dax in the Ryan Report. He was convicted in 2003 for the sexual assault of a sample of 25 boys in Letterfrack. Tobin spent two stints in Letterfrack from the late 1950s to the 1970s. He usually worked in the kitchen and on the poultry farm. There is a chilling account of his sexual sadism in the Ryan Report. A former inmate of Letterfrack, who was there in the 1960s, described how he used to work in its kitchen. One day Tobin asked him to stay back after everybody else.

> Br Dax [Tobin] calmly poured a cup of tea then took his penis out and forced the boy to give him oral sex.
>
> 'He sat me down, made me a cup of tea, well, poured a cup of tea, and then he took his penis out . . . And he pushed my head down on to his lap, and I had to give him oral sex . . . I got back up, sat up straight and he started opening my trousers then, but I wouldn't so I resisted him. He got angry with me then and he smacked me with a teapot. There was a teapot and he just hit me on the head.'[19]

Another former inmate recounted his experiences of being sexually assaulted by Tobin over a period of about 10 weeks. The abuse happened on Saturday mornings when the boy would have to go to Tobin's bedroom to clean it. Tobin would rub talcum powder around his neck while he mauled and kissed him.

> ... he'd lie on top of me and sexually ... he would have his penis between your buttocks and moving himself about and ejaculated and that's it.[20]

John Brown got off lightly when it came to sexual abuse in Letterfrack. He thinks his height protected him because the Brothers tended to prey on the weaker and more fragile boys.

> They'd walk around the bed at night and you'd have to leave all your clothes at the end of the bed and you'd have to make sure your underpants was included in the clothes so that gave them free access to start meddling.

John left Letterfrack in May 1969 when he was 16. He started off working in odd jobs but gradually he got involved with republican paramilitary organisations. At different stages he was a member of the INLA and the Provisional IRA. His underworld activities with those organisations landed him in deep trouble. Over a period of several years in the 1970s and 1980s, he was involved in various bank robberies. At one stage he was convicted for seven years in Portlaoise after a shoot-out with the Gardaí during the armed robbery of a pub.

> It wasn't a case of the money as such; it was being able to do that to the society.

Ironically, John believes he was treated better by the Irish justice system as an adult than he had been as a child even though there was no comparison in the crimes he had committed. In the end he turned against the paramilitary organisations.

> When you look at some of these people's behaviour it's distasteful and the kind of things that was going on. And the whole lot of it was riddled with informers so it would be only a matter of time before you'd end back up in jail with somebody informing on you. As well

as that I didn't entirely agree with some of the acts that they done. Some of the acts was totally brutal to people even to their own. And the filth regarding the hierarchy of it. It was a kind of a cliquey thing. If the Army [regular] was after going doing something, he gets taken out and at best he gets knee capped and could get knuckled in the bleedin' head. But if it's the uppity people, people with the ruling hands in it, they didn't get beaten up.

John passionately believes he would not have pursued a criminal career if he had not been sentenced to time in Upton and Letterfrack. The schools were breeding grounds for criminals in his view because the religious orders treated them as such. During our interview he rattled off the names of some of Ireland's more notorious criminals who had been incarcerated in industrial schools like Letterfrack when they were children. There's no doubt Irish prisons have been populated over the years by former inmates of religious industrial schools. John's opportunities for a successful crime-free life were stymied as soon as the guards caught him with the few pigeons in the derelict house.

You had a grudge against society regarding people that you were meeting afterwards . . . When you did come out of these places and you went for a job, they wanted to know where you went to school. And as soon as you said an industrial school — 'Good luck!' You couldn't get into the likes of CIE or the Council or Corporation or any Government body. If you wanted to become a guard or a screw in the prison, you were blocked from them all. When they asked you where you were educated as soon as you said in an industrial school that was it, good-bye to you, they looked upon you as a criminal. If you're being looked upon as a criminal, you might as well be one.

When the stories of child sexual abuse in the religious institutions exploded in the 1990s, John began to delve into his past. The ghosts of Upton and Letterfrack returned and he used to wake up during the night screaming and sweating with fear. It was during this time that he began to take a number of legal cases against the Christian Brothers and the Irish State. That meant raking through the abuse he had endured in the industrial schools. Those traumatic recollections ultimately resulted in a nervous breakdown in 2001.

It was like having a monster locked in the cellar for years and I opened the cellar door and let the monster out thinking that I was capable of taking it on. But within a year of going into it, I had a nervous breakdown. I thought I had the ability to handle it but it took the legs from under me.

I got so engrossed in it that I rang him [psychiatrist] one day and said, 'You're going to have to hypnotise me. I'm back in there and I can't get out.'

John Brown is still angry at the abuse and injustice he suffered as a child and the role the Irish State played in his incarceration. He believes the Commission to Inquire into Child Abuse has been a whitewash because it never properly investigated how and why Irish judges were able to hand down lengthy sentences on young boys like him for minor misdemeanours. The negligent conduct of the Department of Education, in its failure to supervise and inspect schools like Upton and Letterfrack, reinforced John's cynical view of the Irish State.

I became very aware of what a dirty, filthy state we live in. I knew that I wouldn't get full satisfaction and I wished that this thing had never been opened. I'd have rather kept the monster locked in the cellar.

Today John survives on social welfare and he gets a disability allowance for a heart condition. He is married and has four children.

Chapter 7 ∾

MARIE THERESE O'LOUGHLIN AND GOLDENBRIDGE

On Wednesday, 10 June 2009, three weeks after the publication of the Ryan Report, a silent march of solidarity for the victims of religious institutional abuse took place in Dublin. From before noon, crowds began to gather at the Garden of Remembrance in Parnell Square at the top of O'Connell Street. People mingled in the heat in their short sleeves, light trousers, dresses and sandals. The sunshine seemed perversely out of place as it gave a carnival veneer to the day's sombre proceedings. An unwitting bystander could have mistaken the pre-march buzz and activity for the launch of a summer festival. But the troubled faces of those milling around revealed something more disturbing.

A man with a large handlebar moustache wore a black T-shirt with the words 'Artane 1954 The Boy with the Broken Arm' emblazoned on it. A woman hugged a man wearing cumbersome bicycle gear who was sobbing like a child. He clung to her awkwardly as his legs straddled his bicycle and he tried to keep his balance. One man held aloft a crucifix with locks and chains twisted around it. Another dishevelled soul with a lost vacant stare shuffled uneasily. He looked lonely and bewildered. An attractive young woman with long brown hair and a sad wistful demeanour clutched a tiny red shoe in her hand.

The highly charged atmosphere was like a cocktail of traumatised emotions. This was the first time many survivors of religious institutional abuse publically expressed their pain. Their accounts of their miserable childhoods in industrial and reformatory schools had been dismissed for decades as the powerful Catholic Church in Ireland had hoodwinked their Congregations into disbelieving such abuse could be conducted by God's holy men and women.

Up until the day of the march, many inmates of industrial schools had kept their pasts locked away for fear of releasing the genie of their broken childhoods. The publication of the Ryan Report blew that fragile façade apart and forced thousands of survivors of religious abuse to face their demons. The march of solidarity gave many of them their first opportunity to collectively acknowledge their stolen childhoods.

A woman handed out tiny white ribbons twisted around a lapel pin. Bystanders pinned them on their tops as a mark of solidarity. A line of guards tried to keep some order over the march but a few of the protesters got stroppy and complained about being herded into groups. 'Don't be shoving us back,' one agitated woman shouted. 'We haven't come here to be treated like cattle.' After years of being ignored, these survivors wanted their day of recognition. Shortly after noon the marchers began to walk slowly down O'Connell Street. Those heading the group carried wreaths and a large white banner with the words 'Cherishing all the children of the nation equally' — an extract from the doomed 1916 Proclamation of Independence.

A couple of survivors in wheelchairs moved in front of the main body of marchers. Garda cars cleared the streets and curious onlookers stood by uneasily as the long lines of silent people progressed down O'Connell Street. They seemed unsure how to respond. Their unease reflected a national embarrassment at the length of time it had taken the Irish State and people to acknowledge the systematic abuse that the religious orders had carried out against the children in their care. Some bystanders clapped their hands, others bowed their heads in silence. A few shuffled awkwardly on the streets, their perturbed faces reflecting a confusion about how best to express their sympathies with the survivors.

A plethora of photographers and television crews filmed and snapped around them as the crowds eased slowly through Dublin's main artery. Reporters with pressing deadlines grabbed snatches of stories from brief conversations with former residents of abusive institutions. They rapidly recorded vital details and tried to squash a lifetime of horror into a few soundbites.

I talked with one of the women being pushed in a wheelchair. She had cropped black hair that was sprinkled with grey and she was holding a piece of cardboard on her lap. Written on it were the words 'No 54, Mary Harney St Finbar's Industrial School, Good Shepherd Convent, Sunday's Well, Cork. Incarcerated 1954–1965'. With a slight American twang, Mary Harney told me she had flown in from the US especially to take part in the march. She carried a child's tiny red shoe in her hands — a symbol of the awful abuse she and her fellow marchers had suffered as children. As we gradually twisted our way around Trinity College she spoke calmly about the loveless childhood she had spent at St Finbar's. Her life there was marked by starvation, physical and sexual abuse, humiliation, loneliness and lies. The Good Shepherd Sisters, who had subjected her to years of horrific abuse, had led her to believe she was an orphan when, Mary feels, they knew all along her mother was alive and well.

When Mary went to investigate her background many years after leaving St Finbar's, she discovered that her mother was unmarried when she became pregnant. Mary's fate was sealed when her mother decided to forfeit her baby for the sake of staving off moral outrage at the child's illegitimate conception. She kept her pregnancy a secret and handed over her newborn baby to the nuns. Mary told me how, as a child, she had fantasised about her mother and imagined her to be a glamorous beauty like the movie star Rita Hayworth. Those illusions were shattered to pieces when she eventually met the small, plain, dumpy woman many years later.

Another wheelchair-bound survivor recounted the abuse she had suffered as a child in the 1930s — 83-year-old Kathleen Dunne, who was being pushed by her daughter Maria, described how her life was nearly destroyed from the time she spent at an industrial school in Tralee from 1933 to 1936. Although her incarceration happened a long time ago, the snow-white haired lady recalled with piercing clarity the hunger and beatings she was subjected to by the Daughters of Charity. The damage done to Kathleen Dunne during her early institutionalisation passed through the generations. Both her daughter and son also ended up in industrial schools where they too were abused.

About an hour later, we finally turned onto Molesworth Street where a truck with a make-shift stage was parked by the footpath. Molesworth Street juts onto Kildare Street where the Irish Parliament, Dáil Éireann, is located. For decades this narrow road has been a popular venue for angry protesters voicing their opposition to government policies. The atmosphere on that unforgettable day in June 2009 was a sobering cocktail of sadness and outrage. People stood with tears in their eyes as they remembered their awful childhoods in the industrial schools. Men and women carried memorabilia of the harsh religious regimes that ran the institutions. One man, in a shabby brown suit, had an old leather strap with a coin embedded in the bottom of it. It was typical of the straps used by the Christian Brothers to lash the boys in their care.

Representatives of the main victims' groups began to address the marchers from the podium. The crowd had swelled to around 5,000 and Molesworth Street was throbbing with emotion as the survivors unwittingly participated in a sort of disturbing group therapy. Some of them struggled to contain their sorrow as they revisited their pasts. Others were angry at the way the Irish State had colluded for decades in the incarceration of children like them in abusive institutions. The mood was a mix of anger, sadness, pain and relief. For decades these former inmates of industrial schools had been ignored and their stories of cruelty dismissed. But they felt vindicated when the Ryan Report was published in May 2009. It validated their accounts of abuse and with it came a long-overdue acknowledgment by the Irish public of the magnitude of the abuse that had been carried out for decades by religious orders.

Adult men and women cried as Christine Buckley from the Aislinn Centre addressed them from the stage. 'We have been silenced for so long. I wish we could do this three hundred and sixty-five days a year,' she told the packed crowds in front of her. They roared in approval. 'We believed that this day would never have happened had it not been for you, the public, thank you, public.'

The powerfully charged atmosphere ignited a fireworks of emotions for the adults haunted by their childhoods. At times the atmosphere was menacing. A few people called for the priests and nuns present to stand up on the stage and account for the crimes committed by their Congregations. 'Hang them!' a man shouted. 'Compulsive liars!' yelled another. 'What about the children still locked up in mental hospitals?' demanded an angry man. All of a sudden one woman began shouting and demanding the right to address the crowds. 'I spent two years outside the Dáil and the government didn't listen to me,' she cried. She shouted that she had fallen off a high chair into a burning fire in the Regina Coeli institution and that the Redress Board had never given her the opportunity to seek compensation for her injuries.

The people on the podium shuffled uneasily, conscious that her intense outburst could spark a plethora of demands for the microphone. They shook their heads and sympathised with her and pleaded with her to understand that they did not have the time to hear individual stories. They needed to lay their wreaths, hand over their petition to the government and visit the Irish President at her residence in the Phoenix Park.

But this angry woman refused to be silenced and she kept on shouting. Gradually the crowds began to support her. 'Give her the mike, for God's sake,' people cried. Others criticised the representatives onstage and accused them of hogging the proceedings. 'You don't speak for us,' shouted a few. Finally the organisers caved in. After a brief kefuffle, 59-year-old Marie Therese O'Loughlin was pulled up onto the stage. Her long auburn hair and ruddy complexion gave her a kind of wild look. She pulled her blue cardigan over her floral dress and in a spine-chilling few minutes she gave a brief vignette of her appalling childhood in the notorious Goldenbridge Industrial School, which was run by the Sisters of Mercy in Inchicore, Dublin. 'The children were left, their bodies from head to toe were full of excrement every morning. And children like us from eleven years of age had to clean those children with cold water,' she cried.

She lashed out at those who had for years ignored her accounts of abuse in both Goldenbridge and the Regina Coeli Residential Hostel in North Brunswick Street, Dublin. 'This was a mini holocaust and the government and the religious tried to pretend we weren't hurt in these institutions,' she told the onlookers. Marie Therese's highly charged invective captivated the crowds. People were transfixed as they listened to her harrowing recollections of her childhood.

After several more impromptu speeches from survivors, the main representatives took control of proceedings again and picked up where they had left off. With stark delivery, they read out the names of the 216 institutions where young lives had been shredded to pieces. Black and white balloons were released into the air to symbolise the dead and living victims of institutional abuse. A petition was handed into Dáil Éireann and people tied tiny children's shoes to the gates of the Dáil. Politicians who had left their offices mingled with the victims of abuse. They nodded sympathetically as they listened to their stories and the media recorded their reactions. Gradually the crowds began to disperse and the heightened energy of the day dissipated. I went looking for Marie Therese O'Loughlin and spotted her chatting with a few passers-by who expressed their sympathies with her.

Several weeks later I arranged to meet Marie Therese to conduct a longer interview and to hear a proper account of her story. I had asked her to meet me at a private members' club in the middle of Dublin. I was running late and when I arrived she was already waiting in the garden terrace at the back. She was twitchy and uneasy. She later explained that the large walls surrounding the terrace reminded her of the main yard in Goldenbridge where the children scrambled like animals for scraps of food that had been thrown to them by the staff. She became increasingly uncomfortable sitting on the garden bench caged in by the high grey walls. We went inside and up to one of the large elegant rooms in the back where she relayed the chilling details of her life.

Marie Therese was born in the Rotunda Hospital in 1950. Her mother was unmarried. She had become pregnant by a farmer in Co. Clare but she got no support from him and so she decided to hide her pregnancy from her family. None of them knew she had given birth to a baby girl and shortly after Marie Therese was born her mother took her to the Regina Coeli Residential Hostel for mothers and babies. These mother and babies homes were secretive places. 'No one but no one knew she was pregnant,' Marie Therese whispered to me as she poured tea from a silver pot into a white china cup. 'She was a very secretive person, a bit like myself that told nobody about myself. She told nobody about herself either.'

Marie Therese discovered that her mother had lived with her in the Regina Coeli institution for four years and ten months. Her recollections of that time are vague but documents she discovered later confirmed her mother had stayed with her there until 1955.

All the papers signify that, that she would have been there because the Regina Coeli wouldn't keep you there unless you had your mother.

The conditions there were diabolical. They were Dickensian.

Marie Therese believes her mother must have worked outside the hostel to earn money. It would have been common at the time for the older mothers to go out to work while the younger women took care of their children during the day. When Carmel O'Loughlin met her daughter years later she told her she had suffered from periodic bouts of tuberculosis when she was in the Regina Coeli. She had to spend chunks of time in St May's Hospital in the Phoenix Park.

She was very ill. And one of her lungs collapsed for three years.

Marie Therese's horrific accident happened when she was 18 months old. For years she never knew why she was so scarred as she had no direct memory of the event. She had assumed she had been born with her deformities. At the time of the accident, other young mothers in Regina Coeli were looking after the younger children and Marie Therese's mother was in hospital. That day when she was supposed to be supervised she fell off her high chair into a blazing fire and suffered severe burns. When I asked her what sort of injuries she had sustained she bowed her head and looked away and slipped her right hand out of view. I had noticed several times how she frequently hid her hand in embarrassment. 'My fingers are bad,' she told me as she tucked her right hand under her cardigan.

Marie Therese suffered burns to her face and fingers. She only discovered the truth about the accident years later when she retrieved her medical records at Temple Street Hospital where she had been brought after the accident. 'I had a skin graft on my face there,' she said as she pulled her long auburn hair away from the side of her face to reveal a whiter piece of skin that had been grafted over the burnt flesh. 'That skin was from my leg,' she whispered. Her voice trailed off as she described how her fingers had practically melted away.

In 2005 she pitched a tent in front of Dáil Éireann's iron gates to demand that the government include the Regina Coeli institution in the Ryan Commission Inquiry and the Redress Board. For nearly two years she lived in her tent outside the Dáil where she staged daily protests to get formal recognition for the trauma she had suffered as a result of the accident. Her gruelling campaign forced her to confront her past.

I never acknowledged to myself that I had an injury as well as everything else. I had to come clean about what had happened to me

Boys sewing in one of the workshops at the notorious St Joseph's Industrial School, Ferryhouse, Clonmel. The Ryan Report concluded that the use of corporal punishment there was 'pervasive, excessive, unpredictable and without regulation or supervision'. It also stated that sexual abuse by Brothers in Ferryhouse was 'a chronic problem' and that living conditions there were 'poor, unhygienic, inadequate and often overcrowded'. (*Courtesy of The Rosminians*)

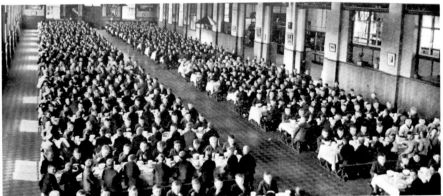

Boys eating their dinner in the enormous dining hall at St Joseph's Industrial School, Artane, Dublin. It operated from 1870 to 1969. Approximately 15,500 boys were incarcerated in Artane during its existence. At its height in 1948 a staggering 830 boys were detained there. According to the Ryan Report boys were ordered to be detained by the courts in Artane for reasons of 'inadequate parental care, destitution, neglect, truancy or the commission of minor offences'. However, Ryan stated that poverty was the underlying reason for why children ended up there. (*Courtesy of The Christian Brothers*)

St Conleth's Reformatory School, Daingean, Co. Offaly, where Noel Kelly was sexually, physically and emotionally abused. The Ryan Report found that Daingean was 'run on penal lines, where repressive measures were the order of the day'. Boys were sent there for several years for committing minor offences. Ryan stated that 'hardened criminals in prisons were not subjected to the violence or deprivation' experienced by the boys in Daingean. (*Photocall Ireland*)

Noel Kelly recovering from burn injuries at St James's Hospital in Dublin after he doused himself with petrol before setting himself alight in May 2001. At the time he had been protesting outside Dáil Éireann. (*Collins Agency*)

Michael O'Brien confronts the Minister for Children at a press conference on 28 July 2009 to lay out the implementation plan of recommendations following the Ryan Report into abuse at State-run institutions. (*Photocall Ireland*)

St Joseph's Industrial School, Ferryhouse, Clonmel where Michael O'Brien spent eight years of his childhood. (*Courtesy of The Rosminians*)

Boys playing in the yard at Ferryhouse Industrial School. (*Courtesy of The Rosminians*)

Boys mending shoes in one of the workshops at Ferryhouse. (*Courtesy of The Rosminians*)

Michael O'Brien [2nd from left] marches with other survivors of institutional abuse through Dublin on 10 June 2009. (*The Irish Times*)

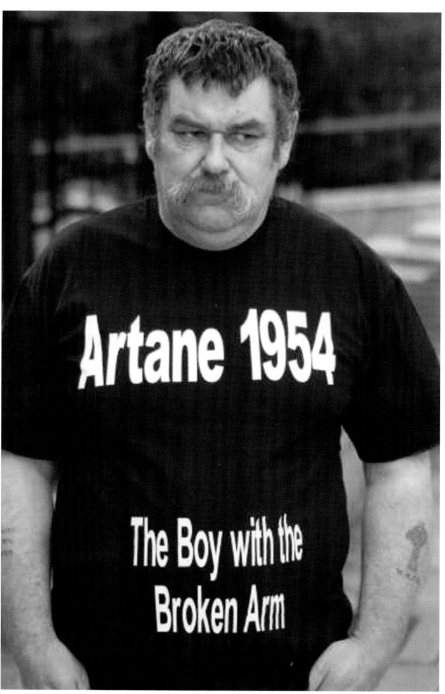

Kevin Flanagan wearing the T-shirt that encapsulates the sad story of his brother Mickey, whose arm was broken in three places in 1954 by a furious Christian Brother at Artane Industrial School. This picture was taken on 20 May 2009 when the Ryan Report was published. (*Collins Agency*)

Kevin Flanagan stands outside the GPO in Dublin on the first day of his hunger strike on 17 December 2009 to highlight the abuse his brother Mickey suffered at Artane Industrial School. (*Photocall Ireland*)

Old picture of St Joseph's Industrial School, Artane, Dublin where Mickey Flanagan was incarcerated as a child. (*Courtesy of The Christian Brothers*)

Old picture of boys at work in one of the workshops at Artane. (*Courtesy of The Christian Brothers*)

Boys working in carpentry at Artane. (*Courtesy of The Christian Brothers*)

Boys working in cloth finishing at Artane. (*Courtesy of The Christian Brothers*)

Boys working in the harness shop at Artane. (*Courtesy of The Christian Brothers*)

Boys working in the Dye House at Artane. (*Courtesy of The Christian Brothers*)

Old picture of an infirmary at Artane. (*Courtesy of The Christian Brothers*)

One of the massive dormitories where boys slept at Artane. (*Courtesy of The Christian Brothers*)

One of the shower rooms where boys would wash themselves at Artane. (*Courtesy of The Christian Brothers*)

Old picture of Letterfrack Industrial School where an estimated 100 boys died from the day it opened for business in 1887 to its closure in 1974. The Ryan Report found that physical, emotional and sexual abuse were systematic there. (*Courtesy of The Christian Brothers*)

Marie Therese O'Loughlin [right] speaks to the crowds of people attending the march of solidarity for victims of religious institutional abuse on 10 June 2009. She is speaking on the makeshift stage on Molesworth Street across the road from Dáil Éireann. (*The Irish Times*)

Crowds of people march through Dublin's city centre to show their solidarity for victims of religious institutional abuse on 10 June 2009. (*The Irish Times*)

A tiny child's shoe is held aloft during the solidarity march for victims of institutional abuse on 10 June 2009. Hundreds of people carried children's shoes that day to symbolise the suffering boys and girls endured in religious institutions in Ireland. (*The Irish Times*)

St Joseph's Industrial School, Salthill, which was run by the Christian Brothers and the place where both Tommy Millar and Gerry Carey were incarcerated as children. (*Courtesy of The Christian Brothers*)

John Kelly [left] joins Christine Buckley on the makeshift stage on Molesworth Street, Dublin, during the march for victims of institutional abuse. (*The Irish Times*)

Gerry Carey as a young boy when he was attending St Joseph's Industrial School, Salthill. (*Courtesy of Gerry Carey*)

so being outside the Dáil was a cathartic experience for me. I was so in pain when all this institutional abuse thing came to the fore. I was so distraught when I discovered that they were going to carve my pain in two and say, 'Oh well we're not dealing with the Regina Coeli.'

Marie Therese endured icy nights, poor sanitation, humiliation, discomfort and derogatory comments from passersby during her long vigil. Tragically her efforts were fruitless as the Regina Coeli hostel was never included in the list of religious institutions investigated for child abuse. Marie Therese was devastated.

The fire to me was like sexual abuse multiplied by two thousand.

At this stage of our interview our tea and coffee had gone cold and our sandwiches were wilting. But there was more to unearth from Marie Therese's complicated life. We had not yet discussed her incarceration in Goldenbridge, where she spent over 11 years. When she was just under five years old, her mother disappeared from her life and Marie Therese didn't see her again until 1978, when the two women arranged to meet at Victoria Station in London.

Marie Therese later discovered that in 1955 Carmel O'Loughlin took her daughter out of the Regina Coeli hostel and brought her to St Vincent's Industrial School in Goldenbridge, Dublin. This awful place was castigated for its cruelty in the Ryan Report. Former residents gave damning evidence about the abuse they suffered there and their accounts caused consternation to the Sisters of Mercy who had dismissed such stories for years.

Goldenbridge first came to prominence in 1993 when Christine Buckley described on RTÉ's Gay Byrne morning radio show the abuse she had endured there as a child. She had contacted the show in an effort to try to find her father. During the interview she talked about her appalling childhood in Goldenbridge. Her frankness opened the floodgates and former residents of Goldenbridge and other industrial schools contacted the programme. The national media then picked up on the story and over the following three years accounts of abuse in religious institutions received sporadic coverage. But it was not until 1996, when a documentary on Christine Buckley's life was broadcast on

RTÉ television, that the spotlight returned to Goldenbridge. The dramatised 'Dear Daughter' documentary contained a number of serious allegations about the school and the nuns running it. The Sisters of Mercy refuted the allegations made in the programme.

Shortly after its broadcast, Sr Xeveria Lally, who was in charge of Goldenbridge during much of Christine Buckley's time there, was interviewed on RTÉ's 'Prime Time' programme. Whilst she admitted that she had been harsh at times, she denied that children were abused there. That denial characterised the Sisters of Mercy's belligerent and dogged refusal to acknowledge their role in the abuse of children in their care. But as more horror stories about their cruelty emerged in the 1990s, the pressure increased on religious orders to own up to their abusive legacy. Their façade of innocence began to collapse in 1999 after the broadcast on RTÉ of Mary Raftery's compelling series 'States of Fear'. The three-part series exposed the astonishing level of past abuse in Ireland's industrial schools. Former residents told how their lives were permanently damaged as a result of their incarceration in religious institutions.

Marie Therese's life in Goldenbridge was a living hell. Throughout her incarceration there she tried to understand why her mother had abandoned her to such a miserable and abusive institution. She put that question to her when they met in 1978.

> I told her what a terrible place it was. She tried to dismiss it. She said she thought I would be safe there and that I would be protected and that it was always her wish that I would come looking for her which I think is a very selfish thing to say to a child.

Carmel O'Loughlin was not the kind of woman you could press for an answer. She remained tight-lipped and insisted that she had no idea Goldenbridge was such a terrible place. In 2005 Marie Therese gave evidence to the Ryan Commission about the abuse she had endured at Goldenbridge. She says that during those hearings she was told that, in 1955, her mother had asked the nuns to mind the little girl for a few months. Carmel O'Loughlin had told the Sisters she needed to go to her brother's ordination and that she wanted the nuns to mind her daughter in her absence. During the hearings Marie Therese heard that the young mother reassured the nuns that she would return for Marie

Therese but she never did so.

According to Marie Therese, this story does not fully add up because she later discovered that her uncle had entered the priesthood only in 1955 and that he was not ready for ordination until 1959. That was four years after Marie Therese's mother had claimed was the date for his full incorporation into the priesthood. Marie Therese was unable to verify this story as she could not retrieve any documentary evidence to support the explanation for her incarceration in Goldenbridge that was given to the Ryan Commission. The full truth remains buried with her mother, who died in 1990. One can only draw conclusions about the inconsistencies in the story but a plausible explanation could be attributable to family embarrassment. It is quite feasible that Marie Therese's mother did not want to jeopardise her brother's chances of joining the priesthood by any revelations that his sister was an unmarried mother. She may have been terrified that someday someone she knew would spot her with her daughter in Dublin. If that news got back to her family, it could have ended her brother's ambition to become a priest. In 1955 in Ireland, a family member with a child out of wedlock could seriously hinder a budding vocation. Marie Therese was to pay a huge price for her uncle's priestly ambitions.

There is another twist to her story. Marie Therese believes her mother did not disappear immediately after handing over her daughter to the nuns. She suspects she hung around Goldenbridge for a year or so and that she had some sort of job there.

> Other people said they saw her coming in during the day and leaving . . . this tall woman.

This part of her childhood is blurred. While she has no direct memories of seeing her mother at Goldenbridge, she gets flashbacks of being pulled away by the nuns after going up to a woman she now believes must have been Carmel O'Loughlin.

> I have traumatic memories of being dragged away by the nun who was Sr Xeveria.

Marie Therese has many reasons to be angry at her mother for leaving her to the mercy of the Sisters at Goldenbridge.

Goldenbridge was a hellhole. I never liked Goldenbridge from the day I went there to the day I left it. And the day that I left Goldenbridge I never voluntarily went back there. I closed the door on that institution.

The memories that I have only came flooding back to me when the 'Dear Daughter' programme erupted and I saw Sr Xeveria's face on the television and Christine Buckley's. I cried and I cried and I know that my counterparts did the same. We all had the same reaction. And we all had that thing about the shame, the fear of Goldenbridge.

St Vincent's Industrial School in Goldenbridge was originally built as a refuge for female convicts who had been serving prison sentences in Mountjoy jail. It opened in 1856 and the Sisters of Mercy continued to run it as a rehabilitation service for former female prisoners until 1883. In 1858 the nuns expanded the complex by building a convent, a national school for the poor of the area and a commercial laundry on its grounds. In 1880 a building within the complex was certified as an industrial school for girls. This was to be St Vincent's Industrial School and it opened with an initial intake of 30 girls. When the original convict refuge closed in 1883 the nuns converted the buildings into additional parts of the industrial school. Over the next two years dormitories, a dining hall, workrooms and extra accommodation were all added. The extra room meant more capacity and within five years of its original certification, St Vincent's was taking in 150 children. This number greatly increased in the 1950s and 1960s up to a high of 193 in 1964. When Goldenbridge closed in 1983 there were 46 children there.[1]

Marie Therese shivered when I asked her to describe the place. She called it the house with the hundred windows. Sr Xeveria Lally was one of the most notorious nuns in charge of Goldenbridge. The children called her Sr Severia. In the Ryan Report she was given the pseudonym Sr Alida. She features heavily in the Report as many of the complainants made direct allegations of abuse against her. In the early 1940s, Sr Xeveria came to Goldenbridge as a newly professed Sister in her mid-twenties. Shortly afterwards, she was appointed as the assistant to the Resident Manager there. The Ryan Report stated that conditions in Goldenbridge were atrocious in the earlier decades of the last century.

The condition of the children was so bad that the School had to be closed down for two weeks whilst the problems of scabies and ringworm were tackled. Bedding had to be removed and disinfected by Dublin Corporation, and all the children's clothing had to be boil-washed.[2]

During Sr Xeveria's early days at the school, conditions were extremely bleak. She told the Ryan Commission that the washing machines were so old and ineffective they were not used. All the washing for the 150 children was done by hand. It was difficult to heat this vast institution and all the clothing for the children was handmade by the older children there. Sr Xeveria admitted to the Commission that the older girls did all of the domestic chores in the house. In 1954 Sr Xeveria effectively took over the management of Goldenbridge and she held that position until 1963. By the time Marie Therese arrived in 1955, she was well into her stride running the place. By then St Vincent's had been given certification by the Department of Education to house up to 165 children. This included a certification for the admission of 15 infant boys.[3]

Marie Therese dreaded the mornings when they would be roused from their beds and frequently lined up for a beating.

Children in Goldenbridge had to line up every single morning of their lives. Children had to line up to be beaten by Sr Severia with her big stick. And she walloped and she walloped children including myself. And I was made to put out the bad hand. I could not show her my other hand. It was the bad hand, you always had to put your right hand out. And she knew I had those injuries.

Many of these unfortunate children were bed-wetters. The 'wet the beds' were treated like criminals in Goldenbridge and most of them ended up in two dormitories. Every morning they would be lined up for a beating for soiling their bedclothes the night before. The children used to dread the sound of Sr Xeveria marching down the corridor with her 'slapper'.

Every morning as fresh as a daisy she would be. And she would be flaying and jumping and shouting. And the froth would come out of her mouth. Everybody in that institution was afraid of that woman.

Public humiliation was part of the bed-wetting punishment. Marie Therese remembers how Sr Xeveria would tell them they were 'dirty things'. The older children were made to hold up their wet sheets so that the damp patches could be seen. Derogatory remarks were made about their family backgrounds. If they were born out of wedlock that 'shameful' fact would be highlighted in front of the other children. Ironically, Marie Therese's own background was never spoken about in public. She never remembers hearing insulting remarks about her own mother. It was only years later, when she discovered her uncle was a priest, that she understood why the nuns remained tight-lipped about her own family.

> The ones that had religious in their family were never spoken about.
> Now I realise it's because she wasn't going to come along and say your mother was this because she'd be kind of pointing the finger at her own society, at herself.

It was common for the nuns to keep critical information about the children's backgrounds a secret. Many of the young inmates at Goldenbridge were falsely led to believe they were orphans with no known living relatives. Some of them discovered only later in life that they had living family members. But while her mother's religious connections were hidden, they didn't protect Marie Therese from enduring physical abuse. She was frequently beaten by the nuns and by Sr Xeveria in particular.

> I was very very unhappy from the time I went there. I never made friends with people. I was always a loner in Goldenbridge. I was always looking out the window at other children getting their visitors and always again on the outside looking in. I felt that I personally was on the lower rung of the ladder and was used to having to do the dirty jobs at Goldenbridge. I was selected specifically for them. And I grew up looking at other children being favoured and going to dancing classes; going to musical classes and I love music, I absolutely love it.

Marie Therese has disturbing memories of the nights she spent in the bleak Sacred Heart Dormitory where the bed-wetters were sent. She became queasy when she began to describe the long rows of beds of frightened children. They used to be terrified at night in case they soiled their sheets because they knew they would get a hiding from Sr Xeveria the next day. 'I'm getting sick even thinking of it,' Marie Therese admitted as she clutched her stomach and bowed her head.

> There were two toilets at the end and we used to be called up when we were very young in the early hours of the morning. Oh God, it's terrible. We'd be called out of our beds, two to a toilet. We'd have to go into the toilet and sit on them at two o'clock in the morning. But children still wet their beds.

The lay staff attached to the dormitory would march into the ward in the early hours of the morning and force the children to get up out of their beds and go to the toilet. Marie Therese is still haunted by the children crying in the wards as they were forced to urinate in the cold, stinking toilets.

> They were clattered and beaten and the toilets would be saturated ... and the stench and everything that came from that dormitory in the morning. That was the dormitory that I had to wash the sheets from. And it was the ones on the lowest rung of the Goldenbridge ladder that you would find that they were in this section. And there were children there that would have wet their beds up to sixteen years of age and they would have been embarrassed about that. So they would have been in the laundry with me doing the laundry.

Marie Therese believes the girls who ended up in the Sacred Heart ward suffered particularly badly and that some of her contemporaries who slept there died prematurely. She recalled how one former inmate she knew, who spent years sleeping in the Sacred Heart ward, committed suicide years later. In its chapter on Goldenbridge, the Ryan Report devotes a significant segment on bed-wetting and the punishments endured by the children who soiled their sheets. The stories corroborate Marie Therese's accounts of the lashings that were given to the children, who were obviously traumatised from being incarcerated in

Goldenbridge as bed-wetting is a classic symptom of trauma. The Report heard from former inmates of Goldenbridge who spoke about the preventative measures that were taken to try to stop the children from soiling their bed-sheets.

> Bed-wetters had their consumption of water restricted in an attempt to reduce the likelihood of an accident at night. Girls were thirsty as a result, and sought sources of water. This included drinking out of cisterns of toilets located near the dormitories. Some gave evidence that children drank out of the pan of the toilet. The attempt to prevent the intake of fluid proved to be largely unsuccessful.[4]

The meagre facilities at the industrial school meant bed-wetting posed a huge logistical challenge.

> The practical problems were formidable. Bedclothes were made of materials such as calico and wool that were difficult to wash and dry quickly. Laundry facilities that might have been stretched in normal circumstances had to handle an increased volume of soiled bed linen. It has to be acknowledged, therefore, that bed-wetting constituted a major challenge to the facilities in an industrial school.[5]

The daily loads of dirty laundry meant the nuns and lay staff took an unforgiving approach to those children prone to wetting their beds. There are several personal accounts in the Report about the lashings given to bed-wetters. One former resident described how she used to wet the bed nearly every night. Her punishment was inflicted on her by Sr Xeveria's predecessor, Sr Bianca.[6]

> When I wet the bed which was nearly every night, she would bring you into this room, it's called the linen room, it was a high room and a narrow room. She just proceeded to put me on the floor on my stomach, she put her left knee on my back, this was the punishment I was getting by the way for wetting the bed, and a big girl, just a big girl . . . again, to me she was about fifteen or sixteen . . . she had to hold my legs down, pull down my pants and Mother Bianca pulled

up my top and proceeded to smack me really hard for a while on the bum.[7]

Another witness described the humiliation she endured.

I remember there was a recreation hall and those of us who had wet the bed on some occasions we had to go into the front hall and stand there and people were coming in and out. On other occasions we had to go into the recreation hall, again with the wet sheets, and the other children were encouraged to walk around and jeer us. They would call us wet-the-beds.[8]

Some of the bed-wetters ended up on Goldenbridge's notorious landing on the first floor. Children were regularly beaten in this cold dark corridor, which lay beside the nuns' rooms. The nuns delivered savage punishments for minor and, at times, non-existent misdemeanours. Former inmates of Goldenbridge have spoken about the time they spent shivering in their nightclothes in the freezing cold on the landing as they waited for Sr Xeveria to march down the corridor with her slapper. In May 2009 Christine Buckley gave a harrowing account of her time on Goldenbridge's infamous landing when I interviewed her on my radio show 'The Wide Angle' on Newstalk. 'I lived on the landing,' she said. 'Every single night. I never knew what I was there for.'[9]

Christine described the ferocious hidings she would get from Sr Xeveria. 'It wasn't a beating, it was a slaughtering. And after the slaughtering she'd chase you into the dormitories so that the children in the dormitories were rattling.' She recoiled when she recounted her ghastly childhood in Goldenbridge. 'The babies were strapped to potties and their little rectums fell down. And all day long you were shoving up rectums. And the damage that that has done.'[10] The Ryan Commission heard testimonials from former Goldenbridge residents who recalled their terrifying experiences on the landing. Many times they had to stand for hours in the cold with bare feet. Sometimes the waiting was worse than the beating itself.

To me, I think we waited two or three hours sometimes. We were just there, it really got late and we were falling asleep, and pushing one another when we heard her coming. You heard her coming eventually, but it wasn't only an hour or a half an hour, she would never come too soon it was always like you were there for ever, it seemed like forever . . . if it wasn't in her office, we were hit on the landing, smacked on the landing . . . just her stick, the one she had everywhere with her. She just used to just bash you, just literally turn you around and wallop you. Sometimes she would hold out your hand, it depended.[11]

The children ended up on the landing for minor offences.

They seemed to be very very menial things, like maybe you stole a slice of bread or you ate out of the rabbit's cage or you drank water out of the toilet . . . There wouldn't have been anything, except my dress tore one time and that was another thing that I remembered.[12]

The frightening ordeal of waiting for Sr Xeveria turned the landing into something akin to William Golding's fictional island in Lord of the Flies, where the chaotic circumstances forced the deserted children to engage in a nasty power struggle. Marie Therese remembers how the older children would push the younger ones to the top of the queue so that they would be the first to receive Sr Xeveria's lashings. By the time she reached the end of the line she would have vented the worst of her ferocious temper on the smaller girls. One witness at the Ryan Commission described how she is still tormented by the screams of the younger children who were first in line for Sr Xeveria's lashings.

When you knew for sure she was arriving, there would be pushing and shoving about who was going first. Honest to God, this is terrible, there would be younger children than you and you would be pushing them to get them to take the beating first. You didn't want to be the one to get the first of the strength. I am sorry, it was horrible, you had to do what you had to do. The screaming of children, the screaming of children will stay with me for the rest of my life about Goldenbridge. I still hear it, I still haven't recovered from that. Children crying and screaming, it was just endless, it never never stopped for years in that place.[13]

Although corporal punishment was still legal when Goldenbridge was operating, rules and regulations set down by the Department of Education imposed limits on its use in the certified industrial schools. The Ryan Report referred to these limits as ones 'which were very restrictive for girls under 15 years, and even more so for older girls'.[14] It also referred to Circular 11/1946, which was sent from the Department of Education to industrial school managers. It stressed that corporal punishment must never be used excessively.

> Corporal punishment should be resorted to only where other forms of punishment have been found unsuccessful as a means of correction. It should be administered only for grave transgressions, and in no circumstances for mere failure at school lessons or industrial training.[15]

These regulations were clearly ignored at Goldenbridge where, like so many other industrial schools in Ireland, the requisite punishment book was non-existent. When Sr Xeveria appeared before the Commission she initially denied any excessive use of force. Whilst she admitted she did use her 'slapper' to beat the children, she told the Ryan Committee that she did not use it to punish children who had wet their beds.

> [The staff] had never any authority to punish children for bed-wetting that I know of, I never gave it to anybody. I don't remember myself taking anybody in the line, beating them for bed-wetting ... I have no recollection of ever having children on the landing for bed-wetting.[16]

When pressed again by the Commission she later conceded that she had indeed slapped children for bed-wetting although she denied ever making the children parade with their wet sheets. The Ryan Report concluded: 'The anguish of those to be punished was increased by long periods of anticipation and by witnessing other girls' suffering. The landing became associated with fear. This system of punishment was cruel and abusive and it contravened regulations.'[17]

Physical and psychological abuse characterised Marie Therese O'Loughlin's 11-year incarceration in Goldenbridge. She lived a bleak, unhappy childhood there. She felt lonely and isolated and constantly lived in fear of getting a beating. Instead of receiving a proper education, she had to endure a gruelling work schedule that began early in the morning when lay staff would march into the dormitories and wake the children up.

> Sometimes the beds would be toppled over. The bedclothes would be dragged off the bed. And you'd be shouted at to get you out of the bed.

She vividly recalled one lay staff member called Margaret[18] whom she remembers as a particularly cruel and sadistic woman.

> She was really, really cruel but she grew up in the system ... she was a perfectionist and she was obsessional.

It was not unusual for the industrial schools to retain former inmates to work as carers in their institutions. In many cases, these people were not able to cope with the outside world. They had been too badly damaged and institutionalised from all the years they had spent growing up in industrial schools. In some cases, they had become brutalised by the very system that was now using them to mind children. Some, like Margaret, were highly unsuited to being in charge of children.

> She worked in the scullery and she was an absolute perfectionist and after lunch the chairs had to be put on top of the table and the whole dining hall had to be scrubbed from top to bottom with boiling sudsy water.

Marie Therese was one of the children who would have to scrub the floors. If Margaret spotted any dirty marks on the floor, she would kick the bucket over and clout the scared child over the ears. Some children suffered from perforated eardrums as a result of her uncontrollable temper.

> She was prone to using a deck brush on their backs. And she would reef the hair off children if they didn't behave. She was very very violent was Margaret.

The children suffered from dermatitis because there was parazone in the water they washed the floors with and it irritated their skin. They were terrified of Margaret, who would be left to mind them when the nuns went up to the convent for breaks or for dinner. The children would have to gather in the recreational hall during these periods. Margaret would make them all sit in silence with their fingers on their lips. 'If children played up, she would come along and she would literally pull the hair out of their heads and the clothes would be nearly pulled off them,' said Marie Therese as she remembered how the other staff members just folded their arms and looked on.

Lunchtimes at Goldenbridge frequently ended in humiliating scrambles for scraps of food in the yard as the starving children clambered for anything that would alleviate their hunger. In what Marie Therese believes was a kind of perverted sport, some of the lay staff used to throw leftover food from their staff room out one of the windows overlooking the former prison yard where the children were sent during the staff lunchbreaks. The leftover bits of toast and biscuits would come from the staff room, which was alongside the kitchen.

> Nobody was allowed in there. That was a small room. And they had sugar and everything and milk on the table. They had normal food. We never had milk or sugar on the table, nothing like that. And there were biscuits laid out and everything and I used to go in there and rob the biscuits when nobody was looking.

The undernourished and hungry children would scramble like animals to get the scraps of food.

> There would be dogfights with the children. And there's even adults who came up to me in later years and said, 'Remember the time we pulled each other's hair out?' It caused a kind of animosity and other lay staff who were there would be laughing their heads off because they really enjoyed that.

Marie Therese remembered one lay staff teacher in particular who used to throw the scraps of food in the direction of children she favoured. She ran her operations at Goldenbridge with an iron fist. Marie Therese bitterly recalled how Ms Murphy[19] had her pets at Goldenbridge who received favourable treatment in her view.

She was the most devious, devious, psychological character and I hated her with a venom.

Every Wednesday night we were all made to sit in the Rec [recreational room] for dancing classes. And Ms Murphy[20] would have the pets that she liked up doing the dancing. Now these would be the very same people that would have gone out to the national school so they would have been to us privileged children to begin with.

On Wednesday evenings Marie Therese and the other children were taken out of the room where they made rosary beads to attend the dancing classes. But, far from enjoying the experience, the young girl was extremely jealous as she was forced to watch 'Ms Murphy's pets' line up and dance while she sat on the benches and looked on with envy.

She would have her pets that went to the outside school up there dancing. And even if they didn't want to dance, they were forced into dancing. Now they would have seen that as cruel. But people like me who were left sitting there were put into this lazy line. So my whole childhood was spent watching other children dancing.

On other occasions Ms Murphy would throw slices of bread and jam to the children begging for food out in the yard. This was usually done around 3pm every afternoon when trays piled high with layers of bread and jam would be brought out into the yard. Ms Murphy was usually in charge of its distribution and she used to ensure any leftover bread went to her favourites.

When everybody got their slice you'd be standing there waiting for more if there was some left on the tray. So the children would put their hand up and shout ,'Miss, Miss.'

The bread would be thrown at a distance into the yard at the children. But you know who they were thrown at? The pets. And then you were left there and she'd ridicule you.

It was not uncommon for lay staff and nuns to have pets or favourites in the industrial schools. Some of the more perverted staff members took sadistic enjoyment in making children jealous of one another. The

Ryan Report referred to the discrimination that was a part of daily life in Goldenbridge. Witnesses told the Commission that children were more likely to be treated better if they received regular visits from relatives. The Ryan Commission heard from witnesses who were in Goldenbridge during the 1960s.

> A complainant, who was aged nine in the early 1960s, described the difference in the way that children were treated. This witness and her siblings were placed in care on the death of their mother, and she noticed particularly how two members of another family were treated so differently that it came as a shock to her to realise they were sisters. Whereas one girl was favoured as a pet, the other was treated with extreme cruelty and was often seen waiting on the landing for punishment.[21]
>
> Another complainant, objecting to favouritism, remarked that the very fact that the nuns and lay staff were capable of forming attachments with certain children demonstrated that they knew how to treat children properly and show them love and affection: ... 'It was wrong there was no need for it, why couldn't they treat us all like pets, why not? That's a choice they exercised.'[22]

Marie Therese was certainly not one of the favoured children in Goldenbridge. During all her time there she said she never received any special treatment from the nuns or lay staff. Her years in Goldenbridge were dominated by an unloving harshness. She still shivers at the thought of the so-called 'painting sessions' when children were made to undress and douse themselves with a stinging pungent chemical that was supposed to eradicate lice and scabies. The chemical was painted onto the children by the staff and nuns. It used to sting their skin.

> I have nightmares to this day about those painting sessions. Children used to have to stand up stark naked with no clothes on them, all ages had to line up to be painted by the staff and the nuns.
>
> Children were violated in my perception. They would have to stand in rows when they were painted and there was newspapers put on the ground. When it came to your turn to be standing up right beside them, you'd be told to spreadeagle your legs and turn around and they'd be mocking.

It's ironic that here they were talking about modesty. We grew up hiding from each other and dressing ourselves underneath our nightdresses. We were told to be ashamed of our bodies. We were so ashamed of our bodies and yet by the same token we were all lining up with no clothes on us.

Children who refused to take part in these perverse sessions would be dragged down to the laundry, where they would be punished severely. Marie Therese was subjected to regular physical and psychological abuse during her years in Goldenbridge. The fact that she had no family members visiting her made matters worse. She was also in a lot of pain because of the injuries she had sustained in the fire accident at the Regina Coeli hostel. The nuns never accommodated her for those injuries when they forced her to make rosary beads in the evening. The burns to her fingers meant the beading process was extremely painful. Rosary bead-making was a thriving industry in Goldenbridge. The Ryan Report states that:

> Sometime in the mid-1940s, Sr Alida[23] was approached by a businessman with the proposition that she might get the children to make rosary beads in return for payment. She saw this as a wonderful opportunity to acquire much-needed funds. In addition, she thought that it would keep the children occupied. So began an enterprise that was to continue until the 1960s.[24]

On most days of the week the children in Goldenbridge were sent to the rosary bead room in the afternoon. For the next few hours they had to string beads on lengths of wire. The wire had to be looped and cut using pliers and each bead had to be attached to the next one until all 10 rows of beads were completed. It was gruelling work that required dexterous skills that were way beyond the capacity of most of the children at Goldenbridge. To make matters worse, the nuns imposed unrealistic quotas.

> The children each had a quota of 60 decades per day and 90 on a Saturday. This meant that, in the two hours of the weekday afternoon allocated for this work, 30 decades an hour had to be made by each child. Not surprisingly, few children reached their

quota in the afternoon, and they had to return to the beads class in the evening and remain there until their 60 decades were completed.

Witnesses described cuts and calluses on their hands as they tried to learn the work.

A child starting would be slow at first, and might never acquire the necessary skill to be able to do it quickly.[25]

If the children did not reach their quota, they were severely punished.

It might happen that, even after going back to beads work after tea and staying there until perhaps 9pm or 9.30pm [some witnesses said even later], the quota would still not be achieved. In those circumstances, the evidence was that the child would be punished by being beaten. If the work was found unsatisfactory, the result was punishment at the hands of the person in charge of the beads room ... It happened occasionally, when a dispatch was due to go to the factory, that some of the children had to stay as late as 10pm to complete an order and ensure that it met the required standard.[26]

Failure to produce the requisite strings of beads frequently resulted in a hiding on the landing. The Ryan Report refers to the opening statement given by Sr Helena O'Donoghue, who represented the Sisters of Mercy. In her statement she referred to the bead-making work 'as a pleasant activity to while away the time, which was enjoyed by the children and often done to music from the radio'.[27] She painted a picture of a happy busy workroom where children chatted as they strung their beads. Her account ran contrary to the overwhelming evidence given by witnesses to the Ryan Commission.

This description of bead making by Sr Helena was inaccurate. The work was hard. The hours were long. While some girls were well capable of doing the work once they had got used to it, for many others it was difficult to master the dexterity required. There was pressure to achieve the quota and to keep to the required standard of work. The work could fail in a variety of ways, including obvious ones like not having the right number of beads in a decade. Less obvious and more difficult to avoid were errors such as having inconsistent-sized loops of wire joining the beads. The atmosphere was not the pleasant group activity imagined by Sr Helena and remembered by Sr Alida. The essential requirement was of quietly, if not silently, getting on with the work; the children did converse but mostly in whispers, and the radio was turned on only occasionally while this work was being done . . . The fact that punishment hung over the activity, for failure to achieve either quality or quantity inevitably affected the atmosphere. The work was relentless, with demanding quotas. This was hard work over long hours during six days a week, for children obliged to do the work with no reference to their capacity to manage it.[28]

Marie Therese O'Loughlin never received any thanks or payment for her bead-making work. The Sisters of Mercy made significant sums of money from the rosary beads that were made at Goldenbridge. The Ryan Report estimated they earned a weekly income of approximately £50 from this highly exploitative industry. But not a single child ever received any money for the slave labour they were subjected to. As Marie Therese relayed her experiences in Goldenbridge to me, I struggled to comprehend the level of cruelty she had suffered there. Her story was typical of many of the accounts given to the Ryan Commission about Goldenbridge. Her incarceration in Goldenbridge scarred her for life. When she left Goldenbridge she went to London, where she ended up mixing with dodgy characters and got into trouble with the law for having drugs in her possession. She eventually arrived at a hostel in central London where the people running it offered to help her. They introduced her to a psychotherapist who held regular sessions with her. Those sessions eventually prompted her to trace her roots.

After many years drifting in London she returned to Ireland in 1978 and looked up a family in Dublin who used to occasionally take her out for visits to their home. She told them she wanted to find out more about her background. It transpired this family knew who Marie Therese's mother was and one day they told her to get into the car because they wanted to drive her to meet her uncle in Wexford. Marie Therese was stunned when she realised this family knew something about her background and it was the first time in her life that she discovered she had living relatives and that she was not and never had been an orphan. When she met her uncle in a pub in Wexford he revealed that her mother was alive and living in England with her husband. When Marie Therese returned to London she arranged to meet her mother. The tall, conservative-looking woman who disembarked from the train was completely different to the person she had always imagined her mother to be.

Despite their reunification, Marie Therese never really forgave Carmel O'Loughlin for abandoning her to a life of hell with the Sisters of Mercy. The two women did not become close and Marie Therese never really got to know her mother properly before she died in 1990. She eventually returned to Ireland but her life continued to be insecure. She still does not have a permanent home and she has struggled over the years to establish a normal happy life.

Chapter 8 ∾

TOMMY MILLAR AND LENABOY AND SALTHILL

Tommy Millar still remembers sneaking into the back of a local pub in Limerick with his older brothers and grabbing a few empty bottles that were lying around. The young lads proudly traded their bounty in the shops for a few pence. Tommy was only a toddler at the time but he was growing up fast. The Millar boys badly needed the few pennies to survive. Things were tough at home. Their unmarried mother struggled to look after her five sons who lived with her in a council house in Limerick City.

Tommy has the odd flashback to his early life at home in Limerick. He remembers sitting on his mother's lap as she washed his hair. Then there was the day she rushed him into hospital after he swallowed a coin. And he can still recall lying on her bed as she raised her lipstick to her mouth for an evening on the town. But his toddler recollections are mostly snapshots of grinding poverty in a fatherless home where the living conditions were basic. Tommy had to sleep with his brothers on a mattress in a raised alcove downstairs. He never knew his father and his mother never revealed his identity to her sons.

In 1965 Tommy's life imploded when he and his brothers were taken from their home and incarcerated in religious institutions. Social workers had got wind of their impoverished circumstances and they removed the boys from their home. Tommy ended up in St Ann's Industrial School for Girls and Junior Boys in Lenaboy, Co. Galway. Several years later he was transferred into the violent clutches of the Christian Brothers who ran St Joseph's Industrial School in Salthill, Galway. Tommy blames his mother for allowing their forced ejection from the family home and a subjugation to a living hell. Years after exiting the gates of his childhood confinement, he tackled her and asked her why she didn't fight harder to keep her kids. His questions were met with a cold, uncaring stare.

> She's never apologised. She has never said that I'm sorry that ye had to go into these places. And anytime afterwards when I've knocked on the door, if I was passing through Limerick, all you'd got was 'What are you doing here?'

Tommy has struggled over the years to comprehend his mother's apparent indifference towards her children. His search for explanations is an attempt to ease the infinite hurt at his mother's abandonment of her child. By all accounts, Mrs Millar did not have an easy childhood herself. Tommy was told her own mother died when she was young and that her father was an alcoholic.

In August 1965 a man from the ISPCC[1] parked his black Anglia car on Tommy's street, walked into the Millar household and informed Tommy and his four brothers that he was taking them for a drive. The young lads were excited at first as they had never been in a car before and it was an adventure. During the journey the man gave them a packet of Marietta biscuits to ease their hunger. They rattled through the countryside for what seemed like hours before arriving in front of a large pair of imposing black gates.

> There was a little house on the right as you went in the gate. And to the left of that there was a big open field. To the right of that was a small wooded area and the further we got down the driveway there to meet us was a big stone building.

Tommy had arrived at St Ann's[2] home for young girls and boys in Lenaboy, Co. Galway, which was run by the Sisters of Mercy. This austere institution would be his home for the next three years. The stern nuns, in their long black habits and veils pulled tightly around their faces, would prove to be miserable substitutes for parents. The young boy had barely landed in the place before he got his first taste of Lenaboy's merciless side. When the boys arrived at the convent doors they were told to get out of the car and ordered to wait inside the hall.

Shortly afterwards, a nun appeared. The starched white rim of her long black veil tightly framed her pouting, angry face. She grabbed hold of Tommy.

> I remember being dragged by the collar of the jumper. And literally being dragged into this hall by this particular nun and told to sit down. I didn't know what was going on but there were a lot of other children in this room as well.
>
> I was told to sit down, keep your mouth shut and wait. Then another nun came along with some kind of a tin mug and in the mug was goody.[3] And of course not knowing what it was, I wouldn't eat it. So next thing the nun came down and said, 'Eat it!' Well, I didn't eat it anyway and needless to say I got the face belted off me because I wouldn't eat it.

Tommy stumbled with the force of the nun's wallop across his face. The stunned little boy began to howl in shock. It was the first time in his short life that he had been slapped with such ferocity. The nun ordered him to eat the stomach-churning gruel. She towered over him with a thundering face as he tried to stop himself from vomiting when he swallowed the thick wet wedges of bread and milk. That would be the first of many punishments he would receive at the hands of the nuns. By the time he had finished his supper, his family bonds were already being dismantled. Tommy's three older brothers had already left Lenaboy with the man in the Anglia. He later discovered they had been taken to St Joseph's Industrial School in Salthill, Galway. His younger brother remained on with him in Lenaboy. Throughout their time there, the two Millar boys wouldn't have any contact with their older brothers even though they were living just a short distance away. Those sibling bonds would never recover from their premature uncoupling.

Lenaboy kept both boys and girls but while the girls stayed for longer, the boys were usually dispersed to other industrial schools after their First Holy Communion. Tommy remembers Lenaboy as a rigid, unloving institution characterised by deprivation and cruelty. The strict religious rigidity of the nuns' lives seemed to have castrated their capacity for affection. They lost their tempers easily and Tommy soon honed his survival skills to avoid being belted by them. An early lesson in survival happened one night when he changed into his pyjamas and left his clothes out on top of his bed. They had disappeared by dawn.

> Unfortunately Lenaboy was the sort of place that if you took off your clothes going to bed you couldn't leave them out because other kids would take them. There would be a lot of bed-wetting going on and younger lads would go to the toilet in their clothes. And of course if you did that you also got a beating for it. So what would happen was that when you'd go to bed at night, if you left your clothes out, you'd wake up in the morning and they were gone. If your clothes were gone in the morning you got a beating regardless of whether Jo Pat was wearing your clothes or not. That wasn't the point. The point was: your clothes are gone, you got the beating. The way they looked at it was: 'They're your clothes, you look after them.'

Tommy trembled with fear when the nun in charge of the dormitory marched towards him for an inspection. All hell broke loose when she discovered his clothes were missing and she gave him an almighty walloping.

> I was brought away and given more clothes . . . and told [by the nun] 'You'll look after them now, won't you?'

From that day on he made sure to hide his clothes under the bed. During his three years in Lenaboy, Tommy was regularly beaten by the highly temperamental nuns. One time he got a lashing from one senior nun for no apparent reason when he was out in the yard.

> I'd asked her for something and, with a blink of an eye, she turned around and she hit me an unmerciful slap with a bunch of the keys across the head and told me to go away.
>   It was like a concentration camp. It was their way or else. When it came to meal times you were lucky to get whatever food was there. The older you were, the more you got.

Hunger was an abiding feature in Lenaboy. Every day the children would be marched into the dining hall where derisory portions of inadequate food were slopped up to them in small plastic bowls. Tommy doesn't ever remember eating meat or vegetables and he is still repulsed by the memory of the thick slices of stale mouldy bread that qualified as a meal. The half-starved young fellow took desperate measures to quell the hunger pangs.

> I can remember going out to where the oil tank was. It was sitting on concrete blocks. And between the tank and the concrete blocks there was black tar. And quite often I used to go out there behind the tank and literally pull up the black tar and eat it. By the time I left the place, there wasn't a bit of black tar left visible under the tank. When you're hungry you'll eat. At one stage I even tried grass.

Humiliation was commonplace in Lenaboy. Sometimes it bordered on sexual abuse. Tommy dreaded Saturday nights when he would have to join a long line of boys and girls who were forced to parade their underwear in front of one of the nuns for inspection. The youngsters were powerless pawns in her chilling game of degradation.

> She'd have all the boys and all the young ones lined up in a row by both sides of the washroom. She'd start from the top corner and if it was a girl she'd have to take off her vest and her underpants. She'd have to strip naked in front of everybody else and walk from where she was down to the middle of the floor and drop her underwear. When she'd be coming down, she'd have to hold them up in both hands, vest and knickers, so everybody could see she actually had a vest and knickers.

The boys on the other side of the washroom would be forced to do the same thing. They too had to strip naked and run the gauntlet of the nun's demeaning inspections with their naked arms outstretched, holding their underpants and vests.

> She'd be standing in the middle and she'd be waiting to see a pair of soiled pants. God love you, and I mean God love you because she would literally give you an unmerciful beating in front of every young child in the laundry.
> This nun would wait until the child was ready to drop the knickers and she'd inspect it and get you to look at it and she'd ask you, 'What's that?' No matter the answer, she would lash out at the

child's face with a slap and then use her fists and keys and stick until she had built herself into a frenzy . . . If there was a bit of soil on it she would beat you in front of everyone.

And you'd be there and you'd be watching this child getting beat like that. And you'd be crying for the child as well.

There was no let up in the cruelty. Tommy vividly remembers the day he was returning from school to Lenaboy on the bus. He jumped off it as it was pulling up outside the convent and he fell to the ground with a terrible bang, tearing his knees and legs along the hard gravel. When he eventually stopped rolling, he was badly bruised and his pants were ripped. He limped back to the orphanage and went to one of the toilets to wipe the blood off himself. But one of the nuns was waiting for him with a face of thunder and her stick in her hand. She grabbed him and lashed him with her cane.

It wasn't the fact that I jumped off the bus and it wasn't the fact that I didn't tell anyone that I was cut. It was the fact that I ripped me trousers. I got another severe beating for that. And I can remember her saying to me, 'That is for ripping your trousers.'

The young lad was already bleeding and in agony from the injuries he had sustained after his tumble but the nun was indifferent to his pain.

There was no one there to put a plaster on or to put their arms around me except this one waiting outside because I had ripped the trousers.

Tommy was profoundly lonely during those bleak years in Lenaboy. His mother rarely came to see him and her infrequent visits left him feeling abandoned and unloved. He is still bitter today over what he believes was her inexcusable desertion of him, leaving him to the mercy of the nuns and later the Christian Brothers. The bonds with his older brothers could not be repaired as he had lost all contact with them during his incarceration in Lenaboy. The only real family bond he had was with his younger brother, Lewis.[4]

Tommy Millar stayed at Lenaboy until the day he made his First Holy Communion when he was six. That morning he was woken up and told to put on the brand-new clothes and shoes that had been given to him for the day. As he pulled up his new frilly socks and pants he was oblivious to what was coming: an eight-year incarceration in another religious institution characterised by physical, emotional and sexual abuse. When the Holy Communion ceremonies were over, a nun walked with Tommy to St Joseph's Industrial School in Salthill, Galway. When he arrived there she handed him over to a tall, silver-haired Brother who took him to a large dormitory and pointed to his bed. The bewildered lad had no idea where he was or what he was supposed to do. A bunch of intimidating boys milled around him and demanded to know where he had come from. He was petrified.

> [They would have said] 'Here's a new fella now on the scene.' As they said in *The Shawshank Redemption*, 'Here's fresh meat.' It was the law of the jungle. You were told, 'That's where you sleep' and nothing else. You weren't even shown where the toilets were or where you ate. You weren't shown where you changed your clothes or where to leave your shoes.

That night Tommy cried himself to sleep. It was the first time in his life that he had shared a room with 20 other boys and he was overwhelmed by its size. The next morning, when he went to change out of his pyjamas, he discovered that his Holy Communion clothes had disappeared. In their place were an old worn pair of short pants and shirt, a jumper and a pair of old shoes. It would be another week before he was given underwear. He was put to work before breakfast.

> The dormitory floor had to be swept. The window ledges had to be washed down. We had to make the beds and then we were all moved off out the door and into the chapel for morning rosary and Mass.

Every morning the boys knelt for several decades of the rosary on hard wooden benches while the Brothers had cushions and seats. The young lads were tired and hungry after their morning's work but they dared not leave the church for fear of a flogging by an angry Brother. After prayers they were released for breakfast, which consisted of spoons of lumpy porridge that would be cold by the time it was dished out.

I am under the impression that your man who was in the kitchen, Br Brown,[5] I reckon he used to dish it up in the bowls before Mass. And some mornings you'd get stale green moulded bread.

Fresh bread was made in the bakery in Salthill every day, but the boys got none of it. Instead it was consumed by the Christian Brothers or sold outside the school while the boys were given the stale, discarded loaves. After breakfast they were sent out into the yard regardless of the weather. They would have to stay there until the Brothers finished their own breakfast of fresh bread and bacon and eggs.

Tommy could hardly read or write when he first arrived at Salthill. His poor literacy skills made him vulnerable to ridicule and attack by the Brothers. He wasn't long in Salthill before he had a run-in with Brother Walsh.[6]

He was not a very nice man. He had no patience. He was the sort that if you acted dumb he treated you dumb. More times than often he'd leave you sitting at the back of the class to do whatever you wanted to do within reason. My first experience of that man was when he asked me a question and I didn't know the answer. He asked me the question a second time and I gave him the same answer: 'I don't know, Sir.'

He came down and he laid into me like the sadist bitch above in Lenaboy: the palm of the hand, the fists. If you went down in the ground at all he'd use the boot.

And then he had the cheek to tell me to get off the floor and sit down on the bench. And of course me crying and sobbing with the savage beating that I got off him, he came back down and put a twelve-inch ruler behind me. He set the ruler up in such a way that if I moved slightly it would fall. Now I wasn't the only fella he did this to.

He knew that within ten minutes that ruler was going to fall because your hands and your sides would be so sore from the slapping and the kicking that he gave you. You were bent over, shaking and crying. And he'd say, 'If anyone falls, I'll be back down to you.' And of course the ruler did fall. And down he came again with the leather across the backs of the legs and he'd literally have you in tears that you wouldn't be able to see where you were going with the amount of crying you were doing. And he'd have the cheek to tell you to shut up.

If boys like Tommy misbehaved, Walsh would send them to the small cellar near his classroom where the furnace was kept. He used to lock the boys in there on their own. Sometimes they would be left there for hours in the dark until break-time. The standards of schooling were completely inadequate in Salthill, and Tommy could barely read or write by the time he left when he was 15. Br Walsh called him a dunce and he frequently ridiculed him in front of the other boys. He would pick on Tommy, and another boy with learning difficulties, to entertain the class with silly antics.

> We were supposed to be the most stupid in the class. I was stupid. I was a gob. We were humiliated by this fella.
>
> He'd call you up and say, 'Do something. Give us a laugh. Do what you usually do. Act stupid.' So what would you do? Rather than get another beating from this guy, you'd act stupid.

The physical and emotional abuse was only a part of the cruelty meted out to Tommy during his eight-year incarceration in Salthill. Within weeks of his arrival there, he was sexually abused by one of the Brothers. It would be the first of several sexual assaults he would sustain there. His main abuser was Br Murphy.[7]

Tommy was first abused by Br Murphy within months of his arrival at Salthill. It was late at night and the young boy was fast asleep. Murphy came into his dormitory and crept up to his bed. Using the pretence of bed-wetting, he shook the boy and told him to wake up. It was common in the industrial schools for night watchmen or Brothers on duty to wake boys who were prone to wetting their beds. They would march them to the toilets in the middle of the night to relieve themselves. But Tommy was not a bed-wetter and so Murphy's excuse was spurious.

> I can remember him calling me and bringing me into the toilets in St Dominick's. He shut the door. He put his arms around me while I was facing the urinal. He put his hands down the front of my pyjamas and he played with my penis. Now that was the first encounter that I can remember of him.

The young boy was startled and had no idea what was going on when Murphy fondled him. He even thought his behaviour may have been a bizarre demonstration of affection.

You know you're that young. What do you know? Is this right? Is this wrong? I had no idea.

After he had finished abusing him, Murphy ordered Tommy back to his bed. He carried out a second sexual assault when Tommy was sick in the infirmary. The paedophile spotted his opportunity when the nurse in charge went to Mass and Tommy was alone in the ward. Murphy walked in, locked the door behind him and approached Tommy's bed. He pulled down the bedclothes and began to sexually fondle the boy.

Down came the pyjamas and he started with my penis again. I was standing up on the bed at this stage with my back to the wall so that when he was facing me he could see the door.

Murphy closely monitored the main door for the nurse's return. When he had finished assaulting Tommy he left the ward without saying anything. He left Tommy alone for a couple of years until he was around nine or ten. Murphy's third sexual attack on Tommy happened when Tommy was ill in bed in his dormitory.

This fucker was as cute as they came. He came up to the dormitory. Now this is where he started speaking. He pulled down the bedclothes. He sat on the bed. He asked me to sit on his lap and then again he pulled down the bottom of my pyjamas and he was stroking me like a newborn. He had his one hand around my neck and the other between my legs and he was playing away.

Murphy was stopped in his tracks when the door swung open and another boy entered the dormitory. He quickly told Tommy to pull up his pyjamas and he warned him to say nothing.

That young fella said, 'What was he doing here?' And of course I told him and he turned around and he said, 'Look, he's doing the same to me.' That confused the issue then again. Is it right or is it wrong?

Or is this part of life? If he's doing it to him it must be a part of life.

Murphy made another move on Tommy shortly after but this time he was violent when he assaulted him in the Hurley hall.

> I went in there to get something. Maybe it was a jersey. There was a few lads queuing up to get jerseys as well. He gave them their jerseys. He told me to wait in the inner room of the Hurley hall and he pulled out the door so nobody could see me in there. He locked the door and put the latch on the door. Now he was the only fella with a key to it. He came into the inner room where I was. He stood behind me. He put the hands down me togs again. Down came the togs. He had me slightly bent over and yet again he was playing with my penis. And after a minute then he started moaning and groaning. Now whether he penetrated me or not, I don't know.

When Murphy finished masturbating, he pulled Tommy's pants up and checked the window to make sure the coast was clear before ordering him out. The young boy was completely confused. He didn't know whether the abuse was normal or not. His confusion was exacerbated by the fact that a couple of the older boys in Salthill were also dabbling in sexual abuse. Tommy believes they had probably been assaulted by Murphy, or one of the other Brothers, and they were mimicking the abusive behaviour. One time he was caught by an older boy who ordered him into a room.

> This fella actually laid me on the floor and pulled down my pants and started playing with my penis. And I mean he was rubbing it. And while he was doing that, he was masturbating and I believe he did ejaculate on me. And when he was finished, then it was up with the trousers and out you go.
>
> Another fella was in charge of the classrooms in the evening. And he called me over to the corner. And he said to me in a very very low voice, 'Have any of the Brothers played with your willy?' And of course straight away I said yes to him like a fucking eejit. So he got me in the classroom, down the pants and started playing with the penis again.

Tommy remembers being sexually assaulted by Br Murphy six times during his incarceration in Salthill. The fifth attack took place in the projector room attached to the makeshift cinema where the boys would watch films. It was a Saturday afternoon and a cowboy movie was playing. Murphy called Tommy into the projector room and told him he needed some help.

> He came down and he said, 'Come on, I want you to give me a hand in the projector room.' So yet again the cinema was dark and the only light that was in the cinema was coming from the film and the projector. And of course everybody was fixed on the cowboy movie. So I went in like an eejit, didn't I, thinking that I was actually going to give him a hand because this guy had a way about him. He was so sweet-talking. In the projector room he pulled down the pants and started playing with my penis and yet again he started moaning and groaning and he got as close to me as he possibly could be.

Murphy made Tommy bend over so that he could wrap himself around him. After he had finished masturbating he told the shocked boy to get out. Murphy usually said very little to Tommy when he was assaulting him. Although he was very physically violent towards him in the classroom, he was usually more passive when he was sexually abusing him. That was until the final assault when he became extremely aggressive. This attack occurred in the store where the boys' clothes were kept.

> I was given a pair of shoes about a week before that: a pair of black slip-ons and, through no fault of my own, they fell apart. He called me in and locked the door. He asked me what happened to the shoes. I told him they just went like that and then that's when he started frothing. That's when the beating started. He started off with the slaps with the palm of his hands on my face and the backs of the legs. Then it went from that then to the closed fists on the face, the back, the stomach. Then he told me to get up on a lot of blankets. They were all lying on the table. I got up on that with the tears streaming down me. He had the fucking cheek then to take down me fucking pants and slapped me on the fucking backside and then start fucking interfering with me. And the same thing he got me in

as close as he possibly could and the same thing happened again once he got me to bend over the way he wanted while he was holding me with one hand on the shoulder. There was a lot of moaning and groaning coming from him again.

Murphy's sexual abuse of Tommy Millar would have a devastating impact on his life. It would leave him sexually confused for years after leaving Salthill.

I didn't know whether I was straight or gay or what way I was.

Before Tommy went into therapy in the 1990s, his relationships with women were crippled by his past.

The kissing part of it was grand but if it went any further than that, Murphy appeared. Murphy was in the head straight away. Then I would have to stop.

Murphy's menacing presence overshadowed Tommy's dreams for years. He suffered from frightening nightmares that would jolt him out of his sleep roaring and shouting in a sweat. Those deeply disturbing memories were easily activated.

If I saw a priest walking down the road, it would trigger it off straight away. If I saw a nun walking down the road, it would trigger it off.

Tommy's adult life has also been tormented by the flashbacks of physical brutality that was a systematic part of life in Salthill. He vividly remembers one ferocious beating from Br Sebastian,[8] who lashed out at him like a monster consumed with a wild, uncontainable fury. At the time Tommy feared the Brother was going to batter him to death. It was one of the worst physical assaults he suffered in Salthill.

It was time for bed and we were all down in the hall and of course lads being lads, they mess to a certain extent. When we got up we were supposed to push the chair back in and everything else and I didn't straighten a chair to the way he liked it. And when he asked me to straighten the chair again I went back and I don't think I straightened it. I even made it worse from the way it was. With that he came over to me and he thumped the living daylights out of me. I went up the stairs crying and got into the bed crying and all you could hear from him was 'Millar, shut up.'

The more Sebastian shouted at Tommy, the more he shook with fear and uncontrollable crying. Sebastian became incandescent with rage when Tommy wouldn't stop howling in his bed and he roared at him to shut up.

> All you heard was 'Millar, if you don't shut up, I'll come down to ye.' Of course I still couldn't stop. He dragged me out of the bed and yet again used the leather, his hands and fists and once I fell on the floor he started using his feet and when he was finished then he shouted, 'Get back into the bed.' And within two minutes it was the same thing again. He shouted, 'Millar, shut up.' I couldn't. He was waiting to say the so-called night prayers and waiting for the night watchman as well. So he came down to the bed a second time and the same thing again. And the more he hit me and the more he kicked me and the more he thumped me, the worse I was getting. But he being so fucking high and mighty and stupid, he didn't realise this, I suppose. So I managed to crawl back into the bed and I thought he'd finished. He came back a third time all because I wouldn't shut up. And out of the bed again. At this stage, I was in bits on the ground. I could have had broken bones for all he cared. He didn't care. He was like the rest of them. Third time: out again. Same thing again and only for the night watchman coming in when he did, I'd probably be dead now because he was beating me so much.

Tommy Millar broke down in tears when he recalled that terrifying night. He vividly remembered how the furious Brother pulled him out of his bed and battered him to a pulp, his mouth frothing with rage, his face contorted with a boiling red anger and his body consumed with such a ferocious energy he unleashed a frenzied cascade of blows on Tommy, who was screaming with pain on the ground. As he passed in and out of consciousness he could hear other boys crying in the dormitory.

Tommy believes he was saved from death that night by the night watchman whose entrance into the dormitory snapped Br Sebastian out of his uncontrollable fury. Tommy painfully climbed back into his bed and tried to find a position that gave him respite from the piercing pain that shot through his battered body. He struggled to go to sleep and he tried to make sense of the awful savagery he had been subjected to. He realised that, had the night watchman not entered the dormitory, no one would have come to his rescue.

Life in Salthill was a miserable assembly of cruelty and hardship during Tommy's eight-year stint there. The only respite came during the holiday breaks when he was discharged to various families around the country. His happiest memories from that time are the holidays he spent with the Cronin[9] family in Dublin, who treated him like one of their own children. He will never forget their kindness and love.

> On the first Christmas that I was with them they received a parcel from America. And of course inside this parcel there was smaller parcels. There was parcels for their kids and there was parcels for the mum and dad of the house and rather than have me left out of this, Jim[10] and Eileen[11] took something from each of the kids' parcels and parcelled it up for me. The love in that house was unreal. I was never treated strange. I slept in the room with either the two boys or one lad at a go. They took turns.
>
> When it came time to have a bath I was in there on my own. They weren't hovering around waiting. When you'd go to Mass with them on a Sunday morning, there was no such thing coming from them, 'Well, this is Tom from an orphanage, we have him for a couple of days or a couple weeks.' There was none of that. I was treated as one of the family.

Despite their kindness, Tommy never disclosed anything about the brutality and sexual abuse he was subjected to in Salthill because he felt they would not believe him.

> The majority of these people that I went to on holidays, they were all good church-going Catholics. A priest could do no wrong. A nun could do no wrong. A Christian Brother could do no wrong. They're feeding you. They're clothing you and if it wasn't for them where would you be?

Tommy was also afraid that if he said anything about the abuse to the Cronins, the Christian Brothers wouldn't allow him to return to them.

Tommy Millar stayed in St Joseph's until 1977 when he was 15. By then he was severely traumatised. The excessive physical, sexual and psychological brutality had left him crippled with depression. He had severe difficulties holding down a steady job and establishing normal sexual relationships with women. It would take him many years before he would be able to begin building a more normal life.

Tommy drifted for a while after leaving Salthill. Initially he received some training at ANCO, which was then the State training agency. When he was 19 he joined the Navy and was posted to the Irish Navy headquarters at Haulbowline in Cork. He stayed in the Navy for seven years working in a variety of posts from training as a medic to helping in the kitchens washing dishes and laying tables. Tommy's poor education at Salthill limited his professional opportunities. Throughout this time he was confused about his sexuality because of the sexual abuse by Br Murphy and he suffered from frequent bouts of depression. At one stage, it was so bad he thought about shooting himself in the Navy base.

> I was on guard duty down there one night and I got into one of my moods. I had a rifle and I just asked myself, 'What's life all about?' I started thinking back. I was inclined to cock the rifle and put the rifle up to my gob and just pull the trigger. That's what I wanted to do.

In the end, Tommy didn't pull the trigger. Instead he dropped the rifle and walked away. It was the first time he had contemplated suicide. He was subsequently dispatched to Collins Barracks in Cork to see a doctor but Tommy remained tight-lipped about the reasons for his depression.

> Even then I still could not speak about the abuse because I still thought I was the only one that went through it and I didn't want anybody knowing my business.

In 1987 he left the Navy and drifted into an aimless life in Galway, living on social welfare and being incapacitated by intense bouts of depression. Sometimes he would just spend the whole day in bed, crying, and go without washing or eating.

I'd go for days when I wouldn't even go outside the front door. I'd go for days unshaven. I'd stay in my room for days.

During this time his relationships with women were, to a large extent, dysfunctional as he was still struggling to understand his own sexuality. Then in February 1995 Tommy got a phone call out of the blue from a social worker who was based in the West of Ireland. He told him he was investigating Salthill and that he wanted to know if Tommy had any stories to share with him about his time there. The social worker never mentioned anything about sexual or physical abuse, he merely said he was looking into stories about the place and that he was keen to talk to Tommy.

I was surprised that he was tracking me down and of course I wanted to know why he was tracking me down.

Tommy agreed to meet the social worker and a colleague of his. The two men arrived at his house shortly after that initial phone call. He was extremely careful about revealing details of the physical and sexual abuse he had suffered in Salthill and it took him some time to open up to the men. For years Tommy had believed he was the only boy who had been sexually assaulted in Salthill. A combination of shame and fear had kept him from speaking about the sexual abuse.

If it was done to Joe Blogs he never spoke about it. If it was done to me I'd never tell Joe Blogs. You had this fear that if it had got back to them, you would have been left for dead. They would have literally beaten the living daylights out of you. That is what I would have feared most above anything else because back then, these guys could not do wrong in society's view. Even for the people that we went to on holidays these people [Christian brothers] could do nothing wrong.

It would take a second visit before Tommy would finally open up to the men and with painful recall describe how Murphy had sexually abused him. It was around this time that he began to see a psychiatrist in Galway. It was an enormous relief to be able to offload the burden of shame and guilt that had shackled him to his abusers long after he had shut the gates in Salthill.

As he continued with his therapy, Tommy's life started to stabilise and he began to hold down jobs working as a chef in pubs. Gradually, through intensive therapy work, he became more comfortable with his sexuality and he realised he was a healthy heterosexual man who was unfortunate enough to have been targeted by a paedophile. By then, more stories were emerging in Ireland of clerical and institutional child sexual abuse. The country was waking up to the legacy of its religious paedophiles who had operated with impunity behind the high walls of their abusive institutions. Tommy began to realise that his own experiences were not unique.

Over the following few years he slowly began to confide in close friends and reveal what had happened to him as a boy. Those revelations lifted the heavy burden of secrecy about his past that he had carried for years. His life took a turn for the better when he met his future wife. At the time he was working as a chef in a pub in Co. Galway.

> She came into the pub one day on her own and she asked for mashed potatoes, no vegetables and a breast of chicken with no gravy. And of course curiosity got the better of me and I had to go out to see who this was for.

Tommy went on to form a relationship with the woman who had asked for that meal on that day. The couple eventually married in 2006 when he was 44. His wife already had one child when they met and they went on to have two children together. His relationship with his wife has given him the love and security that was absent in his childhood, but those precious, innocent years that were stolen from his youth will never be replaced.

Chapter 9

MARTINA KEOGH AND CLIFDEN AND THE MAGDALENE LAUNDRIES

Martina Keogh is a gutsy lady with a strong personality. She's wary of adults and prefers instead the company and unconditional love of her family of cats and dogs who share her pleasant corporation home in inner city Dublin. She's had a tough life that began when her stepfather sexually abused her. Martina has lived rough on the streets, engaged in petty crime and endured abuse in religious institutions that include St Joseph's Industrial School in Clifden, Co. Galway, and one of Ireland's most infamous Magdalene laundries in Gloucester Street in Dublin. Her incarceration in these wretched institutions fostered a rage within her that took years to subside.

I interviewed Martina in her comfortable home in October 2009. A cacophony of barking dogs responded to my knock on Martina's door but the tiny creatures scampered away as soon as she opened it. I was immediately struck by the large white-rimmed glasses that dominated her face and which she wore throughout our interview. She told me afterwards that they eased the pain of conjunctivitis, from which she suffered.

Scented candles were lighting in her spotlessly clean kitchen, which led into an equally pleasant living room. We first chatted about the dog that she had just rescued the night before. He was nearly dead when she found him on a street and she was trying to raise €1,500 for a life-saving operation for him.

Martina Keogh was up against it from the beginning. Her father was killed in a car crash in England when her mother was pregnant with her.

The couple weren't married and her mother wasn't able to cope with the pressure of looking after Martina when she was born as she was already struggling to take care of her son. She decided to put both of her children into care and Martina ended up in an institution run by nuns in Kilkenny. She doesn't remember much about the place other than sporadic flashbacks of relatively happy times.

I remember sitting playing with a friend of mine. I remember sitting at a red table and a black cat on it.

She spent the first three years of her life in Kilkenny. Then her mother decided to take both her and her brother out of care and she brought them back to live with her in a flat in Dublin. By then she had married and had a baby daughter. The family household gradually expanded over the years but Martina's trouble began when her stepfather sexually abused her.

I stayed there for a while. Everything was OK. I was going to school. Then my father started abusing me so I started getting very uneasy, running away and getting picked up by the police and getting brought home.

Martina thinks she was probably around seven or eight when her stepfather first sexually assaulted her. He tried to rape her but didn't succeed so instead he used to fondle her in an inappropriate manner. He was a nasty piece of work who resented caring for his stepchildren.

He was always saying to my mother them two bastards are yours. He would always be threatening. He was a very violent, arrogant, domineering man. The mental abuse he gave my mother was dreadful. He'd call her a whore, tramp, terrible names. He'd fight with her all the time. At half six at night you'd have to shut your mouth, if he'd go to bed because he had to be up at five. Nobody could make noise. It was a very stressful place.

Her stepfather's sexual abuse had a dramatic impact on Martina's life. She began to run away from home and sleep rough on the streets. The guards would pick her up and bring her back to her mother. But the

guards' patience diminished over time and they warned her she was
getting out of control. After several abscondences, Martina was
committed to High Park Orphanage, which was run by the Sisters of
Charity. When she left High Park, she was sent back home but the cycle
of abuse began again and her stepfather would touch her and force her
to have oral sex with him. The young girl was too terrified to tell her
mother as he had warned her to keep her mouth shut. Martina believes
her mother had been ground down by his incessant verbal abuse and
she consequently lost interest in her children.

> She didn't care. I think he was giving her such a hard life I don't
> think she cared about anything anymore. I think that she was a
> woman who was just existing. He never gave her enough money to
> live on. She had to go and work in hotels. She was always short of
> money. The cheque man used to come and she'd be hiding from
> him.

Martina's mother had given birth to more children and making ends
meet was nearly impossible. The situation was so desperate, she used to
pawn her husband's clothes. On Monday mornings she would take his
suit out of the wardrobe and bring it to a pawn shop where she would
exchange it for some money to keep her going until Friday. She would
then retrieve the suit and put it back in the wardrobe for him to wear to
the pub that evening.

> He [stepfather] had a plot and he used to grow vegetables and she'd
> sell all the vegetables. And she used to go over to the dealers and one
> of the dealers would give her ballroom dresses and me ma would
> give her veg. And me ma would rip all the ballroom dresses and
> make dresses for us. God bless her she was brilliant with her hands.
> She'd be on the machine and she'd have four dresses done by the
> weekend for the four girls.

Life at home was so intolerable Martina ganged up with other children
who were also escaping abusive homes and they started living and
sleeping rough on the streets.

> I ended up starting to pick up animals and sleeping with them in

sheds. A few of us used to all sleep in car sheds. We'd sleep anywhere ... We'd depend on robbing the milk outside the shops. We used to rob that for food. Then the police would pick us up and we'd be brought to court and told we were out of control again.

Martina's circumstances deteriorated rapidly one day when she was caught trying to steal a swimsuit in a shop in Dublin. She was around 10 at the time and it was a hot summer's day. She and her pal wanted to go for a swim in Sandymount but she didn't own a bathing suit so she decided to steal one from a mannequin in a store on George's Street. She was caught red-handed by the shop's female security guard.

> Your woman skull-hauled me into the back of the shop and the police came. I was just getting off the window and she skull-hauled me. If I had been cute I wouldn't have got on the window to take the bathing togs. I didn't realise they sold them down in the back of the shop. I could have gone down and took them there but I just liked the ones on the window and I took them off the doll.

Martina was hauled into court and brought in front of a judge. Like so many poor working class children, she had no legal representative and stood little chance of receiving a sympathetic hearing. The Irish judicial system shamefully facilitated the incarceration of thousands of children from poor backgrounds by putting them on trial without ensuring they had proper legal support. Few middle class children ended up in industrial schools.

> You'd be standing there and she'd [the Judge] be sitting up there. And you'd be there and all the benches would be here and the police would be there and you'd be this size. And she'd be roaring down at you and she'd tell you you were out of control and that she'd put you somewhere where they'd keep you in control and put manners on you.

The punishment for her crime was unwarranted. Martina was given a two-year sentence to be served at St Joseph's Industrial School in Clifden, Co. Galway. It was an unjustifiably harsh sentence. After her conviction, she was taken by train down to Galway where a couple of

Sisters met her and took her to the remote institution 50 miles west of the city. Martina was terrified as she had never been outside Dublin and had no idea where she was going. The veiled friendliness that the nuns had displayed when they first met her off the train with her probation officer rapidly vanished once they entered the convent gates.

All of a sudden their attitude changed. I got me clothes taken off of me. The cuddly toy I had was taken off of me. They reefed that off of me. They weren't nice at all . . . It was just one big grey building and it was cold and dark and dull. It was horrible. It was really now a scary place. And we were put to bed. And I woke up the next morning and I just seen hundreds of kids. I'd never seen so many boys and girls.

Clifden was a miserable place that was run like a military prison by the Sisters of Mercy. Affection was non-existent there but physical and psychological abuse was present in copious measures. Martina's day would begin with an early alarm call at 6.30am.

First when you'd get up you'd have to go into this room and there'd be basins. There was a big long table and there'd be about ten basins on one side and ten basins on the other. There would be freezing water and you'd have to wash yourself in that. And you'd be lined up to wash and you'd be all using one another's water. The nun would check your neck and if you didn't wash yourself properly she'd clatter you and make you wash again and nine times out of ten, she'd do it just for fun. I think they got their kicks out of beating kids.

Then you'd go downstairs in your knickers and vest and you'd go down and put your shoes on and your clothes on, an old jumper and an old skirt. It wouldn't even fit half the times. There'd be holes in the jumper and the skirts would be hanging out of you, you'd have to tie them. The shoes never fit you properly. They'd either hurt you or you'd be kicking them, they'd be too big. And when they'd be giving you the shoes they'd be all thrown out on the floor and it would be tough luck to pick them. Every night you'd have to leave them down in this big room with your clothes.

Breakfast at Clifden consisted of scraps of bread and watery tea served up in plastic mugs. After breakfast Martina and the other children were put to work. There was no time for fun or play as their work day began immediately with a thorough scrubbing and polishing of the floors. The Sisters' irrational obsession with cleanliness meant the children had to get down on their hands and knees until the wooden floors shone with wax. Protesting against the work would inevitably incur a punishment.

> You'd be on your knees. And Sr Mary[1] would come along and she'd give you a smack of something across the back of the head . . . You'd have to polish the floors with your hands. You'd have to go down and wash all of the clothes in the laundry. You'd be standing on big wooden planks high enough to get onto the sinks and you'd wash them off the boards. Sometimes your knuckles would be red raw because if the cloth missed, your fingers would rub off the boards.

Martina bitterly remembers having to wash and starch the nuns' habits until they were spotless. She didn't get any education at Clifden because she was a juvenile offender and so her day was filled with laborious tasks. After cleaning the floors and laundry she would be sent out on the farm to clear out the chicken and pig sheds and the cow barns. An old lay worker used to hang around the children making lewd gestures.

> He was a dirty old bastard, he was. He was a horrible fat ole thing. He lived in Clifden. He'd be up to everything; feeling you and everything and giving you brown pennies to give him a feel and he'd feel you. Or if he caught you robbing the chicken house he had you there. He used to set traps for us. He'd never report us but we'd have to give him a feel rather than have him report us.

Martina had to use her wits to keep herself nourished as she was half-starved for most of her time in Clifden. Her experiences scavenging on the streets when she was sleeping rough helped her to survive.

> I'd go down and get into the chicken house and rob about eight eggs. Sally [friend at Clifden] would take all of the skins of the potatoes out of the bucket and she'd wash them under the tap. Then we used to go into the bakery. They had their own bakery and they used to do

beautiful buns but we'd never see them. And we'd give Anne the girl that worked there eggs and she'd roast the skins of the potatoes for us and she'd do an egg each for us and she'd give us a loaf and then we'd give her about six eggs. That was her way of surviving as well.

The girls would also rob cocoa, which was stored in bags in one of the sheds, and they'd eat it raw. Ironically, Martina became a more accomplished thief during her time in Clifden and she developed unorthodox ways of feeding herself.

They'd send you down there [Clifden] for robbing stupid little things but they actually learned you to be a good criminal. You'd come out twenty times wiser than you went in. They put you in there for robbing a lousy pair of bathing togs yet I spent the length of time that I was there robbing for my food. It was a joke.

A crushing oppression characterised Clifden's regime. It was as if the nuns there were running a totalitarian state where love and affection were forfeited for control and power. One particular nun used to threaten to lock the children in the pantry attached to the kitchen.

One thing always stood out in my mind with her. Every time you'd go into the pantry to get water we'd look into this room and there'd be lobsters crawling all over the place. The fisherman must have delivered them. There'd be about twelve or fifteen of them and they'd be huge. And I'm terrified of crabs even to this day. But she'd threaten to lock you in there with them. And one day she locked me in with them and I nearly had a heart-attack ... I think she just done it because she knew you were afraid of them. She did it just to get kicks.

The children were terrified of the nuns. Martina remembers three Sisters in particular who beat the children with canes and whacked them on the head with large sets of keys.

They were very cruel. They made examples of beatings with children. You'd all have to look at them beating kids and you wouldn't want it to be you. Unfortunately your turn would always come. If they were passing through, it was like as if you had to bow down to them. And if you didn't get out of the way. I remember Sr Eily,[2] many a time she'd hit you with keys across the back of the head or the shoulder and you'd be crying with the pain and you'd get another clatter for that. They had no compassion.

Martina is still scarred today from one frenzied attack by Sr Mary. On that unforgettable day she had gone out into the fields with another boy from the orphanage. They were looking for a donkey that had recently given birth to a foal. Martina was crazy about animals and she'd developed a relationship with the donkey that she used to feed with apples and potato skins. The children had to trek a long distance through the meadows before reaching the donkey and its foal. Their enthusiasm for the animals meant they forgot all about the time, and their decision to pick blackberries on the way back further delayed them. The children were horribly late returning to the orphanage and, by the time they reached it, Sr Mary was on the warpath, brandishing the dreaded cane in her hand. Her face was bright red with anger. It was a facial disposition she frequently displayed, earning her the nickname 'Tomato Face' from the children.

> She was standing there like a lunatic and we knew she was going to beat us severely. And we dreaded it. She brought James and myself into the pantry and there was a table there. She went and pulled his pants down and she whacked him out of it with a black leather strap. I said there's no way she's doing that to me. So when she said, 'Pull you pants down' I said, 'No!' I didn't care at that stage because I was punch drunk with the beatings I got and any more beatings didn't matter. And I wouldn't take them down.
>
> So she started pulling and pushing at me. So whatever way I pulled her, didn't her veil come off. So didn't she get me and push me but the way she pushed me there was a door and there were two panes of glasses.

When Sr Mary pushed Martina, her hand went through one of the glass panes and she banged her chest hard up against the doorknob. She was in agony. Pieces of glass were stuck in her arm and she could barely breathe from the force of the knock against the door. Sr Mary got hold of Martina and threw her out into the kitchen where some of the other girls helped to take the glass out of her hand and wrap it in cloth. A few days later she started feeling a piercing pain in her chest, which had become very black and blue as an infection was setting in. Martina's right breast began to swell and she innocently thought at first that it was a part of her hormonal development. But then the pain became increasingly intolerable.

> I remember one night I was crying with the pain it was so bad. And Sr Mary said, 'Take off your nightdress and let me see' just as I was getting into bed. But because there was boys there and there were glass partitions through each dormitory, I wouldn't take it off in front of the boys so she beat me with the stick. I was still sobbing and Sr Regina[3] came in and she brought me into the toilet. And I'll always remember the word she used was 'Oh Jesus!' I only found out afterwards she was a nurse.

Sr Regina rushed Martina over to the doctor where she was kept overnight. The next morning she was brought to a hospital in Galway where she was operated on. The surgeon had to cut open her breast to remove the poison. Martina was so terrified of the nuns she didn't tell the medical staff at the hospital how she had sustained her injuries.

> Once the nuns came up to see me and told me that if I spoke about the home or spoke about anything that went on there, they would find out because the doctors and nurses would tell them and I'd be really sorry when I'd go back. And anytime the doctors and nurses would ask you what happened you'd be afraid. You'd say you fell or something.

The hospital staff failed to investigate the reasons behind her injuries and they sanctioned her return to Clifden. Martina Keogh was certainly not the only child from an industrial school who ended up in a hospital following a physical assault by a Brother or Sister. Had medical staff been more vigilant and properly investigated the explanations for the children's injuries, they may have exposed the brutality in the religious institutions and prevented thousands more children from being abused in them.

To us they were so vicious. They weren't people. As far as we were concerned, they were animals. Animals wouldn't do that to the young. They were sadists. And they beat you for little or nothing. They humiliated you. They used to say that our mothers didn't want us. Our family didn't want us. We were there because we weren't wanted. Nobody wanted us. They were the only ones that were going to look after us and that's the reason we were there.

This twisted propaganda was extremely effective and it turned some children like Martina against parents and family members.

You look around and you see all this and you really begin to believe that nobody wants you and nobody cares about you. And then you begin to get this hatred. As a child it's beat into you and it's a hatred for everybody. You just hated everybody and you rebelled against everybody because you trusted nobody. They made sure you trusted nobody.

Martina began to believe her mother didn't care about her and she started to turn against her. She was also highly suspicious of the school inspectors who would call to Clifden periodically. She didn't trust them enough to tell them about the abuse she was being subjected to. The Sisters were adept at disguising the harsher realities of life in their institutions. Children who displayed bruises from beatings were hidden away during inspection time and the nuns transformed the school into a bogus illusion of happiness. Inspectors working for the Department of Education frequently failed to see through these false depictions.

Everything would be laid out. It would be fabulous. You'd get a beautiful dinner. We got massive new clothes. Everything looked so perfect and the nuns were running around like as if they were our best friends.

They never said, 'What is it like here but no matter what you tell us we won't say anything?' so you didn't trust them. You just said great and you didn't say anything.

The corrosive erosion of Martina's self-esteem permanently damaged her sense of self-worth and her trust in adults. To this day she remains suspicious of people in positions of authority and she prefers instead to seek sanctuary in the company of animals. She will never forget how badly the nuns treated her.

> They were nasty. They were very, very cruel to us. They beat you for no reason. Their verbal abuse was dreadful. They made you feel as if you were nothing. They spoke to you that bad I can't even describe the way they made you feel. It's like as if you were nothing. You were dirt. You were just there as a piece of dirt for them.
>
> There was no laughter or love or care. It was always cold. You were cold. You were hungry. You were starved. You were never given any affection. You were never told you were nice. You were always just told you were there because the devil wanted you. You were a sinner and you wouldn't know what you done. You were bad. Nobody liked us. Nobody wanted us.

During the winter the children were frozen with the cold from the lack of heat and poor clothing. At night Martina and two other girls in her dormitory would pull their beds together and huddle under their combined threadbare blankets but they always ran the risk of getting caught.

> Nine times out of ten we were always caught. But we had to do it because we'd be cold . . . We were forever getting chilblains because we were always made to wash our hands in cold water. And when you'd be out in the field, your hands in the rain would be that cold that we'd go into the kitchen and we tried to put them under hot water to heat them up. But we always had chilblains on our fingers.

Babies were also kept in Clifden but poor staffing levels meant they were not cared for properly and they were deprived of love and affection. The older girls in the orphanage looked after them but they lacked the essential maternal skills to give the babies adequate attention. Martina remembers how tiny babies were tied to their potties because there weren't enough staff to change their soiled nappies.

> I always remember them sitting on potties and out of their little back passages they'd be big red lumps coming out of them and the

girls would make us help them to push them back up. And the poor little things would be screaming and their little hands would be blue with the cold.

There was no let up in the gruelling workload at Clifden. On Saturday mornings Martina would have to clean the nuns' graves, even on bitterly cold winter days when her thin clothes offered little protection against the harsh weather. Her work was closely supervised by one of the nuns.

You'd be picking the weeds up and no matter how cold it was, you'd be out doing it. And she'd be standing there like a big Sergeant Major wrapped up and you'd be out and you'd be on your hands and knees picking the papers and all the leaves off the nuns' graves and putting them into sacks.

When Martina eventually left Clifden she returned to her mother's home initially. She could hardly read or write and she had become as tough as nails from her time in the institution. Her mother noticed a terrible change in her daughter.

Clifden destroyed me. The beatings I got there destroyed me . . . When I came out of Clifden I was just like a wild animal. I used to do terrible things. I would kill the kids. If strange kids went to hit me, I would literally tear the roots of their hair out of their head. I would bite them. Clifden just made a complete animal out of me. I hated adults. I couldn't bear an adult to touch me. I hated them. I just thought everybody was cruel. I went into a world of me own with the kids I ran away with and animals because they were only the kindest creatures. I had no respect for any adult, none whatsoever. Any adult that came across me I just turned my back on them.

There was to be little respite from Martina's harsh circumstances. Shortly after she left Clifden and returned home, her stepfather began to sexually abuse her again. She ended up back on the streets where the guards picked her up for minor offences such as stealing food. She soon descended into a cycle of petty crime that led to her committal to institutional remand centres in Dublin. Large shops such as Dunnes

Stores were popular thieving grounds for Martina and her runaway accomplices.

> We'd get three of the girls in Dunnes to go in the front way and start running a scene and the security would be there sorting them out. So we'd run around the side door robbing the biscuits, the lemonade and the sweets. And we'd be running out the back door because they'd [security guards] be in the front with the three of them. So then we'd come around and they'd see us, then they'd walk off so the security fellas would go back in and we'd pass and go down the lane and we'd eat all the sweets and biscuits and lemonade.

During this time Martina's gang of runaway friends became her adopted family. She had little contact with her mother and she didn't want to return home because of her abusive stepfather. The girls used their wits to seek out safe places to sleep in at night. The pram sheds in Dolphin's Barn made for ideal makeshift bedrooms. Young mothers would park their prams in the small sheds at the bottom of their houses so that they would not have to haul them into their homes. Martina and her gang of girls would lock themselves into the sheds at night where they could shelter in safety.

> We'd sleep there and we'd have blankets that we'd rob off the lines and we'd always keep them in there when we needed to sleep there.

A couple of the local women took pity on the teenagers and fed them whenever they could. One woman used to give the children a big breakfast when she came across them and another mother of a large family would generously feed the runaways with portions of stew that she used to cook. The survival skills she had honed at Clifden had turned Martina into a skilled thief when it came to stealing much-needed food. The girls would watch other homeless boys robbing the stores on Grafton Street in Dublin. They'd wait until the security men chased the boys down the streets and then they'd go into the shops and grab food before the security men returned. Martina discovered other ingenious ways of surviving. At one stage she was shown how to sneak into the mortuary of one of Dublin's hospitals where she would steal coins that people had put on the eyes of their dead relatives. She was told that the money was laid on the eyelids of the corpses to keep them shut.

> We done everything to survive. To us this wasn't robbing the dead. It was robbing to survive . . . we found out that there was money there. And there was always about five bodies in the morgue at the one time. So we'd go in and rob the pennies off the eyes.

Martina slept rough and lived by her wits during the years immediately following her release from Clifden. She spent sporadic spells in detention centres when the guards caught up with her. But the streets became increasingly more dangerous and older men began to intimidate her with their demands for sex.

> You know when you're bigger, then fellas would be wanting to go with you but you wouldn't want that. You'd just want to stay on your own and do what you had to survive. Then it was getting really rough.

At this stage of our interview her phone rang and she began to make arrangements for the dog she'd rescued to have his operation in a veterinary hospital. She enquired about doing a radio interview to see if she could raise funds for the beleaguered animal's treatment. After her phone call, we resumed our conversation and Martina returned to her childhood recollections. Her life took another tragic twist when she was around 15. She ended up in one of the dreaded Magdalene laundries in Dublin after being charged with robbing with violence. Her incarceration capped a childhood characterised by unremitting hardship. Martina says she was an innocent accomplice to a crime she did not commit.

> One day I met two girls I knew from Kilmacud and I was talking to them and out of nowhere the police came and skull-hauled the three of us into the back of a squad car and I hadn't a clue what was going on. I just said, 'What's going on?' and they wouldn't tell us and every time you'd open your mouth the copper would give us a punch but I'd end up jumping and giving him a punch back.

It later transpired that Martina's two acquaintances had got into a row with another woman. A fright broke out between them and the woman's watch fell off. She later accused the girls of stealing it. Martina was unlucky enough to be hanging out with the suspected thieves when the guards came along. The three girls were all convicted of robbing with violence and Martina was sent to the Magdalene laundry on Gloucester Street in Dublin, which was the last Magdalene laundry to close its doors, in 1996.[4] She ended up spending two years in this prison of misery, which was run by the Sisters of Our Lady of Charity. During her time there she was forced to wash and clean clothes that were sent to the laundry from various hotels, hospitals, schools and other places in Dublin. This backbreaking work was stringently supervised by the nuns, who marched up and down the laundry corridors to ensure the women didn't stray from their tasks.

> If you were on the compressors they were really horrible. I'd often seen the compressors coming down on the women's hands and the big lumps of skin on their hands. Oh it was dreadful. Or you'd be on the steamer and you'd be exhausted because the steam would be coming out into your face and you'd be just so tired from it and you'd be sweating. And if you didn't hurry up the nuns would be roaring and screaming at you.

Martina vividly remembers the older women who worked in the laundries. They had been institutionalised from a young age and were incapable of coping with life beyond the rigid control of these awful slave factories. Some of them had grown up in religious institutions and they had been transferred to laundries without their consent. These women became invisible victims of institutional cruelty who were abused and exploited by the nuns and abandoned by the State.

A pregnancy out of wedlock was such a calamitous event it could result in some unfortunate woman being turfed into a Magdalene laundry to repent for the sin of her child's illegitimate conception. Ireland's moral police castigated unmarried pregnant women and they were treated like cast-offs and left to rot in the laundries for the sin of an illegitimate conception. In some cases babies were taken from unmarried women at birth and the women were sent into the laundries to redeem their moral virtues. Some of their babies were adopted by couples living in other countries, including the US. Other laundry inmates ended up there because of minor offences for which they were unjustly punished. Martina hated her incarceration in the Gloucester Street laundry and when she first went in there she was terrified of the older women.

> You'd be frightened of them but you wouldn't realise God love them that the nuns was after doing that to them. We never sat back and took that into consideration. And the young few ones of us there would be calling them mental.

Some of the older women, who had become embittered by years of imprisonment in these contemptible workhouses, used to bully the younger girls. It was as if their minds had been lobotomised from the years of living in these infernal prisons and they began to imitate the nuns' cruelty. But Martina's experiences surviving on the streets had toughened her and she resisted their bullying.

> I wouldn't allow that and there was no way in God or hell would I allow them to bully me at this stage and I used to have murder with them all of time and they didn't like me because I wouldn't take the bullying off them.

Martina proved to be a formidable opponent of any woman who dared tackle her. Clifden had fostered a violent streak in her that was easily provoked. During her incarceration in Gloucester Street, she had two serious violent encounters with two women. One attack nearly resulted in a charge of attempted murder. Martina puts her anger at that time down to the savage treatment she got in Clifden.

> They really were the cause of all the violence I did and the attempted murder that I was nearly up for. They made an animal out of me from the beatings they gave me. You can only beat a dog for so long until it turns on you. It's the same with humans, you can only beat them for so long and they will eventually turn.

Martina's anger surfaced many times during this period in her life and she struggled over the years to control her rage. One day, while she was working in the laundry she broke a girl's leg in two places after she lost her temper when the young woman provoked her.

> One day she was pushing me around and I said, 'Stop pushing me, I'm warning you.' So she said, 'Go on, you're only out of Mountjoy [Prison]' and I looked at her and she pushed me again and that's when I battered her. I had her down on the ground and I jumped on her leg and broke it. I could hear the bone and all clicking. I heard the bone crack and then I jumped on it again and I said, 'You'll never hit me again.'

On another occasion a girl made the mistake of hitting Martina with a brush.

> It was her own fault, she wouldn't stop throwing the brush at me. I asked her five times to stop throwing the brush at me and every time I took the brush up and put it over [by the wall] she'd pick it up and throw it at me so I just lost the head and went over to her and smacked her across the top of the head with a big heavy mug. And all I remember is she just hit the deck and I walked away and left her there so the nuns got the police who tried to charge me for attempted murder.

In the end, Martina was not convicted of attempted murder but it would take years for her anger to dissipate to such an extent that she was able to control it more effectively. She spent two years in the laundry sweating in the stifling steamy rooms cleaning the huge volume of clothes that would come in from outside every day. The nuns carefully scrutinised the women's work and applied strict disciplinary procedures for any slackness on duty.

> They were like Gestapos walking around sitting at tables. You'd get these big baskets full of ironing. I hated the priests' habits. At one stage I just left the iron on the habit and walked away and it burnt right through. Then they put me into the steam room and I wouldn't do it anymore then because I saw a girl get her hand caught [in the compressor] and when they lifted it up Oh Jesus! the skin and all came off. The compressor had come down [on her hand].

Martina spent her time feeding wet bed-sheets, blankets and bedspreads into the huge roller drying machines. Then she'd fold the bedclothes and put them into trolleys to be carted off.

They'd be really heavy and you'd have to do that and I was tiny for my age and the nuns didn't care once you got the work done. You'd be knackered all day.

Other work consisted of folding shirts and packing and labelling the clothes to be taken away. It was a thankless task that Martina passionately despised. She felt trapped in this claustrophobic institution, which shamelessly exploited the Magdalene women and traded their slave labour for their own financial reward.

We never got a shilling for doing the laundry. And I remember one nun saying to me when I said it to her, 'Well, didn't you get fed?' The cheek of her. That knocked me back for six. But they were getting paid for me off the State. And they were getting a huge big income from the work we were doing. We never saw a shilling for that work we done. It was a full day's job like an employee's job from nine to five.

The grinding work didn't always stop at 5 pm. On some evenings, the women would have to make rosary beads or sew Celtic designs on traditional Irish cushions that the nuns sold to shops. They would get a small percentage of the profits from these tasks while the nuns took the rest of the money. Throughout her time in the laundry, Martina was effectively kept as a prisoner. At night she slept in a dormitory with individual cubicles above the laundry, where she would have to stay until the morning. The laundry's harsh regime prohibited any bonding between the women and Martina never developed any friendships with her fellow inmates there. She was determined to get out of the laundry and she vowed she would not end up permanently incarcerated there like the older women.

A lot of these older women were mentally tortured as well in them places. Them old women looked on them nuns as their mothers. And it was like if you didn't do what you were told, they didn't give you a treat. They'd give it to the other women and cause fights. They played mind games even among the women themselves and enjoyed that power. And to me that would be like a mother favouring one child and not giving another child something, the child is going to react. They really had that power and they used it even if they didn't have to beat them. They played terrible mind tricks with them. I think that was horrible. They had the power to hurt them and humiliate them.

After leaving the Gloucester Street laundry, Martina led a transient life. Over the years she drifted from place to place and did whatever she could to survive. She found it difficult to settle down and get a job. Her deep suspicion of anyone in a position of authority meant she rebelled against any bosses who ordered her around.

I remember getting a job in one place and there was one boss kept telling me what to do. And one day she said you make the tea and she kept bossing and bullying me so I fucked the whole pot of tea over her. I could never take the bossing and the bullying because it always reminded me of the homes.

Her emotions had been numbed by the unforgiving regimes in the religious institutions and she found it difficult to trust and to love to such an extent that she was left with a residual suspicion of people.

I wanted to be completely cut off from people altogether.

Gradually, as she got older, Martina's life began to stabilise and she learnt to control her anger. But the abuse she suffered in Clifden and Gloucester Street left her permanently wary of other people and today she prefers to seek comfort and love from her family of cats and dogs and the stray animals who wander into her life.

I wouldn't have cared what I would have done to a human being. If I'd killed one it wouldn't have bothered me. And I would have been capable of doing it and probably would still today. If someone is threatening to me to an extent that rage could come back in from the nuns. That's why I don't mix a lot with people because that rage would be still there and I would worry about that rage. And if I couldn't hit them I would get them one way or the other.

STILL LOOKING FOR
JUSTICE: JOHN KELLY

The permanency of childhood damage is a thread that links many of the stories told in this book: when a childhood is destroyed, the adult is also irrevocably damaged. Children who were abused in industrial and reformatory schools found it almost impossible to fully recover from their childhood abuse. Not one of the survivors I interviewed for this book has been able to move beyond the shackles of their blighted childhood to lead a normal life. Every single one of them is still injured in some way and many of them remain angry at those responsible for the theft of their childhoods. When the love and trust and secure, nurturing nature of a happy family unit is smashed to pieces and replaced with an abusive regime, the children affected will struggle to lead happy lives as adults. Former inmates of Irish industrial schools and reformatories have suffered from alcoholism, depression, poverty, distrust, unemployment, homelessness, relationship problems, marriage break-ups, mood swings and numerous other difficulties that stem from their childhoods. Some hapless survivors of institutional abuse drifted into a life of crime as they felt all other career options were closed to them.

But one remarkably positive feature most former inmates share is their extraordinary ability to survive. They had to delve deep within themselves to find the strength to deal with the abusive tyrants who were making their lives a living hell.

When the Ryan Report was published in 2009, thousands of survivors of institutional abuse felt vindicated. Ryan's significant report reinforced their own stories, which Irish society had ignored for decades. But not everyone was happy with the Report. John Kelly, coordinator of the Irish branch of SOCA (Survivors of Child Abuse), is critical of the rules that established the Commission to Inquire into Child Abuse. Those rules granted full anonymity to the religious men and women named as abusers by witnesses who gave evidence to the Ryan Commission. John Kelly believes that the Inquiry should have allowed for charges to be brought against suspected abusers investigated by the Commission. He is outraged that crucial evidence supplied to the Commission about sexually abusive Brothers and priests was granted privileged immunity. John Kelly insists that any damning evidence should have been sent to the Gardaí to enable investigations of suspected paedophiles. He wants the Irish State to allow access to those files so that charges can be brought against the perpetrators of abuse. He argues that this is the only way justice can now be done as the waiver signed by survivors who accepted redress ended their chances of taking their own cases against former abusers to court.

I first met John Kelly when I interviewed him several years ago for Newstalk radio when he discussed religious institutional abuse. He had spent 18 months in Daingean Industrial School when he was 13. He described Daingean as the San Quentin of Irish religious institutions and a repository for the rotten apples of the Oblate Brothers.

John Kelly was born in Dublin in 1951. His home life was dysfunctional from the beginning because of his family's poverty-stricken circumstances. John's father worked as a carpenter on building sites in England but work was sporadic and Patrick Kelly struggled to send enough money home to his wife, who was trying to raise their 10 children on her own. Things got worse after John's brother Patrick Jr died of kidney failure. Rose Kelly was inconsolable and she was barely able to look after her children.

> My mother found it difficult, especially after my older brother died. There was ten children in total and you have to understand the times as well, there wasn't any work here and my father was back and forth to England.

The Kelly children lived like nomads, moving from place to place and depending on handouts for their survival. They would periodically end up in various hostels and institutions around the city when they had no other place to seek shelter.

Sometimes we'd stay in hostels overnight and I remember we used to sit in Heuston Station for the heating because we didn't have any home. We'd no house . . . We were homeless for various periods. It was something like *Strumpet City* because she [Rose Kelly] couldn't pay the rent so we used to go between various families. I remember staying in my granny's for a little while. We used to go to various families during the day and then go to hostels at night. But we couldn't keep doing that especially when my mother got ill a few times, then we were put into homes for short periods of time, not for really long periods because our mother would get us back out again. But it was like a revolving door thing.

John's home life deteriorated when he was around 10 after his parents separated and he had to depend on relatives to get enough food and shelter to survive. But then life started to improve when his sister got a job and enough money to rent a house in Dublin. For the first time in his life, John had the security of a home and enough food. But those essentials didn't last long. Catastrophe struck one day when he decided to travel into Dublin's city centre with his brother and a friend. By then he was 13 and he had already left school. When the boys arrived in town John was ordered by his older brother to remain on the side of a street and wait for them while they went off on a mission. He had no idea what they were up to but he later discovered that the boys had stolen chocolate and money from the till of a small kiosk in Ballsbridge.

When they came out they gave me some chocolate and I took it. Now one could consider that to be an accessory to a crime but you'd have to know about it in the first place.

John was delighted with the chocolate as it was a real luxury back then and he was innocent of its illicit acquisition. He would later recall with bitter irony how those few bites of chocolate would play such a critical role in influencing the rest of his life. That night the guards came to his house and told his sister they were looking for John and his brother in relation to the theft of the chocolate and the money.

I was arrested then and charged with being part of this but I was never part of it all. What happened is they caught the other chap, I think he was a guard's son, and he implicated my brother.

John was found guilty of the charge of breaking and entering. He initially appealed the conviction but was unsuccessful and on 1 June 1965 he was sentenced to 18 months in St Conleth's Reformatory School in Daingean, Co. Offaly. He was to stay there until 4 February 1967. It was the first time he had ever been in trouble with the law and he is adamant that he was completely innocent.

It was a trumped up charge. I shouldn't have been charged at all because I wasn't near the place.

His brother was also convicted and sentenced to St Patrick's Institution in Dublin. John had no idea what kind of a hell on earth he was being sent to when the guards drove him to the remote industrial school in Co. Offaly. In the Ryan Report, St Conleth's is described as a place where boys 'lived in a climate of fear in which they were isolated, frightened and bullied by both staff and inmates'.[1] Ryan referred to the conditions of 'neglect and squalor' at Daingean where 'dirt, hunger, shabbiness and lack of supervision were all present'.[2] This dysfunctional institution bred a culture where 'gangs of boys operated as a form of alternative government, victimising those who did not obey them'.[3] When John was driven through Daingean's imposing gates, he didn't realise he was entering an institution where sexual, physical and emotional abuse were an integral part of its operations. In fact, his first impressions suggested a more benign picture.

You got this scenery on the way into it. You don't notice the big huge walls around the side. It had this lovely little garden area all grassy and everything else with benches outside. The minute you go through this door that's where the Brothers' quarters are. You go through that and then that's where the beatings and all happened. But even still it doesn't hit you.

The Oblates of Mary Immaculate ran the Daingean reformatory for teenage offenders with brutal effect. A common instrument of control was the substitution of a number for a name. It was all part of the twisted psychological process of stripping the boys of their identities

and driving wedges between themselves and their families. John was
known as number 253. This dehumanising tactic reinforced the stigma
of criminalisation.

John's first two weeks at Daingean passed without any major
incidents. He was sent to a small classroom for some basic teaching. On
reflection, John believes the teacher, Br Markus,[4] used this initial
schooling for Daingean's new entrants as an opportunity to identify
vulnerable boys who could potentially be preyed upon by the school's
sexual predators.

> I didn't take this guy seriously at all because he was so camp and he'd
> be laughing and giggling and he'd be prancing around the room.
> There was a sinister side to him as well. He'd put his hands up your
> short trousers and giggle.

John suspects Markus was a paedophile who would be jailed today for
his behaviour in Daingean but back then the boys just thought he was
a weird fellow and they dismissed his odd behaviour. Daingean's sinister
side emerged within a month of John's arrival there.

> The violence would start early in the morning in the washroom
> where wallops and floggings would be administered for the slightest
> misdemeanours. Br Seamus[5] usually supervised the boys as they
> washed themselves.
>
> You'd get washed in cold water and all of a sudden for whatever
> reason, he'd find a way to wallop you. You were always alert but he
> was dead clever and he'd walk by you and if you looked around you
> were in trouble and this guy would hit you, into the ribs and back
> again.

John remembered one morning, about four weeks after his arrival in
Daingean, when he witnessed a horrific assault on a young boy shortly
after breakfast.

> There was tin plates with gruel and tin mugs. It was like *Oliver*. You'd
> then go out to the yard and then around 9am Br Stain[6] would stand
> in one corner and he'd clap his hands and everybody would line up
> and he would detail you for jobs. You could go to the bog, the farm,

the laundry, the leather shop. And I remember then he'd put you into line. And I remember this young boy who was giggling and he wasn't in line. So he [Br Stain] got this child and he hit him and beat him to the ground. I noticed the way he would put his knuckles and get them where you could get pinpoint precision to inflict the blows so that his knuckles would be in such a way he actually knew the areas in which to hit the child. The child had been knocked out and I had never seen anything like this in my life ... This guy didn't stop hitting until he was exhausted.

Br Stain had expended so much energy flogging the boy he practically buckled on the ground from exhaustion and his arms went limp, as if weakened from the force of the violence he had used on the poor young fellow. Physical violence was only one element of the abuse that was systematic in Daingean. The Ryan Report concluded that sexual abuse of boys by staff took place there and it also found that sexual behaviour between boys was a major issue that was exacerbated due to the lack of effective supervision throughout the institution and particularly during recreation. Ryan stated that Daingean's unsafe environment caused some boys to seek protection through sexual relationships with other boys in order to survive.[7]

John was sexually abused shortly after his arrival at Daingean by Br Brown,[8] who was a notorious paedophile there.

I remember one day I was detailed to go out on the bog. Brown didn't usually go on the bog ... I was sent out this particular day and I remember it was raining. It was wet anyway. He [Brown] pulled me off the digging detail. I was pushing the wheelbarrows actually with the turf on it and he asked me to help with putting jam on the bread and there was brown baskets and there was like a tea towel over them and that was in the cab of the lorry. And he said, 'Look at the dirt of you and you're putting your hands on that food.' This was pre-planned. Then he used it as an excuse to put his hands down on my trousers and that was sore. And then when I went back out it was like everyone had got their bread and jam and I think he was playing football. This was in the bog and I was involved in it [football]. And he pushed me into a ditch deliberately and I was soaking and I was made to wait there for a while until we went back at 4 pm.

When John and the other boys returned to Daingean, Br Brown ordered him up to the shower room. As soon as John started to wash himself, the Brother slipped in beside him and began to sexually assault him. He penetrated John from behind and a piecing pain went through the young boy. To this day, John is not sure exactly how he was penetrated. It may have been with some sort of object or Brown may have simply raped him. When it was over, John was left bleeding and doubled up in pain.

> He actually was quoting God and the Bible to me. I was crying. I was saying to him that 'I'm sore, I'm hurting' and the blood was there. He said, 'A little bit of blood! What about Christ and the bit of blood that came from Christ when he died on the cross? What about him for the likes of you?'

John was dazed after Brown's sexual assault. The paedophile slithered out of the washroom as if nothing had happened and John limped down to the dining area for his supper where Brown was hanging around.

> After this thing happened I remember I was in agony. Looking back now, he was an evil bastard, I swear to God. I remember going down and into the main area immediately after and this guy was laughing.

John, who was extremely shocked, began to cry. Brown taunted and mocked him in front of the other boys.

> He said, 'Give Kelly some sausages there now. He's like a wimp; we have to feed him. Look at him, sure he's a wimp, he fell into a ditch and now look at the state of him.' It was all about control and mind control as well. He'd get the kids to laugh at you so that if you said anything he'd say, 'Ah Kelly's a wimp. Give him some sausages, he needs building up.' . . . But that's part of the process of covering up or discrediting me.

That public humiliation was effective enough to stop John from telling the other boys about Brown's sexual assault of him.

What you don't want added to your physical pain is humiliation by the other boys and being taunted and everything else.

About six weeks after this assault, Br Brown ordered John to take laundry over to the Brothers' quarters. On his way there, he was stopped by Br Rory,[9] who worked in the bakery. He seemed to be waiting for John, as if he already knew the boy was coming his way. He grabbed John and pulled him by the head into the kitchen and slapped him around the face. He pushed the terrified lad down onto his knees, shoved his head under his cassock and forced John to give him oral sex.

He was doing something I could feel this thing in my face. I had to wipe myself. It was unbelievable . . . what was traumatic was that this guy could do it with a compulsion and with no feeling of remorse, feeling nothing as if he had an innate right to do it. That's the shock I got rather than the physical thing, maybe because he couldn't do much worse than the other previous bastard had done.

John was sexually assaulted yet again when he was sent to Br Brown's room. This time the Brother's attack had a pernicious, perverse twist to it. He sat on the bed and made John fondle his own genitals first. He then demanded that the boy perform oral sex on him so that he could masturbate. John believes that Brown was playing a sinister psychological game with him and that he wanted him to believe that he was a willing participant in his own sexual assault. It was Brown's devious way of dehumanising his prey: a calculating instrument of psychological control that sees the victim acquiescing and engaging with the abuser in his own abuse.

The same act is happening but what you do is you don't want to be beaten up and you hope the terrifying aspect of it isn't going to happen; the penetration and that so you go along with the psychological game if you like. It's easier. I know it might sound very strange because it looks like you're doing it for real but you're not. He has coerced you into such a way with the control that he gives you the impression that you're doing it with him and you actually feel that and then you feel dirty and filthy but the alternative to not going along that way is to go along the first way [have him rape you].

They've got you where they want you. It's not as if you're in a house and you can run and tell somebody next door. You have forty-foot walls. They own you. They control you.

It seems bizarre but John Kelly was relieved after this particular sexual assault because Brown didn't bash him to a pulp or rape him but instead he displayed a depraved form of affection.

He now begins to treat you like a human. That doesn't make sense I know and all of this has paradoxes and contradictions but from my psychological thinking he was being nice.

Br Brown's manipulation of John's vulnerable situation was a cynical ploy to control his mind so that the boy would be grateful for his affections even though they were a manifestation of sexual abuse. John suspects that Brown had a powerful control over some of the boys in Daingean, who would voluntarily go to his room to perform oral sex. There was a mutual interest in the abuse. The boys were starved of love and affection and Brown's interest in them filled that void in a deeply perverted way because he also craved affection.

He had a need for you to somehow love him and be affectionate to him, that's what he really wanted and then to do the acts. Maybe he felt a little bit contrite that he didn't want to do the penetration that maybe he thought to himself, 'If I do this gently enough and you do this gently enough to me in the way I want it, then willingly we can lead up to something again like that. And then in that way I'm not committing the sin that I'm really committing.'

Daingean was a paedophile's paradise. John Kelly suspects several Brothers were a part of a paedophile ring there and that they were aware of one another's sexually abusive proclivities. A combination of factors effectively gave them a licence to sexually assault the boys without fear of censure. Daingean's remote isolation and its repressive regime magnified the overwhelming power the Brothers held over the boys. Their elevated status in Irish society fostered a grovelling attitude that placed them beyond reproach. This was exacerbated by the suppression of complaints of abuse and a failure to investigate them. The fact that the boys mainly came from poor backgrounds and were therefore vulnerable to exploitation made matters worse. When John Kelly was there in the 1960s, few people would have believed him if he had revealed that a number of Brothers were raping and sexually assaulting boys in Daingean. It would take many more years before Irish people finally accepted that clerical paedophiles were abusing children and that the Church had protected them and covered up their crimes to safeguard its own reputation.

John Kelly blames the recruiting system the Brothers used to attract boys to the Order for contributing to the abusive behaviour.

> The Brothers were taken in as young as fourteen, some thirteen. They're indoctrinated as children and the very first thing they're taught is that you must divorce yourself from your family and all that family life. If they're taught that, then clearly it's inappropriate for them to be in charge of children. Not growing up within a family setting but with a group of men it is likely they're going to have sexual and physical frustrations. It's no surprise to me that they would then take it out on children. So I think there's a contradiction between their calling to God and their sexual and physical frustrations.

John Kelly believes the Irish State bears a significant responsibility for the abuse of children in institutions like Daingean. The capitation fee paid to the Congregations for each child sent there was an incentive to get as many boys incarcerated as possible. As long as reformatory schools like Daingean existed, there was little pressure for the State to establish more progressive ways of dealing with juvenile offenders. The Department of Education's failure to properly inspect Daingean, or to act on critical reports when it did receive them, illustrates its negligent collusion with the Church in the abuse of children.

> The Church had its power but it was only given the power by the State. The State abdicated its responsibility totally.

The combination of the sexual and physical abuse had a profound impact on John Kelly. His tormentors in Daingean have never gone away. They are like executioners of misery who hover around their victims rattling the cages of their broken spirits.

> You realise then that you weren't human. That is what bothers me to this day. That form of dehumanising to me strangely is the worst thing that's ever happened to me. You can get over these things to some degree but what you can't get over is that you're not part of the human race . . . They'd broken my spirit. They'd broken my humanity. Any feeling or connection I had with humanity was gone. I was worthless.

John Kelly still has moments today when he doubts if he's a full member of the human race. When he left Daingean in 1967, he couldn't shake off the stigma of being labelled a criminal. The fact that he was innocent of the crime he was imprisoned for was irrelevant. The shame stayed with him and he has struggled over the years to shed it.

> I always felt that all these things happened because I took that chocolate from my brother. I feel guilty, humiliated and ashamed that what happened is down to me.

John moved to England after leaving Daingean and he stayed there until 1994, when he returned to Ireland. He later got married and had a son. In 1999, when the then Taoiseach Bertie Ahern apologised to the survivors of institutional abuse, John began to revisit his past. He wanted justice for the abuse he had endured and he was desperate to see the Brothers who had sexually assaulted him in Daingean put on trial. On 31 August 1999 he went to the guards and made a statement about the abuse he had suffered there. It was around this time that he got involved in the establishment of soca with other survivors of institutional abuse. The costs incurred in establishing soca, and his own efforts to get the Oblate Brothers charged, meant he ran up significant bills and he had to sell his house in Dublin to get extra money. He ended up living in a flat with no heating for a while.

> I was willing to go to any lengths to get justice . . . I wanted to go into the court and expose the extent of what these places were like and more to the point how they dehumanised me. It was my way to get back into the human race and say, 'Now I'm vindicated.'

The Gardaí investigating his case sent a file to the Director of Public Prosecutions. But in 2001, the DPP stated that charges would not be brought against the suspected paedophiles named in John Kelly's case. He was devastated. He suspects that the DPP may have been influenced by the establishment of the Redress Board, which was going to compensate survivors of institutional abuse. When the Board was set up, Bertie Ahern said it would save survivors from the trauma of adversarial cross-examinations in court and he emphasised that the passage of time would make it very difficult for them to prove their allegations of abuse. But John Kelly was determined to see his abusers in the dock and he held out the hope that he could achieve justice through the civil courts. In the end, his solicitors advised him to go to the Redress Board and in 2005 his case was processed and he was awarded redress. That meant he had to sign a waiver against taking any further action against the abusers named in his redress application. John Kelly is still bitterly disappointed that his Daingean tormentors have never gone on trial.

> I was looking all my life for normality and to be treated as a normal human being and that's what I want and I don't think I am. I don't want retribution as such . . . I want to be able to walk out [of the courts] and say look he has been exposed for what he did to me physically, sexually, emotionally and everything else and what has also been exposed is the type of system that they operated. Like Hitler's regime it wasn't just the gas chambers, it was how they went about doing what they did to the human race and what they did to Jews. That's been exposed and now I can walk back into the human race.

In 2009 John Kelly discovered that Br Brown was still alive and being cared for by the Oblates in Dublin when a journalist contacted him and told him he had tracked Brown down. Brown's ability to live out his retiring years in the safe and comfortable surroundings of the Oblate Order raises huge questions about the inability of the State to pursue allegations of sexual abuse in these religious institutions. John believes the Redress Board enabled paedophiles like Brown to get away with their abuse.

I'm still trying to look for acceptance. Why is nobody giving me justice for what happened to me? The guy's still alive, one of them.

John Kelly is doubtful he will rest until the perpetrators of abuse go on trial. His psychiatrist once told him that when he comes to see her, he is not on his own. She told him that two people enter the room — the child and the adult — and that John is still trying to protect the child and get justice for him. The psychiatrist advised him to let go of the child in order to move on but for John Kelly letting go will only happen when justice is carried out in court against the men who abused him and thousands of other children in Daingean and elsewhere.

What do I need to help me get back into the human race? Once I know that this child is protected but how can I know that when this child hasn't got justice? I need closure.

Chapter 11 ∿

MAUREEN SULLIVAN AND THE MAGDALENE LAUNDRIES

aureen Sullivan hates the dark. It makes her nervous and she breaks out in a claustrophobic sweat. That's why she always sleeps with the curtains open and her bedroom door ajar and she rarely stays in hotels because she would have to lock the door. That would mean a restless night marred by nightmares that stem from her committal to a Magdalene laundry when she was a young girl. Back then, she slept in a large dormitory in St Aidan's Industrial School in New Ross, which was attached to the large Magdalene laundry that was run by the Good Shepherd Sisters. Maureen was terrified of the darkness that would engulf the dormitory after the nuns closed the curtains and locked the children into the large room. She can still hear the clang of the key twisting the lock shut. The girls would have to tap on the door if they wanted to go to the toilet.

Maureen's childhood evaporated on the day she entered the gates of the Magdalene laundry in New Ross in the 1960s when she was just a young girl. It was illegal for the Good Shepherd Sisters to put Maureen Sullivan to work in the New Ross laundry as she was a minor and entitled to a childhood and an education. Her committal to their religious workhouse drastically limited her future opportunities.

Maureen spent four years in two Magdalene laundries when she was a young girl. During her incarceration in these sweatshops, she worked from Monday to Friday in the laundry and spent her Saturdays and Sundays down on her knees polishing the floors of the church and the convent corridors. These religious workhouses were harsh, unloving institutions where the Magdalene women suffered in silence as they ironed sheets and tablecloths, pillowcases and clerical vestments in a melancholy daze. Women who had spent many years in the laundries were broken down over time and their spirits had been crushed by the harsh rigidity and religious dogma of the Sisters who ran the laundries.

Today Maureen Sullivan struggles to comprehend the cruelty the nuns inflicted on these unfortunate women.

> It was disgraceful, disgusting. They were treated like animals really. You wouldn't do to an animal what they done to them.
>
> Every night I wake up and I think of these women and their faces are in front of me. They were so disturbed. The desperate look on their poor faces. It was just horrible. It will always haunt me for the rest of my life.

The Magdalene laundries were originally established in Ireland in the nineteenth century for 'fallen women' deemed to be leading inappropriate lives. They were designed to rehabilitate prostitutes but that ethos changed considerably as the Catholic Church founded and expanded its own Magdalene institutions. Women were incarcerated in these religious sweatshops for spurious reasons such as being illegitimate, pregnant out of wedlock, the victim of abuse in the home, or the subject of a court order. The moral police of Catholic Ireland went even further in influencing incarcerations. Young women perceived by Catholic zealots to be wayward or promiscuous were imprisoned in these sanctimonious factories and abandoned to the mercy of their religious masters. Unmarried pregnant women, who gave birth to their babies in other institutions, were sometimes incarcerated in Magdalene laundries against their will to repent for their perceived evil, immoral behaviour. They were supposed to cleanse their sins through hard labour and penitence in these austere workhouses.

According to some reports, even a beautiful face and precocious behaviour could incur a committal. Peter Mullan's searing film *The Magdalene Sisters* (2002) portrays a fictionalised account of 1960s Ireland when the Catholic Church ruled with absolute authority and the Magdalene laundries were repositories for 'fallen' women. The film centres on three women who were incarcerated in a Magdalene laundry in 1964. Margaret's crime was to be raped by her cousin. Bernadette's good looks and flirtatious behaviour with boys got her incarcerated and Rose was committed by her parents for bringing shame on the family by having an illegitimate son. In the film, her newly born baby boy is taken from her and given away for adoption. Rose's own parents arrange for his adoption along with her forced committal to the laundry. The film illustrates how the religious orders wielded enormous influence in the God-fearing Catholic Ireland of the recent past where its people swallowed the Church's ludicrous notions of morality.

An estimated 30,000 women are believed to have been incarcerated in the laundries during their 150-year history. The story of the Magdalene women who were enslaved in these grim workhouses is incredibly sad. Many of them became so institutionalised they couldn't function beyond the high walls of their inhumane prisons. They remained in these self-righteous sweatshops for most of their lives, working every day doing mindless tasks in silence and in fear of the nuns who supervised them.

Maureen Sullivan's story illustrates the power the religious orders had in dictating how children from poor or troubled backgrounds should be handled. She was born in Carlow in 1952. She never knew her natural father as he had died from a combination of tuberculosis and pneumonia six months before she was born. She lived with her two older brothers and mother in Bennekerry, Co. Carlow, for the first three years of her life. Then the family moved to Carlow town when Maureen's mother remarried, to a Mr Whelan.

Mrs Whelan went on to have a second family but Maureen's home circumstances were profoundly challenging. There is much that cannot be told about her childhood during this period but it was dysfunctional and there was abuse in the home. As a result, Maureen became withdrawn and quiet. When she was around 13 the head nun in the local primary convent school expressed her concern and asked for a meeting with Mrs Whelan. During that meeting the nun discussed Maureen's melancholy disposition and the abuse in the home was addressed. The nun told Maureen's mother that she had a solution. She proposed sending the young girl to another school in New Ross that was run by the Good Shepherd Sisters. Maureen was told she would love the school and that she would be happy there.

Sr Mary[1] said, 'We've a lovely school for Maureen and she'll get educated' and she said, 'You'll be very happy there.' I'll never forget them words because I even agreed to go. And she said, 'Would you like that?' and I said, 'Yea that would be lovely.' You could see the happiness on my mother's face that something was going to be sorted . . . She [Sr Mary] said, 'You can come home whenever you want and if you're unhappy you can write a letter and your mother can come and get you.'

Maureen was excited about going to her new school and escaping her home circumstances. The night before she left for New Ross she packed her new copybooks and pencil case into her small suitcase, which was tied together with a string. The next day a man driving a large laundry van came to her home and picked her up. There is confusion about the exact date when Maureen was taken to New Ross. She believes it was actually some time in 1964 when she was only 12. However, the Good Shepherd Sisters have disputed that date and claimed she came to them in 1965 when she was 13. During her journey to New Ross, the driver of the van stopped in several locations and picked up large baskets of laundry. When they arrived at the convent gates they drove into a yard where Maureen was met by one of the nuns in charge of the laundry. She instructed one of the Magdalene women to take Maureen's luggage.

She told this woman to take my suitcase and school bag and she took me into the laundry and she showed me all around. I thought that was strange and I thought I was important that they were showing me all over the place and they were very nice. And she was saying, 'This is the calender and this is the iron and this is the starch.' And an old lady came over to say hello to me and I thought it was very cruel the way the nun pushed her away and she said, 'Don't talk to them.'

The young girl was puzzled by the tour. She had no idea that the laundry would be her new workplace and that she would be denied an education throughout her time there. Maureen Sullivan will never forget the eerie silence of the laundry and the sad demeanour of the women who barely looked up at her as she walked past them. They appeared to be almost catatonic; they were lost in their own world of broken spirits with all life pummelled out of them. When Maureen reflects on that time she thinks most of the Magdalene women were aged between 40 and 70 and that there was a smaller number of younger women in their twenties and thirties.

> You'd never forget their faces because there was something strange about the look on them. It was of total sadness and institutionalisation. They didn't know how to communicate. You never heard them talking and every day I used to go down there I used to say that this place is weird. Nobody was allowed to talk. It was terrible. And there was a few women who went around in a daze, you know, like you'd see in a mental hospital.

The New Ross laundry was a thriving business in its heyday. The women worked non-stop washing and ironing the large volumes of laundry that came in every day for cleaning. Maureen was stunned by the sheer size of the place.

> There was a big, long, grey-looking room with ironing boards not like the ironing boards that we use. The ironing boards would be like big tables down along the whole wall and there'd be irons plugged in everywhere that would be going down along one wall. Then over on the other side you had the calender that you'd feed the sheets into, and you had pressers that you'd pull down to do the shirts. Then you'd have more ironing boards — these huge yokes that you'd put the priest's gowns on. Then there was the place that the laundry came in from the hotels that was called the sorting room.

When the laundry was sorted it was then washed in huge machines in the washroom and taken to the large ironing section. That's where Maureen spent her unforgettable two years in the laundry. She used to feed the sheets through the massive calender, which had large rollers that pressed them. Two girls stood on the other side of it and folded the sheets as they came out of it. The sheets were then packed into baskets or cloth bags and returned to their owners.

After her tour of the laundry on the day she arrived at New Ross, Maureen was taken to St Aidan's Industrial School, which was a part of the Good Shepherd convent complex. She used to walk from the laundry to St Aidan's through a corridor and then down through a passageway that she called a tunnel, which ran underneath the church. A nun brought her to the large dormitory and told her that's where she would sleep at night after her day's work in the laundry. When she enquired about schooling and requested to see the classrooms, the nun stared coldly at her and dismissed her query.

> That evening I said, 'Could I have a look at my classroom?' That's when the attitude all changed. She [the nun] said, 'Classroom?' and I said, 'Yes, my classroom where I'm going to learn and I brought my new books and I'll show you my new pencil case.' I was real friendly that day. She looked at me as if to say don't mention that again. That was her response.

That night Maureen's identity was stripped from her when the nuns gave her a new name. The Sisters told her she would be called Frances from then on. She was warned not to talk to the other girls in the dormitory and not to ever mention anything about her home circumstances or her previous school in Carlow. The nuns threatened a severe punishment for breaching the rules and the little girl soon learnt how serious they were when she introduced herself to one of the girls in the dormitory using her proper name. That girl innocently got Maureen into trouble when she went up to a nun after discovering that Maureen had inadvertently left her facecloth in the washroom.

> The girl said to the nun the next morning that 'Maureen's left her facecloth on the sink.' You were supposed to take them back to your locker and I left it behind me. So the nun came in and she was shaking me and pushing me and saying, 'Your name is Frances and you have to get this into your head now that your name is Frances.'

Maureen Sullivan never went to school in New Ross. Instead she slaved away in the laundry throughout her time there. Her routine was the same every day. There were no gentle awakenings in St Aidan's. She was roughly awoken every morning at 6am when a nun would shake her arms and give her a dig. She would have a breakfast of bread and a glass of watered-down milk in the kitchen of the industrial school. A dreary Mass followed breakfast and then she would be taken to the laundry where she changed into the shapeless, drab grey dress that was the

Magdalene uniform. Maureen would then spend the day feeding sheets into the large calender for pressing. At first she couldn't reach the enormous rollers that sucked the sheets in because she was small for her age and so one of the workers from the farmyard made a small box for her to stand on. One of the Magdalene women tried to speak to her on her first day in the laundry but she was brusquely corralled out of the room by one of the nuns.

> An oldish lady came and she said, 'You're only a child, what are you doing here?' And the nun came and pushed her out the door real rough and she was digging the crucifix into her and I knew it was because she asked me why was I there. She was trying to be kind and I knew she got into trouble. So I knew there was something not right there and that there was something terribly wrong. And then a nun came in and she called me and she said, 'Frances' and of course I didn't answer. The nun was looking directly at me and calling me 'Frances' and I didn't answer and you could see all the other women looking at me as if to say, 'That's probably not her name.' They knew that wasn't my name and that's why I wasn't answering. But anyway I was brought out and boxed into the ears while another one [nun] looked on. There was two of them. They pointed out how I wasn't answering to my name and that if one of the Magdalenes spoke to me, I wasn't to answer back and I wasn't to talk to them: 'You just refuse to talk to them.'

The atmosphere in the laundry was one of stony silence. Maureen was too terrified to speak to any of the women in case she was caught and punished. The nuns controlled the Magdalenes by imposing a strict regime of fear. They belittled the women to such an extent that some of them ended up like institutionalised robots who had been brainwashed by years of unremitting subjugation and religious dogma. In *The Magdalene Sisters* this is wonderfully illustrated by one woman in her sixties who enthusiastically imitates the nuns' abusive behaviour. She struts around the laundry bullying the girls with gusto and boasts about being in the institution for 40 years.

Maureen remembers how the nuns in New Ross supervised the women with military precision as they marched up and down the laundry like prison guards.

They were very cruel. They behaved like men. They were very masculine women. You'd be terrified of them. There were no smiles; they were cross all the time. You never got a nice look off them. Every time they looked at you, it was a vicious look . . . All they had to do was walk up and down. We were like little robots. Nothing was done wrong.

The nuns castigated the Magdalene women for the slightest misdemeanours. They would wallop them across the head with a swipe of their keys or dig their crucifixes into their bellies. The Sisters displayed little sympathy for any injuries sustained during working hours in the laundry.

I often got burnt from the calender. You'd burn your hand and you'd ask them for a bit of cream that the burn was so painful you'd be holding your hand. You could get a box for that. They wouldn't help you; you wouldn't get a bit of cream or nothing.

It is difficult to comprehend the inhumane behaviour of the nuns towards the women. Their perception of the Magdalene women as somehow immoral or depraved seemed to have given the nuns a licence to treat them with disdain. Compassion was in short supply here. This harshness was starkly demonstrated for Maureen one day when a Sister cut off all her hair when she discovered the little girl had lice.

I couldn't sleep the night before and I was very tired and when the nun got me up the next morning I said, 'I'm so tired. And she said, 'Why are you so tired? Why don't you go to sleep and you won't be so tired?' And I said, 'I couldn't sleep because there're all sorts of crawlies in me hair.' And she still brought me down to me breakfast and brought me down to Mass and then down to the laundry. And of course I was standing there tearing my hair. My head was cut from me tearing so much and they [lice] were crawling down around me and they brought me out of it [the laundry] and the nun came down and she looked at me and she came over. She must have seen them crawling and she took me over to her room and two of them held me down and chopped my hair off in big chunks. And one nun held me head in between her legs and squeezed me and me two ears and me head was raw when I got back up. And I was screaming and I was crying my eyes out and I was saying, 'How could you do such a cruel thing? Look at my hair?' And they said, 'Now you won't have lice. That's what you get for having creepy crawlies.'

Maureen's scalp burned from the searing pain of the chemical the nuns rubbed all over her raw, bleeding head. It was a hugely traumatic event for the little girl and she couldn't understand why they were treating her so badly. Head shaving was used by the Sisters to defeminise the Magdalene women. In Peter Mullan's film there is a dramatic scene when one of the main protagonists, Bernadette, has her head shaved after attempting to abscond from the laundry. Blood oozes down her face as the Mother Superior pulls back the young woman's shiny black hair and cuts into her scalp in her dogged determination to chop it off.

There were very few breaks from the daily grind in the laundry. Dinner, at 12.30, lasted for just half an hour and it took place in an atmosphere of complete silence. And while the Magdalene women were served plates of inedible gruel, the nuns ate sumptuously at the top of the dining room. Maureen remembers the delicious aromas that used to come from their tables.

The smell of their food was completely different. You could hear some of the women saying, 'They've got steak!' They used to get a lot of roast beef because you'd hear the girls in the kitchen talk about it. And we'd get just sloppy stuff. All the time it was sloppy — like stews.

The whole place was so sad. To me it was worse than a prison. At least in a prison people had recreation and you could read books or do something.

Although the laundry stopped operating at 5pm every day, the exploitation continued when the sweatshop moved to the recreational hall. After a supper of bread and dripping, the exhausted women were then forced to make rosary beads and Aran sweaters for several hours. Maureen had to learn quickly to knit jumpers and string rosary beads. As usual, their work was strictly supervised.

There'd be a nun up at the top watching you. She'd sit up there and she'd be reading a book and she'd be looking out under her glasses. Nobody talked.

The women were given targets and ordered to complete a certain number of rosary beads and sweaters. Failure to reach those goals guaranteed the wrath of an angry nun who would humiliate and lash out at the slow achievers. The intimidated women were so petrified they worked frenetically to finish their tasks even though they were nearly collapsing with exhaustion. Maureen detested stringing the beads.

The rosary beads was hard because you had wire and you had these little pinchers and you'd put on a bead and then you'd have to turn the wire in and then you'd have to connect the wire and put on another little bead. It was quite sore on your fingers.

This delicate task was tortuous for those Magdalene women who did not have nimble fingers. They frequently cut themselves with the wire and pinchers and their eyesight suffered as a result of the intensity of the work. The women were never thanked or paid for the hours they spent knitting and beading but the Sisters would have made a tidy profit from their work and the tourists who bought the beautifully made Aran sweaters or rosary beads were probably oblivious to the exploitation behind their creation.

They used to go out in big boxes and they used to have lovely tissue paper. They'd put this lovely paper in between them and they'd be folded over and packed into boxes. Boxes and boxes of them went out.

The profits gained from the Magdalenes' 'recreational' work topped what must have been a significant income from the laundry. Maureen Sullivan remembers it as a very busy place where large volumes of clothes were washed and ironed every day. She reckons about 60 women worked there during her two-year incarceration in New Ross. When she finished for the night, she was taken back to the dormitory in St Aidan's where the other girls would already be fast asleep. Maureen pressed the nuns several times about attending school and demanded to know why she wasn't able to receive an education, but her queries were dismissed.

> The nun brought me into the office one day and she told me, 'If you bring up about going to school again we are going to get very annoyed with you and you're going to end up in very serious trouble.' So I just looked at her and I just walked out when she told me.

The little girl desperately wanted to tell her mother about the nuns' refusal to send her to school. One day she decided to write to her mother to explain her grievances. She handed her letter to one of the Sisters who assured her it would be posted that day. But to her horror, Maureen later discovered her letter had been shredded.

> I handed the letter in on a Saturday and on the Sunday I went into the Nun's office with another girl to clean it out. My letter was tore up in the bin.

It was common for the nuns to destroy any damning letters that Magdalene women wrote to people outside the laundry while letters posted to the women were frequently read by the nuns and destroyed if there was anything unacceptable in them. Maureen was rarely visited by her mother during her time in the laundry as it was difficult for Mrs Whelan to travel to New Ross, but one particular visit stands out in her mind. Maureen was excited about her mother's impending visit and she warned the nuns that she would tell her that she wasn't receiving an education in New Ross.

> I told the nun that 'I'm going to tell my mother that I'm not going to school.' Well, they gave me such a beating, they thumped me into the stomach. I was so badly beaten in the stomach that I couldn't stand up straight. It was horrific and she [the nun] told me, 'You'll never see your mother again if you keep this up about school. We're sick of it at this stage listening to you about school.'

A Sister sat in the room and supervised Mrs Whelan's conversation with her daughter throughout her visit. When she asked the nuns how Maureen was getting on they painted a rosy picture of life in St Aidan's and reassured her that Maureen was receiving excellent training.

> The nuns was saying, 'Oh yes, she's very good and she's coming along great and she's getting great training and tell your mother about the lovely Aran sweater that you done', not *sweaters*! And I was thinking, God how many have I done at this stage? And my mother was saying, 'Can you do an Aran sweater?' She was all excited because I was able to knit an Aran sweater. I think she really didn't know that we were knitting Aran sweaters late at night after a day's work. The Laundry was never mentioned.
>
> My mother was a real Catholic and she trusted them. The nuns was important to her; she'd nearly bow to them.

The Sisters' halcyon depiction of life in New Ross was a devious distortion of the reality. Maureen's incarceration there obliterated her childhood and left her emotionally crippled for years. She has never received a satisfactory answer from the Good Shepherd Sisters explaining why they forfeited her education and stuck her in the laundry to work as a child slave. A possible explanation is that they wanted to hide her troubled family background and that meant shutting her up in the laundry away from the other girls in St Aidan's. The protection of the conventional family unit in 1960s Ireland was of paramount importance to the Catholic Church and stories of family abuse were shoved under the carpet. Another possible explanation could be one of expediency. The laundry was a thriving industry when Maureen arrived there in the 1960s and the Sisters may have required extra hands to get the work done. They would have known that she was vulnerable because of her family circumstances and unlikely to have angry relatives calling them to account. The emotional fall-out of her incarceration in New Ross was enormous. She became withdrawn and unable to communicate properly.

> I think I went into myself something terrible because even when I went over to London when I did come out of them places I was terribly bad at communicating with people. Even in London they used to call me the quiet one. Even when you'd go into a pub, you just sat there and they'd say to me, 'How are you, Maureen?' and I'd go, 'Fine' and I wouldn't make conversation with them and you

never trusted anyone.

Generations of women who entered Magdalene laundries never left these pious prisons. Death was the only release from the shackles of the Sisters who ran these exploitative institutions. The constant babble of perverse religious dogma numbed the women's minds and castrated their independent spirits. Those unlucky enough to have been incarcerated by their own families were doomed from the beginning as they had few people on the outside fighting for their release. Maureen Sullivan could never understand why the Good Shepherd Sisters dehumanised the Magdalene women. She will never forget one poor woman who was forced to eat her dinner off the floor like a dog.

> I came up one day to go to the toilet and the recreation room had a door into it from the toilet and I could hear a woman crying. And I went out onto the corridor and the windows of the recreational room was along it and I went out to look in to see what was wrong and I could see them make her eat it. 'Eat it!' they were going, 'Eat it.'
> . . .
> They had dinner off a plate and she [nun] was hitting the plate off the wooden floor emptying the food onto the floor and she said, 'Eat it. Eat it.'

Maureen recalled how the nuns had forced the frightened woman down onto her knees and tied her hands behind her back. They then made her lean down and eat the food off the floor. She was crying inconsolably. Maureen later met another former inmate of the New Ross laundry who confirmed that the same thing had happened to her. She too had been shoved down onto her knees and forced to eat her dinner off the floor.

The Sisters were adept at the art of humiliation. Bed-wetters got the full brunt of their degrading tactics. Maureen sometimes wet her bed during her time in New Ross. When the Sisters would discover her wet mattress, they would summon her from the laundry and haul her back to the dormitory to take her moist mattress down onto the schoolyard for a public parade.

It was the only time I'd ever go back over to St Aidan's during the day if they found out that my bed was wet. You were brought back over to carry your mattress around the playground in St Aidan's in front of everybody. You could even see the nuns looking out at you. You'd have to drag it [the mattress] down the stairs and they'd be watching you. You'd not get one hand with it, not one bit of help. And you'd drag it on down the steps and you'd go down one step at a time and bring your mattress with you. And the only time they'd ever give you a hand is when you'd be trying to get it up on your back. If you were a bit stooped you'd get a grip and you could hold it better.

When Maureen was 14, she was transferred to another Magdalene laundry in Athy that was run by the Sisters of Mercy. The New Ross laundry was closing down and the nuns wanted to move the Magdalene women to other institutions. For Maureen, Athy was like a mirror image of New Ross. Although its laundry was smaller, it was equally grim and severe. She left Athy when she was 16, and was then sent to Dublin to work in the laundry of a school for the blind that was also run by the Sisters of Mercy.

My mother came up to see me and Mammy asked, 'Maureen, do you not think that really you should be getting wages now?' So I went back and said about the wages and that was me out. I had to pack me bag and they gave me £5 and they left me at the train station.

Maureen returned to Carlow where ironically she ended up working in a laundry in the town. But within a short time she left for England where she spent the next 30 years. She went on to have two children. Her daughter was born when she was only 19 while her son was born 15 years later. Maureen got married in England in 1987 when she was 35 but she found the intimacy of the relationship difficult to handle.

I loved being on me own. I'd like a certain amount of time on my own. I used to love going off to the parks sitting on my own. Well, that doesn't work in a marriage. You were so used to people not talking to you [in the laundries] and then too many people talking to you it would kind of flutter you. And if my husband wanted to bring his family around I wasn't able to deal with it in case things would come up in a conversation. You could get caught. You're going to be asked about your school and 'Where did you go to school in Carlow, Maureen? What's Carlow like?' It starts off with the simplest little things and the next minute your school is into it ... You had to create a completely different image of yourself altogether.

Like so many survivors of institutional abuse, Maureen kept her background in the Magdalene laundries a secret from everyone except for one close friend in London. She didn't discuss it with her husband Jimmy when they lived in England and instead she kept it bottled up inside her. She regrets not revealing to her husband the full details of her bleak past.

I wish I did tell him. I didn't want him to know that I was in a place like that or anything like that happened to me. You were ashamed of it.

You never had any confidence. Anytime school came up ... you'd just sink into yourself. You'd wish the ground would open up and swallow you because you can't have a conversation. Anytime anything about Leaving Cert. came up your heart just thumped because you had to get out of that conversation somehow so you'd end up creating a different person than you were. Your stories that you used to tell people was completely not you at all.

I remember one night in a pub in London and a girl came up and said, 'What about your Leaving Cert.?' You'd tell a load of lies and say, 'Oh yea, we done this and we done that.' You're creating yourself as a different person.

Maureen returned to Ireland in 1995. Her husband also came back but the couple lived apart although they saw one another regularly. Maureen stayed in Carlow while Jimmy moved to Westmeath to be close to his relatives. He died on New Year's Eve in 2005 when he was just 50. Today Maureen acknowledges that it was impossible for him to get close to her.

It wasn't his fault and he told my mother, 'I always loved her but I could never ever get close to her. I never knew her.' God love him. And he did try. And he said, 'I could go up and have dinner with the woman and I could have a lovely time and the next minute, she can't wait to get me out the door.' I could never help that you see. I could never ever get that close to anyone. And that's something that's going to stay with me. It's not going to change now.

When Maureen returned to Ireland her background caught up with her and she had nightmares about her time in the laundries. Those flashbacks coincided with an increasing number of stories appearing in the media about the abuse of children in industrial schools and reformatories. The pressure of the past pushed Maureen to the brink and she was on the verge of a nervous breakdown when she decided to seek counselling. That propelled her on a journey of healing and gradually she opened up to other people and talked about her background. That process has been extremely cathartic for her. She no longer feels ashamed of her childhood experiences because she now realises she was never to blame for the circumstances that led to her incarceration in the Magdalene laundries, or the abuse that she endured in those institutions.

In 2009 Maureen Sullivan featured in a documentary made by the young Irish film-maker Stephen O'Riordan. *The Forgotten Maggies*, which was shown at the Galway Film Festival that year, told the stories of four women who were former residents of Magdalene laundries in Ireland. It followed Maureen's struggle to get compensation from the Residential Institutions Redress Board, which was established in 2002 to give redress to survivors of religious institutional abuse. The Magdalene laundries were never included in the list of religious institutions because the government said the Irish State never had any responsibility for the laundries and that it never sent any women or children into them. This position was reiterated in a statement in 2009 from the Minister for Education, Batt O'Keeffe. 'The Magdalene laundries were privately-owned and operated establishments which did not come within the responsibility of the State. The State did not refer individuals to the Magdalene laundries nor was it complicit in referring individuals to them.'[2]

That defence has since been disputed by James Smith, author of *Ireland's Magdalen Laundries and the Nation's Architecture of Containment* and associate professor at the English department and Irish Studies programme in Boston College. He has insisted that the

State was complicit in its referral of women to the laundries. 'The Irish courts routinely referred women to various Magdalen laundries upon receiving suspended sentences for a variety of crimes, and I have archival documents detailing communication between judges and mothers superior of a number of convents arranging such referrals.'[3]

Former Magdalene inmates were justifiably angry at their exclusion from the scheme.

When Maureen initially applied for redress she was told she would not be entitled to it because she was a former resident of a Magdalene laundry and not an industrial school. However, she insisted that, although she worked in the laundry during the day, she slept in St Aidan's Industrial School at night and that she was only a child when she was sent there. The Good Shepherd Sisters resisted her attempts to get redress and they insisted she never went to St Aidan's and that she was a resident of the laundry throughout her time in New Ross. After a long struggle, Maureen's case was finally accepted when the Redress Board acknowledged that there was enough evidence to suggest she had slept at St Aidan's Industrial School and therefore was entitled to redress.

Up to the time of the publication of this book, the Magdalene women were still fighting for redress and for the right to have their stories documented in a forum similar to the Commission to Inquire into Child Abuse that resulted in the Ryan Report.

Maureen Sullivan believes their exclusion from the redress scheme is tantamount to an act of State betrayal.

> I think it's terrible. I think it's very, very wrong. And I think there will never be closure until them poor women get redress. It's terrible that they're left out in the dark and I'd say they suffered more and worked more than anybody did. They got terrible treatment.

Today Maureen lives in a pleasant home in Carlow, which she shares with her lovely retriever dog. Her son is attending college in Cork and her daughter lives in England. The journey of healing and recovery that she has made over the last decade has had a profound impact on her.

> I think I definitely feel different. I feel stronger. I let a lot go. I'm a different person and a lot of people that would have known me in

England that I went back to see they said it's like I'm a new person. Definitely it changed my life. It does help to get it all out and you do become stronger.

Many former Magdalene residents are still too traumatised to talk about their past. Their exclusion from both the Commission to Inquire into Child Abuse and the redress scheme has prolonged their suffering. They believe the Irish State and the religious orders who used them as slaves in their laundries are still refusing to accept full responsibility for the role they played in destroying the lives of thousands of Magdalene women.

Chapter 12 ∿

FROM HOMELESSNESS TO
HOPE: GERRY CAREY

When Gerry Carey opened the door of his flat in central Dublin
on a cold November morning, he immediately thrust a mug
of steaming coffee into my hand and showed me into his
neat, cosy living room. He'd transformed his council flat into a snug
home, adding individual touches such as the ornate fireplace in the
living room that was laden with photographs and mementos. Gerry's
white hair and round face gave him a kind of friendly fatherly
appearance. As we chatted on his sofa, he spoke about his ambition to
open a centre in Galway for victims of abuse. Gerry Carey is well-placed
to offer advice on abuse.

A survivor of religious institutional sexual and physical abuse, he
ended up an alcoholic and his wife and children threw him out of the
family home. He became a destitute vagrant living in a hostel for the
homeless and begging on the streets for a pint until he hit rock bottom
one day after a massive alcoholic binge. That overdose of booze set him
on a path of recovery and he managed to turn his life around when he
confronted his past. Gerry's ability to deal with the abuse of his
childhood is an inspiration.

Life was tough from the beginning. He was born in Tullamore in
1958. His father was a turf cutter and a chronic alcoholic who would
drink his wages in the local pub. His mother had a stroke early in life
that left her with a paralysed arm and leg and she found it difficult to
cope. Their first home was a bungalow in Esker, Co. Offaly. Gerry went
to bed hungry many nights as his dad was easily enticed into the pub,
where he spent all his money.

He was known as about the best turf cutter, cutting it down himself so everyone was looking for him to cut their turf first. They were cute, the people down there, at that time. They used to take him to the pub and pay him in the pub.

The neighbours would ply Gerry's father with pints and food such as cabbage and potatoes in lieu of payment. He was so drunk he would stagger home penniless, forcing Gerry and his brothers to find innovative ways of feeding themselves.

I remember that there was a family living down the road, who were brother and sister, and they were in their early fifties or sixties and they owned a little farm. And because there was very little food in my place, in my father's house, I used to go up the road to them and help them feed the little lambs and sheep and run around their fields bringing in the cows. There was a dog there that used to walk me home at night-time.

These kind neighbours gave the young lad food and shelter and a respite from the hardship of his own home. Gerry's drunken father frequently lost his temper with his children and they dreaded the nights he'd stagger in the door and remove his belt to give them a lashing.

Every time he'd come in with a bar of chocolate on a Friday, the little thin skinny bars of Milk Tray, if he had drink taken, he'd hit us.

One night, when Gerry was four, his father arrived home stinking of booze. He told the children and Mrs Carey to pack their bags as he had lost the family home to another man during a gambling session in the local pub.

He lost it in a game of cards and your man took it off him. He came home and he told my mother, 'Look what I have in the yard.' It was a kind of camper van on wheels and he said, 'That's our new home.' So we had to drive up the road about three miles to a sandpit and he parked there and he made that into our house. We all had to sleep on bunks.

The loss of the family home was devastating and life in the caravan was miserable. Gerry escaped from it as much as possible by visiting his neighbours down the road.

> I loved it down there. I used to get out of that house as quick as I could and then the dog used to walk me home at night-time.

The Careys depended on handouts from relatives and friends to survive and Gerry's mother used her sewing skills to make trousers out of potato sacks for her young sons.

> They were short trousers but they were all right to me. I didn't know I was dressing wrong until I went to the school and they started fitting me up for shoes and clothes.

Gerry and his brothers used to scavenge in the forests for provisions to heat the caravan's wood-burning stove, which was the only source of heat.

> We used to have to go up into the woods and break the sticks even in the wintertime. I remember my brother's hands bleeding because it was so cold when we had to get the sticks for it. We had to get water from the sandpit and we had to try and sweep around the caravan so that it was kept tidy.

The Careys' precarious existence was eventually brought to the attention of social welfare officers. One day in 1964, a man from the ISPCC pulled up in an Anglia car outside the Carey caravan and told Mrs Carey he had instructions to remove four of her sons. Gerry later discovered that the neighbours he had visited so frequently were distraught when they heard he had been taken away as he was like a surrogate son to them.

> If they had known, before I was taken away, they would have took me in and they didn't know until I was gone.

Gerry was six when he was plucked away from his mother, who stood helplessly by her caravan door as the strange man told the boys he was taking them out for the day. Gerry was initially excited at the thought of the drive, but he was puzzled by his mother's obvious distress. She cried uncontrollably as her sons were driven off.

I could look out and see she was crying. I was just waving and saying, 'We'll be back, we'll be back.'

The family bonds began to disintegrate from the moment the boys were taken from their mother. The Carey brothers would never be able to rebuild their sibling ties after that traumatic uprooting from the family caravan. That night Gerry was taken to an elderly people's home in Tullamore.

The next morning they came over with porridge to us and I remember it well because it was very salty. I couldn't eat it and it was lumpy.

After breakfast, the boys were driven to St Joseph's Industrial School in Salthill. The man in the Anglia told Gerry and his younger brother to get out of the car while the other boys stayed in it.

He took me and me brother out and knocked on this huge big black door. And this Brother opened the door and said, 'Oh these are the two children I've been waiting for.'

By now Gerry was extremely confused and he had no idea what was happening. He was brought down a long corridor and into the office of the head Brother, who told him he was to get washed and ready for supper.

He brought us in and got us washed. I suppose we had lice and we had all that stuff because we were living like mountain men [in the caravan].

Gerry was given clothes and a pair of shoes and brought into a large dining room that was teeming with children. He was shocked at the number of boys milling around as he had never seen so many children gathered in one place. That night he tucked himself up into a ball beneath the thin blankets of his metal bed and cried himself to sleep. The loneliness was unbearable. Even though life in the caravan was bleak, he desperately missed his mother and other brothers. The next day the other boys laughed at him when he insisted he was only there for a short break. They cruelly told him he wouldn't be leaving Salthill until he was 16.

> I was devastated when I finally believed it. Then every night after that, I wet the bed for many years. There was punishments for that. You'd get mocked and called 'Pissy bed'. All the other children would laugh at you, and scream at you watching you washing your laundry. And there were a good few of us washing our laundry. I was in my late twenties before I stopped [wetting the bed]. Even when I was taken out on holidays by people, I used to get up in the middle of the night to wash the sheets. But she [mother of the family] caught me and she said, 'Gerry, you don't have to do that, I'll do it for you. Don't be worrying about doing them.' I thought she was going to hit me or slap me because I was used to getting that. But she said, 'No, Gerry, while you're here, just sleep.'

Salthill was typical of other industrial schools run by the Christian Brothers. It was a cruel, harsh institution where severity and sadism were deployed with staggering frequency.

> I can't remember many days that went by that I didn't get beaten.

Gerry will never forget one physical assault when he was around seven. It was a hot summer's day and he had taken his shirt off and fallen asleep on one of the playground walls. He lost track of time and didn't notice his body burning up. Br Brown[1] went ballistic when he saw Gerry's red-hot skin. He shouted at the young fellow to go down to the infirmary and get the nurse to put some ointment on the burns. When he reached the infirmary, the nurse was in a thundering mood.

> She ran a bath of cold water and she told me to get into it. I stood into the bath because I was naked and she got a scrubbing brush that you would do the floors with and she scraped every blister off my body and she told me to stop screaming or she'd send me back up to

Brown. I remember I screamed for ages and I was so sore I don't know whether it was the cold water or the scrape marks that were left on my body from the deck brush that she was using that you used to clean potatoes or floors with. And that memory stands out as one of the worst for me because when I went back up to Brown crying, and when he seen me crying, he hit me more.

Brown kicked and punched Gerry and warned him to stop behaving like a baby and to get up to bed. That experience left him with a lifelong phobia of baths so much that when he moved into his council home years later, he asked for the bath to be taken out and replaced with a shower. He was petrified he'd go into a shock and have a seizure if he stepped into the bath.

I can't have a bath because of the sunburn I had and the way she took it off my skin. I have to stand up and have a shower.

Br Brown was a vicious thug who picked on Gerry throughout his time in Salthill.

He had this white foam that came out of his mouth every time he was angry. And every time he moved his lips you could see the spit following it. And we knew to just keep away from him because he was angry. But we couldn't because he picked out the same few fellas all the time and beat the crap out of us.

One day Brown thrashed Gerry because they had performed badly during a football match against another school. The boys were pulled out of the shower and told to stand beside the sinks because Brown was coming down to see them. Gerry smelled the stench of alcohol from his breath as soon as he walked in. Brown was seething.

He took a swing at me with the long squidgy that they used to wash the floors with to get the water off and because I moved to stop it from hitting me, it broke the sink and that's how much power he was using on our legs with that. And because he missed and because he broke the sink he got me the second time with anger.

Brown used to teach in Salthill and he regularly beat Gerry, who struggled with some of the subjects such as Irish. He had little patience for children with learning difficulties and he used his full physical force against them.

> He'd use the window poles, he'd use his leather strap, he'd use his fists, he'd use anything at all to hit me. There was a child in my class who fainted every day in class with the fear of Brown. He absolutely passed out.
>
> He'd call me a dunce and put me into a corner and I had to face the wall crying of course. I was bawling my eyes out until he told me to 'Get out!'

Gerry believes Brown had a pathological hatred of children. When the boys played hurling on the pitches, he would run up and down the sidelines like a psychopath and hit them on the ankles with his hurley. He would force them to stay out until late in the evening even in the middle of a freezing cold winter's day.

> If you couldn't keep up, he'd run behind you and hit you. That's why I was only nine stone seven, because I was fit.

The physical beatings Gerry endured in Salthill damaged his hearing and eyesight and left him with bad veins in his legs.

> I was punched so many times by Brown that there was times I think I ended up being unconscious.

Gerry remembers Brown as a medium-sized man with glasses and black hair that shone with hair cream. He was a control freak with a foul temper who would explode in anger for little reason.

> I wanted the fucker to burn in hell because we were taught about the fires of hell.

Apart from physically abusing boys, Brown was also a sexual predator. Gerry's first sexually abusive encounter with Brown happened when he was around nine and he was taking a shower. By the time he had

finished, Brown had entered the washroom. He told Gerry to go back
into the shower and wash its walls properly.

> I got into the shower and as I was in the shower he walked into the
> shower behind me with his long robe on and he said, 'I have you
> now.' I'd be pushed up against the wall and the next thing is, his
> hand would be down onto my thing [penis]. Then he grabbed my
> hand and put it on his thing [penis]. I was facing the wall and you
> could feel this thing getting hard but mine wasn't. He was breathing
> his alcohol on top of me. He was stinking. I was stroking him and he
> was mauling me. That used to happen about twice a year with
> Brown. When he felt himself coming he'd have a white hanky. And
> he'd use the white hanky and all you could hear was the sigh. And
> he'd say, 'Now clean that shower and don't open your mouth to
> anybody or I'll get you again.'

Brown also engaged in other lewd behaviour in the washrooms when he
would conduct bizarre investigations of the boys' teeth.

> When we stepped out of the shower, we had to hold out our
> toothbrush. We were naked. He'd walk around with a tube of
> Colgate and he'd put a little bit on each brush. Everybody got a bit
> of it. Then we'd walk over straight to the sink and we'd stand there
> and we'd brush our teeth. He'd be walking behind us, checking our
> ears, checking in between the cheeks of our arses, and this was all
> forms of sexual abuse. And then when we turned around we had to
> show him our teeth and we had to open our mouth to show we
> swallowed the toothpaste, and he'd check our ears and he'd lift up
> the willy to see was that clean. He was getting great satisfaction out
> of all of this.

Brown also used his own office to abuse the boys when he would bring
them in on false pretences and lock the door behind them.

> I remember sitting there one time and he'd be telling me how bad of
> a pig I was. And the next thing, you'd see him masturbating behind
> the chair, rubbing himself up, and then you'd see the hanky coming
> out cleaning it off. 'This is what you make me do. It's your fault.

You're the devil. You're useless,' he'd say.

During some of these assaults Brown would warn Gerry never to go near women, saying they would infect him with fatal diseases. He also told the boys to keep away from alcohol even though his own breath was stinking from booze. Not all of the Christian Brothers in Salthill were paedophiles, but their silence and lack of action facilitated child predators like Brown who abused with impunity.

Brown was not the only paedophile in Salthill. Br Murray[2] was another predator who assaulted Gerry one day in the gym.

> I was told to roll up the mats that we used to roll on. And when I was putting the mats away he came behind me and he told me to lie down. And I was lying on my back and he told me to turn over and do push-ups. And he was showing me how to do the push-ups. As I was doing the push-ups, he pulled down my shorts, and I don't know what he put in me but he put something in me in the back area.

The boy was in extreme pain after Murray penetrated him. He warned him to keep his mouth shut.

The Christian Brothers woefully neglected the children in their care in Salthill. The food they slopped up every day was almost inedible and Gerry frequently went to bed on an empty stomach. He remembers eating rotten potatoes and mince with bits of grease floating in it. It was so disgusting it used to make him retch. While the children were fed miserable scraps of food, the Brothers dined on the best produce available. Gerry saw their delicious food when he got a job in the Brothers' kitchen washing dishes and sweeping floors. They had their own cook who used to make mouth-watering meals for them every day.

> They'd get the best of food. They'd get roast beef, ham, bacon and cabbage, vegetables, pork. She [cook] made lemon meringues once or twice a week. She done apple tarts, pies. She done everything for them.

The delicious aroma of food made the young boy weak with hunger and he devoured the leftovers when the Brothers had finished eating.

Anything that was left on their plate I was eating it before I brought it into the sink to wash . . . The most important people in the school were them [the Christian Brothers]. The one thing that they were sure of was to never go hungry and feck the education that the children were supposed to be getting, and feck the clothes they were supposed to be wearing, feck everything else that they were supposed to have. I think a lot of the food that they were giving us, vegetables and stuff, was going out of date. It was donated by fruit markets and the potatoes were soft and going off, and I think they just put out the poor mouth around Salthill, they got donations and out of the money that they were getting paid by the State, and some of the parents, was feeding them and looking after them.

While the Christian Brothers enjoyed the meals of their own cook, the boys in Salthill were forced to eat the miserable rations dished up by the Brother in charge of the children's kitchen.

He was a filthy no good for nothing dirt bag. At times we used to see him in the kitchen putting his finger in his ass and then stirring the soup with the same finger.

All the time you had to be one step ahead of them to survive. They used to give you this greasy crappy-looking mince and I couldn't eat that. But the way I'd survive is that I'd swap my mince for a potato.

Gerry stayed in Salthill until he was 15. He remembers his parents visiting him only once during his entire incarceration there. Their absence had a profound effect on him and, for many of his adult years, he struggled to comprehend their negligence when he was a child.

I had always been blaming my mother. How could any mother let her child be taken away? I was forgetting that my father was an alcoholic because it suited me to forget.

The original court order had determined that Gerry should stay in Salthill until he was 16, but a nasty confrontation with Br Brown led to his early discharge. Gerry snapped one day after yet another flogging by Brown and he threatened to kill the Brother.

Brown was coming down the corridor and empty bottles were in the corridor. I picked up a coke bottle and I broke it on the wall and put the broken bit to his neck and I said to him, 'You're never going to touch me again or I'll kill you.'

He was scared shitless. I seen the fear shitting him. I was shaking too because I had lost it. I wanted to kill him. I couldn't take him anymore. I took so much of him.

Gerry was thrown out of Salthill two and a half weeks later. He was not even allowed to do his Inter Cert. After his departure, he embarked on a journey of self-destruction that was influenced by the neglect and brutality of Salthill. The sexual abuse left Gerry saddled with paralysing emotional and psychological baggage. It would take him another 25 years before he would have a Damascene conversion that would help him release his childhood demons. When he left Salthill he returned to his parents, who were still living in the camper van. Their circumstances were as dire as ever and Gerry's descent into alcoholism began on the day his father met him off the train from Galway and took him to a pub in Tullamore, where he began his calamitous relationship with drink.

He brought me into a pub and put a glass of Guinness in front of me and put two spoons of sugar in it and said, 'This is the makings of a man of you now.'

That first drink set Gerry on a rapid descent into alcoholism that would eventually leave him homeless and begging on the streets. His first job was with Bord na Móna stacking turf on the bogs. It was poorly paid backbreaking work. He initially lived with one of his older brothers in a converted cowshed on a farm outside Daingean. Gerry stayed there for a year before moving back in with his parents when they were offered a council house in Clonbullogue, Co. Offaly. By then his two other brothers had been discharged from the industrial school they were sent to. The Carey boys were finally reunited but they were like strangers.

In 1975 Gerry's alcoholism worsened when he joined the Army and was assigned a job as a chef in a barracks in the Curragh, Co. Kildare. His daily 4am start, preparing breakfasts for the Defence Forces, meant an early finish at noon leaving him the rest of the day to drink in the Army bar. He frequently drank up to 25 pints a day.

Heaven meant you were in the bar all day drinking because it was only twenty pence a pint. So for every pound you made, you were getting seven or eight pints.

I used to go on the binges where I'd get so drunk I wouldn't even know where I was. I'd go into Newbridge and I'd wake up in Dublin and I'd be too far away from the Curragh. I used to have blackouts. I was drinking for reasons to forget. Every day I woke up, I wanted to forget. Every day I woke up, I remember saying to myself, 'I'll get this done quick. I'll get down and get a few drinks and I'll feel better.'

Gerry's loner tendencies deepened his drinking habits and he tried to drown the misery of Salthill by lunging into an alcoholic oblivion.

I had nightmares all the time about being hit and punched. Anyone that was sharing the bed with me used to say, 'You were covering your face', 'You were covering your hands', 'You were blocking punches', that 'It looked like you were going through a hard night.'

When Gerry was in the Army, he met his future wife. The couple married in 1977 and had three children together. But money was tight and so he left the Army to become a seasonal driver with Bord na Móna. He was drinking heavily at this stage and struggling with his marriage. After his second child was born, he ran away with a woman he met in Dublin and went to live in England with her for six months. It turned out to be a disastrous decision.

I started to miss the kids after six months. We were drinking heavy over there as well. Both of us were working and were staying in a Bed & Breakfast. She worked in the B&B so we'd get the rent free. And I was working on the building sites and any money we were getting, we were drinking. She didn't like me drinking because I changed moods. She just came with me to keep me safe.

One day we went into the labour exchange in England and I was ahead of her and I got my money and I walked over to the window and tears started rolling down my eyes for no reason at all. And she came over to me and said, 'What's wrong?' and I just looked at her and said, 'I think we have to go home because I miss my kids.'

The couple returned to Ireland and promptly parted company and Gerry moved back in with his wife in Dublin after promising to commit himself to his marriage. Over the following years, he did odd jobs to earn money for drink but for the most part his wife kept the house together and looked after their children.

I was a total loser. Looking back now, I was a gobshite, but you don't realise that when you're drinking.

Gerry couldn't wait to get out of the house and into the pub from early in the morning.

I've been in every early house in Dublin ... I'd go into town to start work and go in and have a few pints and go to work; come out at lunch time and go for a drink; come out at dinner time and go for a drink and come out at four o'clock in the evening with a couple of the lads and get more drink.

Sourcing the next pint became his main obsession. He did anything he could to fund his boozing lifestyle from washing windows to grabbing bags of turf from the Wicklow Mountains and selling them around the houses in his neighbourhood in Dublin. Sometimes he managed periods of sobriety when his good-natured side would emerge.

I went into a kind of a nice fella then for about five or six months where I'd be starting a GAA club. I'd look after the kids. I'd go to the parent-teacher meetings. Then all of a sudden I'd be back down again.

Gerry admits he was a lousy father whose aggression towards his children reflected his own ravaged childhood, which left him paralysed with depression.

I was no father at all. I couldn't understand what the big deal was. If a kid fell, I'd say, 'Get up'. If they got a cut in their leg I'd say, 'Get up, you'll be all right.' Then they'd come in for their lunch and I'd say, 'Cook it, you know how to make soup.' I didn't care. This would be after a drinking session. They'd come home from lunch and I'd be still in bed. I wouldn't get up. I was in severe depression, I'd say. I think I was blaming the world. Why am I like this? Why can't I be like everyone else? Why can't I have some feelings towards my children? Why is it that I got such a raw deal? All these negatives and then I'd unload on myself so that I could feel miserable and then wait for an opportunity to get rid of the misery.

Throughout most of his marriage, he kept his background of child sexual abuse hidden from his wife. She couldn't understand why he behaved so harshly towards his children.

I wouldn't wash them or shower them because I thought that was abusive. I wouldn't hug them because I thought that was abusive. When I was having washes I was abused so I couldn't separate them. My wife would say, 'Go up and shower your daughter or bath her' and I'd say, 'No! I will not.' To me I'd see a baby naked and that was abuse.

Even when I was doing football with them or training them in Gaelic, I was harder on them than on anyone else because I wanted to show them that life's hard. You're not going to get things handed to you. You have to earn it.

She [my wife] had a miserable life with me. Her favourite statement was, 'When you're good, Gerry, you're great. When you're bad, you're a bastard.' And I was a bastard most of the time.

I got into more fights. I got guns pointed at me. I got hit by cars. I got hit by buses. I got stabbed three times.

Gerry was eventually kicked out of his home in 1995 after he went on a massive drinking binge that left him seriously hungover the next day. His wife and children were so fed up with him they tackled him that morning.

I was lying on the couch and the next thing I seen my suitcase down the bottom of it. And I said, 'What's happening?' and she [his wife] said, 'You're getting out of here. I can't put up with this crap anymore.' So I said, 'I'm moving out? You won't get me out of here.' I said, 'I'm not leaving this house, you'll never get me out of this house, if you do put me out of this house, I'll break back through the window. Where have I to go? I have nowhere to go.' So my daughter came in, she was only about ten and she said to me, 'Dad, please go because we're not happy. You just can't stop it.' And when I heard her saying that I got up and I said, 'OK, if that's what you want.' And I went.

Gerry's situation rapidly deteriorated after his humiliating exit from his home. He ended up in a hostel for the homeless in Dublin eking out an existence on social welfare. His alcoholism was so bad he was sent to sleep in the hostel's basement where the drug addicts and boozers hung out and he ended up begging on the streets for his next pint.

> What I used to do in the day was, I'd tap on the streets, which means you'd sit on the streets begging ... I left the pub scene and went on the street scene. Cider was the main product then. A good tapper knows where money is because you'd hear the change in their pockets ... It used to be embarrassing in case people knew me.

Gerry steadily drifted into a semi-permanent state of drunkenness, sharing his miserable life with other bums who, like him, were boozing themselves into oblivion. Then in 1998, when he was 40, he had a moment of epiphany that pitched him into sobriety and on to a journey of recovery. His life-changing volte-face followed a massive alcoholic binge funded by a windfall repayment of £1,500 that he had received from the Department of Social Welfare. At first, he thought he would use the money to rent proper accommodation. But his good intentions were thwarted when the prospect of a few pints with another drunk from the hostel arose. His homeless companion had also received a refund bounty of £600 and the two men decided to embark on a non-stop orgy of drinking.

> We ended up going out for eight days non-stop from six in the morning. About twelve o'clock in the day, I'd fall asleep in the pub. The barman would wake me up after I'd had a nap and start serving me again.

The two men drank themselves into a stupor, stumbling home at night after spending the whole day in the pub. But on the eighth day, when they were about to spend the last of their money on a final binge, Gerry woke up in a semi-comatose state. When his boozing buddy knocked on his door to rouse him for another day on the lash, he lay on his bed, immobile and speechless.

> I couldn't speak. I'd lost my voice. I was in the bed which was soaking from sweat. I couldn't stand up. I had no power in my legs and my hands were shaking. He pushed in the door and he seen me, and he helped dress me. He got me on me feet and I was walking baby steps trying to walk. And I thought, 'Jesus, I can't keep doing this.'

Gerry's friend managed to drag him down to Temple Bar in central Dublin where the owner of a pub let the two in before opening time and served them a pint each.

> I got it [pint] up to my mouth and I drank it and I drank another one. And I looked across and I said to him, 'That's my last drink. I'm going home.' I wanted to live. Something just hit me in the head that it's time to live now. It was like my guardian angel saying, 'You've tried to die, now try to live.' So I went home. It took me two more days to get the alcohol out of my body.

Gerry had reached that rock bottom moment that can propel alcoholics to sobriety. He never touched a drop of drink again and shortly after that momentous day he signed himself into the Stanhope Alcohol Treatment Centre in Dublin and went on a four-week detox programme.

> I went in very angry in the sense that I didn't think people talking to me to stop me drinking would work.

But that therapeutic work was profoundly effective. It helped Gerry to sober up and tackle his past. For the first time in his life he found some peace within himself.

> I started to live like a human being again. Then I said I want more of that.

The pressure valve of the past had been released and the years of pent up anger, frustration and depression began to seep out. After leaving the Stanhope Centre, he embarked on a year of intensive counselling that allowed him to confront the ghosts of Salthill that had plagued him for years. He stayed on in the hostel for another year but this time he was determined to stay sober. He knew his life had taken a turn for the better when he was removed from the basement and given a room upstairs, where he began to carve out a new future.

I had five things written down to do in the first year. One was to make amends to all the people I had hurt during my drinking. I apologised to all of them. I wanted to get a flat, get a job, go back and visit my old school and face my demons. My fifth wish was to visit the people that used to take me on holidays who I hadn't seen in 35 years to let them know that I was still alive.

Gerry completed his goals during his first year of sobriety. He began to work as a part-time chef and he started to travel around the world. He remained on in the hostel for another year until Dublin Corporation assigned him a cosy flat in central Dublin. He set about converting the one-bedroom apartment into a comfortable home. He was determined to make a go of his life and he began to study counselling to enable him to help other survivors of child abuse. As his life stabilised, his contact with his children was re-established and, for the first time in his adult life, he began to form healthy relationships with his children and his former wife.

When they'd be in here helping me with stuff I'd turn around to my son and say, 'Can I ask you a question?' And he'd say, 'Ya, what, Da?' And I'd say, 'Was I a shit father?' and he'd say, 'Ya, you were, Da, you were a bastard. And forgive me for saying it but we like you the way you are now. You're doing good.' And I'd say, 'Can I apologise for being a shite father but you didn't know about my past and I had a shite life.' And he'd say, 'We know about it now, Da, and we support you a hundred per cent.'

By the time I met Gerry in 2009, he had been sober for 11 years and was hoping to open a centre in Galway for victims of institutional abuse where he could use both his training in counselling and his own experiences to help them to recover from the abuse they had suffered as children. He is hoping to fund the centre from donations given by the religious orders who ran industrial schools such as Salthill.

> I would like to be sitting down in Galway three days a week counselling victims and hopefully making their lives better. I don't want a big car or a big house or anything like that. I just want to know that my time on this life will be just to help people through what I came through.

When Gerry reflects on his past, he acknowledges that he cannot forget what happened to him in Salthill but he is acutely aware of the danger of becoming addicted to victimhood. That destructive attachment can prevent victims of abuse from moving on.

> They think that if they step out of the safe box that they won't be able to cope. They have become dependent and institutionalised in the sense that as far as they are concerned they still feel that they deserve more. They need to be listened to every day about the same thing because they need to think that by telling you that it's going to make them feel better. But they don't know how to let it go because by keeping it, it's keeping them functioning. They need it.

Chapter 13 ∾

THE ABUSERS: HOW AND WHY?

When the full impact of the Ryan Report's sobering details were absorbed over the days and weeks following its publication, the same disturbing questions were asked repeatedly: Why did the religious orders so brutally abuse the children in their care? What turned them into sadistic monsters? Why were paedophiles within the religious ranks able to abuse with impunity and how were they able to get away with the sexual abuse for so long? Other questions were raised about the Irish State's collusion in the incarceration of the children and its negligence in supervising their care when they were in these despicable institutions.

The initial commentary in the days immediately following the Ryan Report's publication suggested a gamut of reasons. The repressive religious vows of chastity, poverty and obedience were blamed for the dehumanising behaviour of the nuns, Brothers and priests. Analysts suggested the vows went against human nature and that it embittered members of the religious orders to such an extent that they took their frustrations out on the children in their care. The unnatural living conditions of convents and monasteries, which required groups of men and women to live cooped up together in grim austere buildings, were blamed for tipping them over to the dark side. Irish people also had to face the unpalatable reality that the lethal mix of poverty, insularity and Catholicism had played a significant role in the contribution of the whole of Irish society to the abuse.

In the heated emotions following the Ryan Report's publication, it was tempting to project a twenty-first century modern and liberal perspective onto the last century when, for most of it, Ireland was poor and the Catholic Church wielded enormous power. That power didn't start to wane until the 1980s. An appreciation of that historical background is critical when assessing Ireland's legacy of child institutional abuse.

There are many reasons why children were physically and sexually assaulted for decades in industrial and reformatory schools and other institutions run by the Congregations. They include: the remote locations of the institutions themselves; the repressive regime within these places; the appalling system of dealing with complaints and reports of physical and sexual abuse; the harsh religious vows of chastity, poverty and obedience; Irish society's grovelling attitude to the Catholic Church and their dismissive attitude towards children sent to the schools; the Catholic Church's perverted theories of sexuality and Irish people's endorsement of their bizarre dogma; the Congregations' recruiting methods for novice Brothers and Sisters; the disgraceful negligence of the Department of Education and its utter failure to properly supervise and inspect the schools; the roles played by the Irish judiciary and the ISPCC; and the capitation fee payment system.

This chapter by no means provides a comprehensive analysis of all of the reasons that led to the appalling behaviour of the religious orders towards the children in their care. Extensive academic and sociological investigations will be required to fully explain this dreadful period in our history. It does, however, give an overview of some of the main reasons behind the abuse.

THE NATURE OF THE INSTITUTIONS AND THE SEVERITY OF THEIR REGIMES

The industrial and reformatory schools should have been disbanded decades before they officially closed their gates. In Britain these Dickensian institutions were being phased out from the 1920s as they were no longer considered to be effective in dealing with children from problem backgrounds. Instead the British began to develop systems of foster care and encouraged the establishment of smaller communities for children. But while the British were winding down these types of institutions, in Ireland they mushroomed following the establishment of the Irish Free State. The religious orders enthusiastically accepted children into these places. In fact, they had a vested interest in ensuring they incarcerated as many children as they could possibly cope with.

The capitation grant system of payment meant the State paid the Congregations for every child taken into their care. Therefore the more children they had, the more money they made.

The remote location of many of the schools facilitated abusive behaviour. Institutions like Daingean, Letterfrack and Upton were situated far away from the homes and families of the majority of the children who were sent there. These places were cut off from the surrounding communities and were extremely difficult to get to. Letterfrack, for example, was located in the middle of Connemara, some 84 km from Co. Galway. The parents of boys who were sent there from cities such as Dublin, Limerick and Cork found it very difficult to travel there to check on their children during their incarceration. That isolation meant the children were virtually prisoners, caged in by their all-powerful custodians who exploited their privileged positions in Irish society to abuse with impunity.

The austere and grim nature of the institutions themselves increased the frustrations of the religious members living there. The buildings were frequently cold and severe and lacking in the luxuries available in more comfortable day schools, convents and monasteries. Their remote locations also meant the religious members were socially cut off from their wider communities and that could have exacerbated their frustrations. A posting to an industrial or reformatory school was seen as a harsh dispatch and it has been argued that the more troublesome or less bright and poorer members of the Congregations ended up there. That lethal mix of institutional austerity and dysfunctional human behaviour made the children easy targets for their frustrated and angry guardians.

Overcrowding was another reason why the Brothers and nuns exerted unnecessary physical violence towards the children. They felt a strong arm was the only way to control the large number of children in their care.

COMPLAINTS PROCEDURES AND TOLERANCE OF PHYSICAL VIOLENCE

The lack of a proper complaints procedure to record and act upon reports of physical and sexual violence contributed enormously to the abuse. Children who reported sexual assaults to religious figures in the schools were generally punished for doing so. The futile attempts made by the people featured in this book who were sexually abused illustrate how a veil of silence was drawn over institutional paedophilia. Irish people inadvertently colluded in that silence as the majority of them would simply not have believed that Brothers and priests were sexually assaulting boys and girls. Such conduct would have been beyond the comprehension of most Irish people up until the time the majority of these abusive institutions closed. The combination of poverty, ignorance, insularity and the power of the Catholic Church blinded Irish people to the awful abuse of children that was going on behind closed doors. It was really only in the 1980s that the Catholic Church's grip on Irish people began to loosen and more progressive and modern views began to emerge.

The lack of accountability when it came to the excessive use of corporal punishment enabled the Brothers and Sisters to beat children without the need to justify the violence. The Department of Education ruled that punishment books were required in the schools and that the religious orders had to keep a record of punishments administered to the children. These rules were largely ignored in the schools investigated by the Ryan Commission.

The Ryan Report's chapter on Artane illustrates how the religious orders abandoned their legal obligations when it came to physical abuse. The Artane chapter has numerous accounts of physical brutality. Witnesses who spoke to the Ryan Commission gave spine-chilling accounts of beatings they sustained during their time there. The Christian Brothers in Artane completely ignored their legal obligations to ensure excessive violence was not carried out or tolerated in the school. Ryan declared that Artane enforced a regime of 'militaristic discipline', that 'corporal punishment was systemic and pervasive'[1] and that 'management did nothing to prevent excessive and inappropriate punishment and boys and Brothers learnt to accept a high level of physical punishment as a norm'.[2] On their abuse of power, in unequivocal terms Ryan declared that the Christian Brothers 'did not intervene to stop excessive punishment by colleagues, and there was a code of conduct between Brothers that prevented criticism of each other's behaviour, even in cases when it was clearly extreme or excessive. All Brothers therefore became implicated in excesses.'[3] Like so many of the other industrial schools, Artane ignored the Rules and Regulations for industrial schools and Ryan concluded that the punishment book

THE ABUSERS: HOW AND WHY?

was not kept in Artane because 'the Christian Brothers chose not to maintain it'.[4]

The violent nature of the industrial and reformatory schools was facilitated by a prevailing view in Irish society that the children who ended up in these schools were troublemakers who needed strong discipline. While Irish people may not have been aware of the extent of the physical abuse in the schools up until the late twentieth century, there was an understanding that physical punishments were justified to control unruly children.

THE POWER OF THE CATHOLIC CHURCH IN TWENTIETH-CENTURY IRELAND

There is no doubt that the power of the Catholic Church and therefore the power of the religious orders running industrial and reformatory schools played a huge role in fostering the physical, sexual and emotional abuse of children incarcerated in their institutions. The religious orders were a pivotal part of Irish society in their provision of education and hospital and other social services and the deferential attitude of Irish people towards them helped to perpetuate their abusive tendencies.

Up until the 1980s, the Church wielded enormous influence in Ireland. Priests, Brothers and nuns enjoyed an elevated status that placed them beyond reproach. The guards deferred to them, the masses bowed to them, the politicians prayed with them and the doctors and lawyers referred to them. A smokescreen of moral perfection disguised a backdrop of abusive behaviour. Every Sunday morning Irish people flocked to Mass to hear sermons from priests dictating the moral compass of their lives. They preached from their pulpits on topics that ranged from the vice of divorce to the immorality of sex outside marriage. We now know of course that some of these priests were preaching about moral values while they themselves were sexually abusing boys and girls in their communities, and they castigated unmarried mothers from their altars while they were having extra-clerical affairs with the likes of their housekeepers and fathering illegitimate children.

The hypocrisy of the Church and its abuse of power went to the very top in Ireland. The 2009 Murphy Report of the Church's cover-up of clerical child sexual abuse reveals a breathtaking example of how the protection of its own reputation was of paramount importance. This took prime consideration over everything else, including the safety of children who were vulnerable to being abused by clerical paedophiles. The Report showed how the Catholic hierarchy in Ireland protected clerical paedophiles by shunting them around from one community and institution to another while blatantly keeping their abusive conduct hidden.

That potent elixir of power and control poisoned the industrial and reformatory schools and influenced a pattern of abuse. Michael O'Brien's story of how the Rosminian priest raped him on a Saturday night and put Holy Communion into his mouth at Mass the following Sunday is a graphic illustration of an utter abuse of power.

The Christian Brothers were experts at creating an illusion of benevolence. They cynically paraded the Artane Boys' Band as a product of their excellent training and duped the Irish nation into believing they were providing a proper education to these deprived young lads. The Band toured the country performing concerts and they even travelled abroad to play in the likes of the United States and Britain. We now know from the Ryan Report and accounts of former members of the Band that the boys were being abused by the very Brothers who basked in the adoring applause of the audiences enraptured by the Band.

THE VOWS OF OBEDIENCE AND POVERTY

The religious orders' austere vows also contributed to the abuse of children. The Ryan Report assesses the impact of the vows on the behaviour of the Brothers and Sisters in the institutions. The vows of obedience led to an unquestioning acceptance of the institutions' harsh regimes. Religious members were expected to carry out their orders without question even if they had grave reservations about the behaviour of their superiors. No distinction was made between the obligation of the Brothers and Sisters to observe their own vows and their own behaviour towards the children in their care. They tended to impose the same rigid code of conduct on the children.

Current and former Christian Brothers who gave evidence to the Ryan Commission spoke about how the vow of obedience 'permeated every aspect of life within the Congregation'.[5] That obligation to bow to the will of their Superior and Congregation meant they were extremely reluctant to criticise senior Brothers and it discouraged and prevented them from reporting abuse or objectionable behaviour: 'In some cases, it inhibited the reporting of suspicions about sexual misconduct on the part of other Brothers'.[6]

One former Christian Brother explained how the vow of obedience fostered a military-like regime.

> I think the vow of obedience was conceived of as being partly like military discipline. Indeed, the priests who gave the Brothers their retreats and so on, and the 30-day retreat we had in the novitiate [were] all from Jesuits, and they'd famously have a military metaphor for what they'd do. I think there was a certain amount of that, this was like the army and you just obey.
>
> But that's not what I understood as the vow of obedience, I think the vow of obedience was an internal . . . an internal resignation of your will to the will of your Superior. The most important thing about obedience was not what you did but how you thought. I certainly would have believed that when I was that age, yes.[7]

That same ex-Brother illustrated how the vow of obedience was tested in young novices in training, who would be subjected to humiliating punishments if they disobeyed their orders.

> The one I remember in terms of work was being told to move a pile of stones in part of the garden, I think, an old shrubbery from there to literally the far side of the table and spending several days doing it with an old wheelbarrow, when it was all finished he came around and said, 'That is very good now. Excellent. Now would you move them all back again please?' You were meant to say, 'Certainly Brother', which I did being a very good boy . . . It was a bit silly really but we just accepted it.[8]

The requirement to exercise daily discipline and remove themselves from the outside world exacerbated the rigidity of their lives.

> They rose early for prayer and Mass, and were required according to the rules of the Congregation to live an ascetic and spiritual life with few comforts. They practised fasting, and mortification of the flesh,

in order to perfect their communion with God . . . The Christian Brothers were obliged 'not to maintain any intercourse with externs' without permission from their immediate Superior. Brothers were not allowed to read newspapers, listen to the radio, visit friends or attend outside functions or sporting events without express permission. Walks had to be taken in the company of at least one other Brother.[9]

The Christian Brothers' requirement to maintain a distant relationship with women from the outside world led to a perverted attitude towards women that fostered dysfunctional conduct within the institutions.

Brothers were instructed to keep all conversations with mothers or female friends of the children in their care to the minimum. One consequence of this was that the Christian Brothers' institutions became all-male worlds. Numerous witnesses gave evidence to the Investigation Committee about the problems caused by the lack of female involvement in the day-to-day operation of the schools.[10]

The religious orders seemed unable or unwilling to differentiate between the harsh vows they had chosen and what was an appropriate way to supervise the children in their care. They imposed equally unforgiving work ethics and discipline on the children and insisted 'on silence in the daily tasks of eating and preparing for bed. Silence was a rule strictly adhered to in everyday life. Whistles were used in some cases to signal to the children when they were to move from one activity to the next.'[11]

Ryan points out that the strict regime imposed in the industrial and reformatory schools led to the children becoming institutionalised.

Many left to join the Army, or drifted into other institutionalised occupations, and far too many ended up in institutions like prisons or in psychiatric care.[12]

THE VOW OF CHASTITY

In the aftermath of the Ryan Report, the vow of chastity was widely blamed for influencing the sexual abuse of children in the institutions. The argument was made that the unnatural imposition of a celibate life led to pent-up sexual frustrations and depraved and sexually abusive conduct within the male religious institutions in particular.

While those arguments are valid, such sweeping explanations are too simplistic and fail to take into account the other factors that helped to foster child abuse. We also now know that the religious orders were not solely responsible for all the abuse. The Ryan Report clearly shows how lay workers and teachers also abused in these institutions. Dr Eoin O'Sullivan has done extensive research into industrial and reformatory schools in Ireland. His collaboration with the journalist Mary Raftery resulted in the publication of their investigative book *Suffer the Little Children* and the RTÉ series 'States of Fear'. Both of these substantial pieces of work exposed the abusive nature of industrial and reformatory schools.

Dr O'Sullivan points out that there is always the risk of paedophilia in institutions where children are being cared for regardless of whether their guardians are religious or lay people. He says Ireland is no different from the rest of the world in this regard.

In residential care across the world this is a problem; in Australia, in Canada, North America and England.[13]

Dr O'Sullivan argues that the dysfunctional nature of the religious institutions enabled the abuse of the children incarcerated there. He dismisses the notion that young males with paedophile tendencies signed up to the religious orders so that they could be placed in institutions where they would have access to children. That explanation is too simplistic.

The sexual frustration argument just doesn't hold because when you look at the spectrum of people who were abusing children, the biggest cases in this country have not been religious people; they've been lay people in the family . . . It seemed to be partly the personality of the individual and the context and the setting [of the institution]. There are a number of examples of people [who were abusive] who left the priesthood and never did anything ever again. They got married, settled down, had a family. That's why I firmly believe it was the context and the setting that drove some of their impulsive behaviour plus possibly fuelled by alcohol.[14]

This argument is reinforced by an analysis of the defence given to the Ryan Commission by the paedophile Br Maurice Tobin, who was convicted in 2003 of sexually abusing former inmates of Letterfrack Industrial School. Tobin gave evidence to the Ryan Investigation Committee who cross-examined him. He admitted to abusing boys in Letterfrack over a 15-year period. Tobin is given the pseudonym Br Dax in the Ryan Report. His explanations for abusing the boys give a chilling insight into his paedophile motivations and his ability to abuse for so long. Tobin used to work in the kitchen and the poultry farm and sometimes he supervised the dormitories. He began to abuse the boys within six months of his arrival in Letterfrack. Most of the abuse took place in the kitchen, the poultry farm and in the boiler room. Tobin told the Ryan Committee that he would abuse the same children regularly and that he could have been abusing a number of children at any one period during his time in the school. The assaults included raping some boys once or twice a week for a prolonged period.

> He said that, as far as he was aware, no adults other than his Confessor were aware of his activities, although he accepted that children who worked in the kitchen would have known about them. He also accepted that it was possible that a wider pool of children would have been aware of his inclinations. He was also asked about his awareness of the risk of detection. He said he could not recall taking any specific steps to avoid detection.[15]

Tobin admitted to the Ryan Commission that it was extraordinary that he had managed to get away with the abuse for so long. He was questioned at length about his motivations for sexually abusing the boys. He said a mixture of overwork, loneliness, a feeling of isolation and his own human weakness led to his abuse of the boys.

> Br Dax confirmed that in his 'human weakness' his way of dealing with loneliness was to engage in sexual abuse of boys. When asked how he would go about satisfying that human weakness, Br Dax simply stated 'Touching, embracing'. Br Dax could not explain why he behaved differently to other Brothers who were equally isolated from their families.[16]

Tobin told the Commission that the abuse was primarily about release for him and that he never formed any emotional relationships with the boys.[17]

Letterfrack's dysfunctional and repressive regime fostered Tobin's paedophile tendencies. If his evidence is truthful, then celibacy alone does not fully explain his behaviour. That lethal mix of loneliness, isolation, overwork and his own 'human weakness' coupled with the harsh atmosphere in Letterfrack made it the perfect hunting ground for paedophiles like Tobin. His position of power over the boys cultivated a fear of reporting to other Brothers and even when they did reveal incidents of sexual abuse by paedophiles like Tobin, we know the Brothers punished the boys for reporting.

THE IMPACT OF THE RELIGIOUS VOWS ON THE NUNS

The strict religious vows taken by the nuns also influenced their abusive conduct towards the children in their care. The Ryan Commission found fewer cases of actual sexual abuse in religious institutions run by nuns. However, evidence given to the Commission by former residents of industrial schools owned and operated by Sisters point to depraved conduct that bordered on being sexually abusive. In Goldenbridge, the Sisters of Mercy subjected the children to humiliating underwear inspections. Witnesses before the Ryan Commission spoke about how soiled underwear was 'paraded on a pole for everyone to see before they received their fresh laundry'.[18] In this book, Tommy Millar recalled how the nuns in Lenaboy made the children parade naked up and down the corridors of the washroom holding up their dirty underwear for everyone to see. While this conduct may not be overtly sexually abusive it certainly borders on a form of depravity. Christine Buckley's story (see Chapter 14, p. 241) of the woman who, as a child in an industrial school, had a ruler shoved up her vagina by a nun beggars belief. That assault destroyed that woman's chances of having children and it raises many questions about the motivations of the nun who so brutally penetrated the girl with the ruler. Was she trying to destroy the little girl's sexuality because she herself had signed up to a life of celibacy? Did she resent having to spend her life in submission to God and her religious superiors? Were the children in her care targeted because she was bitter at the miserable life she had chosen?

In their submission to the Ryan Commission in May 2006, the Sisters of Mercy analysed the impact their religious vows had on their behaviour. They acknowledged that their arduous routine of prayer had the consequence of a regime of strict religious observance being imposed on the children.[19] The Sisters stated that the emphasis on silence 'as a means of focusing attention on God and the things of God' had an enormous impact on their interaction with the children. Their obsession with work, which they saw as 'generous, obedient and self-giving', had the negative effect of circumscribing leisure activities and ensuring that 'everyone was caught up in a system where rest, unstructured relaxation and variety were seen as luxuries rather than necessities'.[20]

The Sisters spoke in evidence to the Ryan Commission about their lack of a display of physical affection towards the children.

> The question of the reluctance to show any physical affection for the children found its roots in a positive understanding of caring for all children equally and of not favouring one child over the other.[21]

However, the Sisters were adamant in their defence that their lack of affection for the children was in no way linked to a nun's choice of a life of celibacy rather than a choice of marriage and motherhood.[22]

On the vow of obedience, they referred to Chapter 7 of the 1926 edition of the Rule and Constitutions dealing with obedience:

> They are to execute without hesitation, all the directions of the Mother Superior: whether in matters of great or little moment, agreeable or disagreeable. They shall never murmur, but with humility and spiritual joy carry the sweet yoke of Jesus Christ . . . They shall obey the call of the bell as the voice of God.[23]

In the book *Responding to the Ryan Report*,[24] a former Sister of Mercy gives her views on how the religious vows affected the behaviour of the nuns towards children in their care. Margaret Lee entered the Mercy Novitiate in 1961 when she was 17. She explains that the religious orders enjoyed significant status in Irish society at that time. They were looked up to and revered: 'It was a world where one had merely to wear a veil and deference was given.'[25] An orphanage was attached to the convent in which Ms Lee spent her postulancy and novitiate. In the book, she refers to the British psychiatrist and psychoanalyst John Bowbly who was writing in the 1950s about the need for a child to have a warm and intimate relationship with his mother or primary care-giver. Ms Lee says it would have been impossible for the nuns to provide that kind of care to children in orphanages or industrial schools because 'the obsession with chastity and bodily purity would have precluded the kind of physical intimacy the child needed'.[26] She makes the point that the nuns would have been unable to understand how children in the orphanage were grieving for their absent mothers: 'How could we given that we were not supposed to be attached to our own parents or families?'[27]

Ms Lee explains how the requirement of a 'common mindset' precluded an individual nun's ability to make her own judgment about how best to treat vulnerable children in the orphanage. She contextualises Irish society's unquestioning acceptance of celibate men and women caring for children:

It is possible that this arrangement was never queried because of people's unwavering confidence in church figures, but it is equally possible that the issue was not raised because people were not interested in what happened to the children consigned to the orphanage and industrial school system.[28]

The former Mercy nun elaborates on why there was so much cruelty in the industrial schools and how men and women of the cloth could have behaved so inhumanely to the children in their care.

One possible reason is that these people were voiceless and without any great status in their congregations and, consequently, within themselves were simmering with anger, frustration and dissatisfaction with life. I believe that they were often alienated from their inner selves. In the religious communities they were powerless but in the world of the orphanage they had absolute power.[29]

RECRUITING METHODS OF THE CONGREGATIONS
The recruiting nature of the Congregations was another factor in creating misfits and bullies who went on to abuse children in the industrial and reformatory schools. In the past, boys and girls were

encouraged to join religious orders at a young age. In many cases joining a convent or monastery was a way to escape from poverty and to get an education. Irish parents were incredibly proud to announce they had a son or daughter in the priesthood or Congregations. Such an exalted position meant enormous pressure was put on Irish children to sign up to a life with God. That frequently meant leaving home at a very young age. A religious vocation was a status symbol that guaranteed respect in the community. It was common for the Christian Brothers to visit schools and encourage boys as young as 13 or 14 to leave home for a religious life. The boys were then sent on to boarding schools that were run by the Brothers where they would study and complete their Leaving Certificate exams. Boys as young as 15 could enter the novitiate, when they would then wear the habit of the Congregation.

That early separation from a boy's or a girl's family for a life with a religious order would surely have been a bewildering if not traumatic experience. For much of the last century, these young recruits would not have been able to see their families on a regular basis. They would have been expected to exchange their former family lives for those of the Congregations. That imposition of enclosure within the Order and segregation from the outside world increased the risk of fostering resentment and dysfunctional behaviour.

THE ROLE OF THE IRISH STATE IN CONTRIBUTING TO THE ABUSE

In 1999, when Bertie Ahern apologised to survivors of institutional abuse, he acknowledged the role the Irish State had played in the damage that was done to thousands of people incarcerated in the institutions. This official acknowledgment of Irish State complicity in the abuse was reinforced when the Residential Institutions Redress Board was established to compensate survivors of institutional abuse. The then Education Minister, Dr Michael Woods, made it clear that the Irish State was extremely culpable for the past abuses and consequently would have to foot a significant part of the cost of the redress bill.

While there was outrage at the Indemnity Deal that was struck with the religious orders that left them paying a fraction of the overall cost of the redress bill, Mr Ahern and Dr Woods were correct to acknowledge the State's appalling collusion in the abuse of the children. The biggest State culprit was the Department of Education, which failed abysmally to supervise and inspect the schools. The Ryan Report castigated the Department for its utter failure to carry out its duties of responsibility to the children in the industrial and reformatory schools.

> The deferential and submissive attitude of the Department of Education towards the Congregations compromised its ability to carry out its statutory duty of inspection and monitoring of the schools. The Reformatory and Industrial Schools Section of the Department was accorded a low status within the Department and generally saw itself as facilitating the Congregations and the Resident Managers.[30]

The Department's inspection system was slammed in the Report. Ryan found that it was fundamentally flawed and incapable of being effective.[31] Inspectors weren't able to insist on recommended changes because they didn't have the support of a regulatory authority. The Report's list of criticisms highlights the Department's utter failure to fulfill its obligations to the children, care of whom it had subcontracted to the institutions.

> There were no uniform, objective standards of care applicable to all institutions on which the inspections could be based. The Inspector's position was compromised by lack of independence from the Department.
>
> Inspections were limited to the standard of physical care of the children and did not extend to their emotional needs. The type of inspection carried out made it difficult to ascertain the emotional state of the children.
>
> The statutory obligation to inspect more than 50 residential schools was too much for one person. Inspections were not random or unannounced: School Managers were alerted in advance that an inspection was due. As a result, the Inspector did not get an accurate picture of conditions in the schools. The Inspector did not ensure that punishment books were kept and made available for inspection even though they were required by the regulations. The Inspector rarely spoke to the children in the institutions.[32]

The Ryan investigations showed that the Department of Education

knew that violence and beatings were endemic in the schools but it did
nothing to prevent them. The Department failed to investigate cases of
children who had absconded from the schools and it did not insist on
finding out why they had tried to escape.

> Cases of absconding associated with chronic sexual or physical
> abuse therefore remained undiscovered. In some instances all the
> children in a school were punished because a child ran away which
> meant that the child was then a target for mistreatment by other
> children as well as the staff.[33]

Even when the Department received complaints of obvious abuse in the
schools it ignored them. Ryan attributed some of the Department's
negligence to its deferential attitude to the Church.

> Punishments outside the permitted guidelines were ignored and
> even condoned by the Department of Education. The Department
> did not apply the standards in the rules and their own guidelines
> when investigating complaints but sought to protect and defend the
> religious Congregations and the schools.[34]

When it came to sexual abuse, the Department of Education was
equally negligent. Ryan found that it dealt inadequately with
complaints of sexual abuse, which were generally dismissed or ignored.
Not only did the Department ignore allegations of abuse, it didn't
bother to inform the Gardaí either so that they could pursue their own
investigations.

> The Department, however, gave the impression that it had a
> function in relation to investigating allegations of abuse but actually
> failed to do so and delayed the involvement of the proper authority.
> The Department neglected to advise parents and complainants
> appropriately of the limitations of their role in respect of these
> complaints.[35]

THE JUDICIARY AND THE IRISH SOCIETY FOR THE
PREVENTION OF CRUELTY TO CHILDREN

One of the major flaws of the Ryan Commission to Inquire into Child

Abuse was its failure to comprehensively investigate the involvement of the Irish justice system in incarcerating thousands of children in religious institutions. Judges had enormous power in committing children to industrial and reformatory schools. We know from stories told in this book that juvenile offenders who committed misdemeanors received draconian punishments. John Brown[36] was given a four-year sentence for taking pigeons from a derelict house. He was accused of causing around £50 worth of damage to the ramshackle building even though he says it was completely derelict and looked as if a bomb had hit it well before he and his brother even entered the place. John had no legal representative to defend him when he appeared before the judge. This was surely unorthodox practice even in 1960s Ireland.

John Kelly was handed down a two-year sentence to be spent in Daingean for being an innocent accomplice to a crime as minor as stealing some chocolate and a small amount of money. His committal to Daingean nearly destroyed him. Non-attendance at school was another juvenile crime that incurred a severe punishment. Mitching school kids were put away for several years in dreadful places like Daingean and Artane. Many of the children who were given harsh sentences from judges were from poor backgrounds, whose families could not afford to pay for any lawyers to defend them. They were vulnerable children whose futures were dictated by the judges they went before. The capitation fee paid to the religious institutions complemented the Irish judiciary's approach to sending miscreant boys and girls to industrial and reformatory schools. As long as these places existed, there was little incentive to develop more progressive ways of dealing with children from problem backgrounds.

The courts were also responsible for sanctioning court orders that allowed for whole families of children to be committed to religious hellholes because of challenging home situations such as impoverished backgrounds or having negligent parents or a mother who may have died and a father who struggled to take care of his children. Michael O'Brien's family were torn apart when the 'cruelty' man arrived at his house after his mother died. When the children were brought to Clonmel's District Court, the judge committed Michael and his siblings to Ferryhouse and other institutions. Michael's youngest sister was only around six months when she was wrenched from her sister's arms and put into a convent until she was 16. There seemed to have been no system that allowed for a review of court orders that sanctioned lengthy committals on the basis of sentences. This was yet another example of how the Irish State colluded in the abuse and disgracefully abandoned its responsibility towards the children.

As already mentioned in stories told in this book, the ISPCC and its predecessor, the NSPCC,[37] played a role in sending children to abusive institutions. The Gardaí were also responsible for arresting children and taking them to court.

While the blame for the actual abuse of children can unequivocally be laid at the doors of the religious institutions and the religious and lay staff who worked within them, such systematic abuse would not have been possible had the arms of the State not enabled it through its negligent and, at times, complicit actions. That lethal cocktail of State negligence and collusion sustained the abuse far longer than would have been possible if the State had properly fulfilled its duties.

Chapter 14 ⁓

ROUGH JUSTICE: THE RESIDENTIAL INSTITUTIONS REDRESS BOARD

On 16 December 2002, the Residential Institutions Redress Board was formally established to begin processing applications from survivors of institutional abuse seeking compensation for the cruelty they had endured in religious institutions. The Board was set up under the Residential Institutions Redress Act 2002 and it was designed 'to make fair and reasonable awards to persons who, as children, were abused while resident in industrial schools, reformatories and other institutions subject to State regulation or inspection'.[1]

The Redress Board consisted of a chairperson and members appointed by the Department of Education and Science. They were to assess each application and decide what compensation should be awarded. Its headquarters were based on Beech Hill Road, Clonskeagh, Dublin 4, while its Review Committee was located on South Frederick Street, Dublin 2. Applications were to be processed in private and the Board promised the strictest confidentiality in its treatment of each application.

Under the Residential Institutions Redress Act, applications for redress were required to be received by the Board on or before 15 December 2005. That deadline could be extended only under special circumstances. The Redress Board carried out advertising campaigns in Ireland from December 2002 to December 2005. Survivors of institutional abuse who felt they were entitled to seek redress were invited to send in formal applications to the Redress Board. When claimants applied for redress they could decide whether they wanted their applications to be processed by way of statements or whether they wanted to appear in front of the redress panel at formal hearings.

The Board assessed each application and then decided whether the applicant was entitled to compensation. If redress was to be given, the Board made an offer to the applicant based on its assessment of the severity of the abuse. That person could then accept or reject the offer. If the applicant rejected the settlement, he/she would then have to participate in a hearing by the Board. The Board stated that the hearings would be as informal as possible. They were to be held in private and were not to be open to the public or media.

By December 2009, the Board had completed the process in 13,743 cases,[2] having received a total of 14,667 applications. A total of 10,188 offers were made following settlement talks and 2,741 awards were made following hearings. Eleven applicants rejected their awards; 814 applications were withdrawn, refused or resulted in no award. Survivors who accepted redress had to agree in writing not to bring a claim for damages in the courts in respect of the abuse and injuries covered by the award.

In theory the redress system was supposed to provide appropriate justice to survivors of institutional abuse and to award them suitable compensation. That was the aspiration. The reality was radically different. Instead of receiving fair and compassionate treatment, many survivors felt shafted by the redress scheme. Unhappy claimants said they were subject to further abuse by another arm of the State that also conducted its proceedings behind closed doors. 'I think every aspect of the redress system is wrong,' said Christine Buckley, founder of the Aislinn Centre for survivors of institutional abuse. 'The whole design of the Redress Board is one of secrecy and one of abuse. It is just a complete and utter continuation (of abuse).'

When details of the redress scheme were originally announced, it was declared that survivors could expect to get compensation payments equivalent to those awarded in the courts for similar cases. That led to false expectations and disappointments as many survivors expected to get far higher awards than they ended up receiving.

Compensation was based on a weighting system, which gave awards on the basis of points accumulated according to the severity of the abuse suffered, physical and mental injuries, emotional and social effects of the injuries and loss of employment and other opportunities, although the Board did not pay any compensation for loss of earnings as such. In exceptional cases, the Board was authorised to make an additional award of up to 20 per cent of the normal redress award. Survivors were also led to believe that the Redress Board would conduct its business in a supportive, non-adversarial way. They thought they would be treated humanely and spared the trauma of the aggressive cross-examinations they could expect if they were to take civil action cases.

But far from receiving apposite justice, many survivors said the redress system failed abysmally in apportioning reasonable redress and that the awards for victims of sexual abuse did not equate to equivalent sums awarded in the High Courts. By December 2009, the average payout by the Redress Board was €63,000 while equivalent civil cases of sexual abuse taken in the High Court led to awards of up to €300,000 to €400,000. In addition, the hostile nature of the hearings' cross-examinations left some survivors angry that they hadn't pursued their cases through the courts. Claimants felt they were not given adequate opportunity to tell their stories of abuse and finally set the record straight and some were despondent at the Board's sceptical consideration of their cases: they felt they hadn't been believed and that was a shattering experience for them.

The redress scheme was flawed from its inception. For starters, the whole process was shrouded in secrecy. Anybody who sought and accepted redress was obliged to sign what amounted to a gagging order. In order to receive their redress payments they had to agree not to disclose any details of their interaction with the Redress Board. They could not discuss anything about the process of their applications or their experiences of a redress hearing if they had appeared at one. They could not give interviews to journalists about those experiences and journalists were not allowed into any of the hearings. In addition, claimants could not disclose how much redress they were awarded. Excessive punishments were threatened for any breaches of the agreement. An initial breach incurred a fine of €3,000 and/or a prison sentence of six months, a more serious breach could incur a fine of €25,000 and/or an imprisonment of two years.

The secrecy and lack of transparency were all the more egregious given that Irish taxpayers were footing most of the bill for the redress scheme and so surely were entitled to know about its inherent flaws. Few people in the country understood how traumatised survivors were by the apparent injustice of the awards given and the distressing impact of cross-examinations endured during hearings. Representative groups of survivors wanted to stop the gagging order from the outset and they voiced concerns about the way compensation was going to be awarded by the Board. But despite initial reassurances, their concerns were not taken into account when the legislation to enact the Redress Board came into being.

Survivors were deeply suspicious about the nature of the awards being given to other applicants. They complained that the system was unfair and that some people were getting bigger awards than others even though it may have seemed that they were incarcerated for shorter periods and sustained less abuse. It's possible those applications were simply more convincing and their accompanying material more compelling. But the suspicions raised inevitable doubts about the fairness of the scheme. Survivors who accepted redress were too terrified to go public with their complaints as they risked incurring fines and prison sentences. Had those misgivings become public knowledge, the Redress Board may have had to account for the perceived discrepancies in the awards and the injustices of the gagging orders. That pressure could have led to a re-examination of the Board's operations.

The legal profession's involvement with the Redress Board also came in for criticism. Solicitors were paid by the Board for each application they processed and some firms made millions from the scheme. The Redress Board's December 2009 Newsletter stated that legal fees had come to €148.5 million up to that point. A number of claimants were unhappy about the way their applications were processed by their legal representatives. Some complained they did not receive proper support and advice and that not enough diligence had been given to their applications. Survivors were aghast that the redress scheme had created a gravy train for those solicitors processing large volumes of cases. That gave the impression that lawyers were making millions from people who had been abused as children.

A number of complaints were made to the Law Society about the practice of solicitors involved in the redress scheme. The complaints included accusations of double-charging. The Law Society investigated the complaints and referred a number of them to the Solicitors Disciplinary Tribunal. Most of the complaints were rejected and only a small number of solicitors were disciplined for abuse of the scheme. Part of the confusion involved solicitors invoicing their clients for part payment of medical assessments that were conducted to support their claims of abuse. The Redress Board paid only a certain amount of the medical fee. The remainder had to be paid by the solicitors who commissioned it in the first place. They then invoiced their clients for the outstanding fee. That created consternation for some survivors who thought their solicitors were double-charging them. The whole affair left a cloud of doubt over the legal profession's conduct in relation to the redress scheme.

The hostile environment of the panel hearings was a huge bone of contention for claimants who appeared before them. Some survivors were completely unprepared for the distressing experience of being cross-examined by members of hearing panels. The panels' determination to scrutinise the legitimacy of claims meant they sometimes engaged in adversarial exchanges with survivors. That approach contradicted Bertie Ahern's reassurance that the redress scheme would protect victims from the trauma of antagonistic interrogations in the High Court. Survivors have described their experiences of panel hearings as 'cold and uncompassionate', 'rotten to the core', 'aloof and unsympathetic', 'aggressive', 'challenging', 'arrogant' and 'the most atrocious model of allegedly dishing out justice that I have ever seen'. They felt they were the ones on trial and unfairly forced to vigorously justify their claims of abuse.

Another troubling and highly questionable procedure was the rule preventing claimants from taking anybody with them into the hearing room apart from their legal representatives. That meant vulnerable, damaged people were on their own defending themselves in a cold, unwelcoming forum. In May 2005, in a letter to the *Irish Times*, the late Consultant Psychiatrist Dr Michael Corry expressed his horror at the nature of the hearings and how he was not allowed into the room where clients of his were being cross-examined. He described the hearing room as a place of secrecy, exclusion and bewilderment. Dr Corry's letter was a startling illustration of the redress scheme's inherent flaws.

I have given evidence to the board on three occasions on behalf of

three patients, all victims of layers of abuse, in particular sexual. Two
of these have been under my care for over 10 years. All will bring
their pain and suffering to the grave. I was not allowed to be present
when they gave their evidence, nor indeed were their partners, a
friend, an advocate, no one of personal significance. They were
alone. Alone in attempting to articulate their exposure to regimes of
unbridled rape and violence which lasted for years, at the hands of
sadistic sexual perverts answerable to no one. Alone in telling about
how their chance of a normal life was diminished from the
beginning. About how they learned to place no value on themselves,
and with their lives totally derailed following their release at 16 years
old, drifted from one crisis to another for the rest of their lives. One
patient was left alone, on the verge of a panic attack due to the
intensity of his fear, to tell the board of a past littered with criminal
behaviour, prison records, substance misuse, dysfunctional
relationships, mistrust of authority, and family breakdown.

I found the discomfort of waiting in a side room to give evidence,
aware of my patients' fears and worries, unbearable. They dreaded
getting a panic attack, a flashback to an incident of abuse, a rush of
uncontrollable anger that would alienate the chairman and
jeopardise the outcome. In giving my sworn evidence I felt under
time pressure, and worse, that I was an unwelcome irritation
slowing down the proceedings. An atmosphere of minimisation
prevailed. It was impossible to present a complete picture.

The 'board' consisted solely of a judge and a medical doctor. On
two occasions that doctor, having had no experience of working
with traumatised or abused children, let alone a qualification in
psychiatry, was nonetheless there for the purpose of contributing to
a judgment on the compensation deemed appropriate for each
victim. Not being a court, it is held in secret, away from the eyes of
the community, and no perpetrator of a crime is ever sentenced to
a punishment. No apologies can be offered as no one is there
representing the religious orders responsible. Justice for the victim
is not the purpose, only financial compensation, which is capped to
a maximum of €300,000 . . . The award is conditional on them
signing a secrecy agreement and a waiver on taking further legal
action. If the victims disclose the amount they were awarded or
discuss the facts of their case in public, they face criminalisation.

The wronged now accused of a crime! They can be fined up to
€3,000 and can face a summary jail sentence of six months. After a
second disclosure, they face a fine not exceeding €25,000 and a two-
year jail sentence. Why the secrecy? It's certainly not for the benefit
of the victim.

There is emerging evidence that the Redress Board re-
traumatises victims. One patient of mine used this analogy. 'An
adult, man or woman, abuses a child. It is their "secret". To make
sure the "secret" is kept the adult will give the child money or sweets.
They buy silence. By making secrecy a condition upon payment, the
board is doing exactly what an abuser does to a child.' The elements
of restorative justice which are required for the restitution of
balance and healing are transparency instead of secrecy, formal
apologies, the punishment of the wrongdoers, and supreme efforts
to compensate for damage done. The Redress Board embodies none
of these. Its role makes a mockery of the legal system, and of the
Goddess Themis, whose scales are the symbols of Right and Justice.
It is my firm belief that the Redress Board contravenes the most
basic of human and civil rights. In short, it represents a crime
against humanity. It should be abolished immediately and replaced
by an open forum where the victim is not only properly monetarily
compensated, but where they can have their perpetrators named,
and the scales of justice balanced.[3]

The concept of being re-traumatised by the Redress Board is illustrated
in the case of one man who visited the Aislinn Centre in Dublin in 2003.
He went there a week before he was to go to the Redress Board. When
he attended the Centre he met its founder, Christine Buckley. He told
her he had been incarcerated in both Artane and Letterfrack industrial
schools. She remembered how he was quite animated about his herb
garden.

He was talking to me about his herbs that he had grown. He was
mad into nature and he wouldn't have tea or coffee. And at the time
we could smoke and of course we were puffing our brains out and
he didn't do any of these things. He was very healthy and very health
conscious and he was delighted with Ballygowan because he didn't
drink tea or coffee. And he was telling me then that he'd a lovely

herb garden and he was going to bring me in some herbs. And he did a bit of art and he said that he was separated.

A week later the man returned to the Aislinn Centre but instead of entering the building he stood awkwardly outside the door in an agitated state. Christine Buckley went out to him and asked him how he had got on in the Redress Board.

> I went out to him and he said to me on the steps of Ormond House, 'I was offered €144,000' and I said, 'How do you feel?' He said, 'Dreadful they didn't believe me.' And I said to him, 'But they must have believed you because they're dreadful up there and they could have given you €30,000 or €40,000.' 'No Christine,' he said. 'They didn't believe me.' He broke down and walked to the right down towards the Four Courts.

The following Sunday evening that man hanged himself in his kitchen. Christine Buckley found out about his suicide when his ex-wife phoned her and gave her the tragic news.

> He had hired a sander to sand his floors. He did all of whatever washing he had to do. He had his suit spotless and he stood up on his kitchen table and hanged himself.

Christine Buckley believes he killed himself because he felt the Redress Board didn't believe his story of abuse and that mattered much more to him than the financial award. She also recalled how another person who attended the Redress Board committed suicide following her appearance at a redress hearing.

The woman was originally from the Irish Travelling community, from which she had been taken as a young child and incarcerated in an abusive religious institution. During the redress hearing a member of the panel put it to her that she had been far better off having heating and clothing in the institution than sitting by the side of a caravan. That woman threw herself in front of a train later that day. No one can say for sure why she decided to end her life as she did not leave any explanation. We can only speculate that her experiences in front of the redress hearing were so harrowing that they left her deeply traumatised.

Christine Buckley remembers one woman who was completely traumatised after attending a redress hearing. She had accompanied the woman to the Redress headquarters in Clonskeagh but as she wasn't allowed into the hearing itself, she remained outside the room while the woman was cross-examined by the panel. This survivor had already supplied the Redress Board with ample medical evidence to support her claim of extensive physical abuse by nuns in a religious institution when she was a child. After a period of cross-examinations, the woman suddenly started screaming and Christine knocked on the door and demanded that the panel stop questioning her.

She had had a ruler rammed up her vagina by a nun because she was giggling on a line. They [the hearing panel] were asking her repeatedly what length of the ruler was rammed [up her vagina]. The evidence was in front of them of the permanent damage done to that woman. She could never have children and she had a solicitor and a barrister who were not protecting her.

The redress scheme was embroiled in controversy from the outset. After Bertie Ahern's 1999 apology to the victims of institutional abuse, it was decided that some form of compensation should be awarded to survivors of institutional abuse. The Redress Board became the mechanism for processing those compensation applications. But before it was formally established, a deal had already been struck that capped the payments the relevant religious orders would pay to the redress scheme. In June 2002, Dr Michael Woods, who was then the Minister for Education, signed a deal with the 18 Congregations involved in the abuse. The deal indemnified those Congregations against all present and future legal claims by former residents in exchange for a payment of €128 million, which was to be made up of cash, property transfers to the State and counselling and other support services for former residents and their families. The indemnity applied to 'all cases which could potentially come within the remit of the redress scheme and would operate for any related litigation which had commenced within three years of the last day for applications to the Redress Board'.[4]

That deal exposed the Irish State to unlimited liability with an obligation to cover the rest of the compensation costs of the redress scheme. It was agreed just a day before Dr Woods stepped down as

Education Minister as a general election was looming in Ireland.

So why did Michael Woods agree to cap the payments from the religious orders given the litany of abuse they had conducted against children in their care? Over the years he has defended the deal by arguing that the Irish State had to finally take responsibility for its role in incarcerating and abandoning children in abusive religious institutions to which it had subcontracted their care. He said that it was always expected that the State would incur a substantial part of the compensation bill and that, at the time of the negotiations, the estimated number of potential claimants was modest and the payment of €128 million seemed adequate. Dr Woods also argued that he wanted to prevent any further delays in establishing the redress scheme to spare survivors of institutional abuse any additional anguish.

Dr Woods is right to acknowledge that the State played a significant role in incarcerating children in abusive religious institutions through the highly questionable operations of the ISPCC, the guards, its judicial system and its incompetent and downright culpable Department of Education. But that surely did not justify a deal that elicited such a paltry sum from the religious orders, especially as Irish taxpayers were left to foot the rest of the redress bill. What's even more astonishing is that the government's original decision to establish the redress scheme wasn't even dependent on any contribution from the Congregations.[5]

Michael Woods radically underestimated the number of people who would seek compensation from the Redress Board. His agreement to cap the Congregations' payments at €128 million meant they would end up contributing just 10 per cent of the overall cost of the redress scheme. In September 2003, the Comptroller and Auditor General, John Purcell, reported on wasteful expenditure of public money. Chapter 7 of his 2002 Annual Report is primarily devoted to the Indemnity Deal. He asks why no government department ever did a detailed analysis of the potential exposure of the State during the negotiations with the Congregations. In his report, Purcell refers to estimates provided by the Department of Education and Science. The earliest estimates suggested that around 2,000 claimants would seek redress and that the total liability would amount to €254 million. But by June 2002, those estimates were way off the mark. Purcell points out that by then, the Department had estimated that the potential number of claimants could be 5,200 or more. Based on those figures he calculated that the minimum liability they should have expected would range from €560 million to €720 million.[6]

Purcell's findings raise worrying questions about the nature of the Indemnity Deal. Why did Dr Woods not commission his own department to conduct a full audit of likely costs to the State before he struck any agreement with the Congregations? Why did he strike a deal with the religious orders based on outdated figures that radically underestimated the likely number of claimants and costs to the State? Purcell also pointed out in his report that the Department of Finance had advised Dr Woods to strike a 50/50 deal with the Congregations but they were unbending in their determination to limit their own liabilities.

The Woods Indemnity Deal meant those religious orders that had abused children in their care were left with minimal liability. By December 2009, nearly €900 million had been paid out in compensation to survivors of abuse and €148.5 million was paid in legal fees. The final bill is estimated to come to around €1.4 billion. The Indemnity Deal caused consternation in the Dáil, with Opposition politicians demanding to know why Dr Woods had signed such a bewildering agreement.

Michael Woods vehemently defended the deal during an interview on the RTÉ 'Prime Time' programme in September 2003. He told 'Prime Time' presenter Miriam O'Callaghan that the deal was about meeting the wrongs of the past and that the State carried the major responsibility.

It's a good deal for those who were abused. I have countless letters from people who were abused in that period who said, thanks be to God I was there and I held out especially against the Labour Party who wanted to delay it and obfuscate, push it back and that's all on the record. And now they're dancing up and down. They should be dancing in favour of those who've been abused. And as far as the country is concerned, the country will be glad in time that this shadow on the people of Ireland will have been lifted because it was done by the people.[7]

There is another twist to the Woods Indemnity Deal. It transpired that the then Attorney General, Michael McDowell, was not fully informed about the deal at every step of the negotiations and he was not aware of the extent of the exposure of the State. In his 2002 Annual Report, John Purcell notes that from October 2001 to April 2002 the Office of the Attorney General was not represented at meetings with the Congregations and had no contact with those negotiating on behalf of the State.[8] He refers to problems the Attorney General experienced during this time in acquiring information from Minister Woods.

> In order to be in a position to offer further advice, following the oral report of the Minister to the Cabinet and the announcement of the agreement in principle, in January 2002, the Office of the Attorney General sought information on the detailed negotiations, including the extent of the indemnity. A letter requesting information was sent to the Minister by the Attorney General on 31 January 2002 and this letter was followed by a further letter from his office on 1 February 2002. As no reply had been received by 13 March 2002, the Attorney General advised the Department that his Office could not participate in negotiations or offer legal advice in the absence of the requested information. As the negotiation details had not been documented the Secretary General prepared a retrospective memorandum on the negotiations conducted by the Minister up to that point.[9]

The Minister finally responded to the Attorney General on 13 April 2002, and he outlined the policy approach he proposed to adopt in further negotiations in relation to the indemnity. According to the Comptroller and Auditor General's 2002 report, in June 2002, the Attorney General indicated that the estimates of likely claimants were conservative and 'he pointed out that the contribution of €128 million might be regarded as insufficient and highlighted the lack of a mechanism for increasing the contribution from the Congregations if the number of cases increased greatly'.[10]

In an interview with 'Morning Ireland' on RTÉ on 1 October 2003, Dr Woods insisted he had kept the Attorney General fully informed about the negotiations with the religious orders in the run up to the deal. That opinion was refuted in a statement issued by Michael McDowell later that day: 'If you're asking me whether the Attorney General's office was involved to an appropriate level at all times the answer is that I have to candidly disagree with the Former Minister.'

Outrage over the Indemnity Deal resurfaced after the Ryan Report was published in May 2009 when the extent of the abuse was revealed in stark detail. More questions were raised about the sweetheart deal Dr Woods had brokered with the Congregations and groups representing survivors of abuse demanded that the government renegotiate the deal and get the religious orders to pay more compensation. Dr Michael Woods was accused of allowing his deep Catholic faith to cloud his judgment. Conspiracy theorists pondered over his alleged membership of Opus Dei and wondered if that had influenced his decision. In a Dáil debate on 12 June 2009 the former Labour Party leader Pat Rabbitte accused Woods of protecting the religious orders and stated that 'it is now established that the "Woods deal" was suspect and is in any case a lousy deal morally, legally and politically'.[11] He went on to say that the religious superiors were confident in their power and that senior politicians and senior civil servants were submissive or worse.

> Perhaps for the first time in our history, public opinion wants an end to the deference and a separation of Church and State. Even in this debate, it has been noticeable that there has been so little craw thumping. There has been a nod in the direction of the good done by some religious, which is only fair because some religious have made an incomparable contribution to our society. However, the Congregations must be told in no uncertain terms by the elected representatives of the people that they are not above the law, and they must pay for the crimes of those in their ranks exposed in such a measured way in the Ryan report. We, in this House, cannot ignore the conclusion that when complaints were brought to their attention 'they chose to protect the institution and the reputation of the congregation rather than the children'.[12]

Dr Woods vigorously defended his handling of the deal during that Dáil debate. He said the Ryan Report had greatly expanded the knowledge of how children were treated in the State's residential schools and reformatories. However, he added that although the government knew in 1998–9 about the nature of the abuse and injuries, it didn't realise the full extent of the crimes committed against incarcerated children.

Some commentators stated and still state that we should have had a full inventory of all the lands, schools, hospitals, care centres and other facilities before accepting the contribution of religious congregations who ran most of the institutions on behalf of the State. This would have resulted in delay and more pain and suffering for the victims. The scheme was based on taking a no fault, no quibble, and no legal context approach. We knew that few cases would succeed in court and, accordingly, the cost of the scheme would be much greater than if cases were contested in court. It was the State's decision to behave at last in a magnanimous manner to those whom it had offended by its actions in placing children in horrific circumstances, grossly neglecting them and ignoring all warnings and reports. The system, which the State ran, was the cause and opportunity for these grievous offences against children.

Others argue we should have taken time to allocate blame to all the parties involved. This, too, would have involved delay and adversarial court proceedings. It would also have placed victims under renewed stress, which the Government was not prepared to do. The Government determined that the redress scheme be provided regardless of the involvement of anyone else. This was done by the State paying full compensation. The issue was regarded as one for society to be dealt with fully and firmly and once and for all. The most effective way the Government could achieve this outcome was to take responsibility for the matter, which is what it did. The scheme was to be fully funded by the State — that was the starting position — and full awards were to be paid.[13]

In May 2009 I interviewed Bertie Ahern in his offices at St Luke's in Drumcondra shortly after the publication of the Ryan Report. He was emphatically supportive of the Indemnity Deal when I asked him about it.

The deal wasn't the important issue at all. What we wanted to do was to find a way that would not create any more trauma. These people were getting old, they were dying, they had suffered huge hardship and if we had got into litigation with the congregations it would have meant that all of these individuals would have to be subject to

cross-examination in court. I was not going to put that on them so
that was the issue.

Survivors who went to redress hearings say they might as well have
taken their cases to the High Court as they were still subject to
combative inquisitions from the redress panel. They believe the courts
would have provided better justice because their cases would have been
heard in public and they wouldn't have been forced to sign gagging
orders. Bertie Ahern was incorrect to say that those who would seek
redress were getting old and dying. In fact many of the claimants who
applied for redress were in their forties, fifties, sixties and seventies and
presumably would have endured delays for a better redress system.
During my interview with Mr Ahern I asked him why the government
had underestimated the likely number of claimants who would seek
redress. He said:

> We had no idea actually at the time how many people would seek
> compensation. We had no idea at all. And what happened ultimately
> was that people who were in the institutions all over the country
> came forward.

Mr Ahern's statement that they had no idea how many people would
seek compensation, at the time of the negotiations with the religious
orders, is puzzling. In his 2002 report, John Purcell states that in
February 2001 the State had estimated that the upper limit of liability
was €254 million. But, he pointed out that by June 2001, a further
Department of Education and Science memo stated the liability might
be as high as €508 million.[14] That estimate came a full year before the
final deal was done with the Congregations. Given the discrepancies in
the estimates, it is astonishing that Bertie Ahern and Michael Woods did
not ensure a thorough audit was conducted to fully investigate the likely
number of claimants who would seek redress. Had they done so, they
would have been able to calculate a more realistic estimate of the likely
costs of the redress system and that would surely have resulted in
securing a higher contribution from the religious orders.

When the Ryan Report was published in May 2009, the Irish public
were aghast at the extent of the abuse suffered by children in religious

institutions. For the first time ever, there was a national acknowledgment of the horrendous wrongs done to children abandoned in these places. Survivors of institutional abuse felt vindicated but they also felt betrayed. The public outcry had come too late for the majority of those who had received redress. By then they had signed the gagging orders and the waivers against taking any future legal action. Their lips were sealed and their anger was palpable. They demanded to know why the Congregations had paid so little to the redress scheme and they called for more money from the religious orders.

The survivors of abuse felt cheated and angry that the very people who had abused them so brutally when they were children had escaped so lightly financially and legally. Once again they felt betrayed by the very State that had facilitated their incarceration in abusive institutions and they accused the government of hoodwinking them into accepting a pittance from the Redress Board. Christine Buckley summed up their frustrations: 'The compensation system was a continuation of institutional abuse. We were deemed as nobodies in those places, we were told we were nobodies and therefore that same mindset was used in the compensation.'

Chapter 15 ∾

A REPUTATION IN TATTERS: THE CATHOLIC CHURCH IN IRELAND

When I was growing up in Co. Cork in the 1970s, I had great fun visiting my two aunts in their convents in Dublin, Cork and Limerick. Aunty May and Aunty Nora were Sisters with the Reparation Order. They used to be known as the Blue nuns because of the light blue and white habits they wore. I and my sisters and brother used to run around the long corridors of their huge convents laughing and playing hide and seek. The other nuns used to play with us and I always remember them as kind, warm women. I used to love investigating the big boxes of dried food stored in the substantial pantries of their large convent kitchens.

May and Nora joined the Order when they were just 17 and 18 respectively. Aunty May was the first girl to leave the family farmhouse in Whitechurch, Co. Cork, for a convent life. My grandfather wiped tears from his face as he watched his beautiful red-haired daughter wave at him from the top of the avenue as she boarded the bus to take her to Cork City. From there she took a boat to England to begin her novitiate. John Coleman was heartbroken because he thought he would never see his gorgeous girl again. Back in the 1940s, women who entered convents weren't allowed out to see their families. They were expected to make the ultimate sacrifice and forfeit their loved ones for the price of being a bride of Christ. The Reparation Order was an enclosed order where the nuns were expected to live the rest of their lives in devotion to God, cut off from the world behind their closed convent gates. Aunty Nora followed May into the Order several years later. Their parents and brother and sisters hardly saw them again for years. Gradually, of course, as Ireland progressed and as the religious orders became more liberal, things changed and Nora and May were allowed out of the convent to visit their beloved families.

My two aunts were wonderful women. They were bright, warm, kind and generous people who always fussed over us whenever we visited them in their convent. I have only fond memories of them. May and Nora were successful Sisters. May became a Mother Superior and Nora was fast following in her tracks before she died. They were progressive modernisers who understood the need for their Order to connect with the communities around them. They recognised that Ireland was coming out of a dark abyss of poverty and famine, that secularism was rising and that the Church would have to loosen its strangulating grip on the nation for it to survive and thrive in a modern Ireland.

Both women are now dead. Aunty Nora was killed when a car crashed into her motorbike while she was driving from Limerick to Whitechurch to see her sick niece. May died after a long illness following brain damage she sustained after a bicycle accident in San Francisco.

If May and Nora were alive today, they would be horrified at how members of religious orders battered, raped and traumatised thousands of children in their care. They would no doubt seek sanctuary in their churches and silently question their own commitment to their faith. They would ask if the sacrifices they had made in their lives for God weren't all in vain. Thousands of nuns and priests and Brothers who never abused and led good lives have equally been betrayed by the abusers within their ranks. There are plenty of good priests, nuns and Brothers who have done wonderful work and contributed to their communities over the years but their reputations have now been badly tainted because of the rotten apples among them. Lay people of strong faith are also feeling tremendously let down. It has been difficult for churchgoers to separate the teachings of Christ from the unacceptable conduct of the hypocrites who have preached from the pulpits while abusing children behind their altars.

The abusive members of religious orders and the priesthood have done enormous damage to their Church and their colleagues in religious communities. The series of damning revelations about clerical child sexual abuse has shaken the Church to its core. Over the last five years three reports into clerical sexual abuse have brought the Catholic

Church in Ireland to its knees. The 2005 Ferns Report and the 2009 Ryan and Murphy Reports have left the country reeling.

THE FERNS REPORT

The Ferns Report in 2005 exposed the shocking details of how 21 priests in the diocese of Ferns, Co. Wexford, abused boys and girls in the community between 1962 and 2002. The Report found that both Bishop Donal Herlihy and his successor, Bishop Brendan Comiskey, placed 'the interests of individual priests ahead of those of the community in which they served'. Between 1960 and 1980 Bishop Herlihy was found to have moved offending priests to a different post or diocese for a while but then he returned the priest to his former position.[1] The Report said that Bishop Herlihy failed to report cases of clerical abuse to the authorities and that he seemed to treat such cases as exclusively moral problems. Bishop Herlihy was criticised for ordaining 'clearly unsuitable men into the priesthood when he knew or ought to have known that they had the propensity to abuse children'.[2]

In Bishop Comiskey's case, he was found to have failed to persuade offending priests to step aside from their priestly ministries if they had been found to have sexually abused children. The Report also criticised the Gardaí. It said that the Garda handling of one complaint of clerical abuse was 'wholly inadequate'.[3] The Inquiry concluded that 'the Church authorities, the medical profession and society generally failed to appreciate the horrendous damage which the sexual abuse of children can and does cause'.[4]

One of the most notorious paedophiles in the Ferns Diocese was Fr Sean Fortune, who abused Colm O'Gorman and other young boys in the 1980s. In March 1999 Fr Fortune committed suicide in his home in New Ross while awaiting trial for 66 charges of the sexual abuse of 29 boys. The 2002 BBC documentary series 'Suing the Pope' investigated Fr Fortune's abusive legacy. Colm O'Gorman, who set up the One in Four organisation for victims of abuse, successfully campaigned to get the Ferns Inquiry established.

THE MURPHY REPORT

The 2009 Ryan Report's searing details of the abuse of children in religious institutions stunned Irish people. But more bad news was on its way. Within months of the Ryan Report's publication another investigation came to equally damning conclusions. In November 2009, the Commission of Investigation into the Catholic Archdiocese of Dublin outlined the extent of the Church's cover-up of clerical child sexual abuse. The Murphy Report, named after the Commission's chair, Judge Yvonne Murphy, reported on the handling by Church and State authorities of a representative sample of 46 priests who had operated in the Archdiocese of Dublin and against whom allegations of child sexual abuse had been made. The period of investigation was between 1975 and 2004.

The Commission investigated how the Church had covered up paedophiles within its ranks for decades. The Catholic hierarchy had ignored allegations of clerical sexual abuse and instead they shunted paedophiles from place to place while keeping their records of abuse secret. The protection of the Church's reputation was of paramount importance and took precedence over every other consideration including the safety of children who were vulnerable to being sexually abused by paedophile priests in their communities.

The Murphy Report stated that:

> The Dublin Archdiocese's pre-occupations in dealing with cases of child sexual abuse, at least until the mid 1990s, were the maintenance of secrecy, the avoidance of scandal, the protection of the reputation of the Church, and the preservation of its assets. All other considerations, including the welfare of children and justice for victims, were subordinated to these priorities. The Archdiocese did not implement its own Canon law rules and did its best to avoid any application of the law of the State.[5]

Murphy concluded that the Church's excuse that it didn't know about sexual abuse until the 1990s was not credible. In fact, Judge Murphy's Report shows that Archbishop McQuaid dealt with child abuse cases as far back as the 1950s and 1960s. The Dublin Archdiocese had actually taken out insurance against legal claims for sexual abuse as far back as 1987. Murphy's investigations revealed that archbishops, auxiliary bishops and monsignors were aware of clerical abuse for many years and that they covered up the abuse to protect the good name of the Church. They used the secrecy and loose interpretation of Canon law to prevent reporting of alleged abusers to the authorities.

The Report listed examples of how abusive priests were protected and shifted to other parishes where they also went on to abuse boys and girls in the community.

FR NOEL REYNOLDS

The case of Fr Noel Reynolds, who was one of the priests investigated by the Murphy Commission, highlighted the collusion between the Church hierarchy and paedophiles within its ranks.

In 1994, when he was serving as the parish priest for Glendalough, Co. Wicklow, concerns were expressed to a neighbouring curate about his behaviour. Complaints were made that Reynolds talked 'dirty' to children as young as 11 and 12, that he encouraged children to swim naked and that he would bring children in his car and have them on his lap as he drove around. He also 'exchanged sweets for kisses'. Some of the children complained to their school principal and those complaints were referred to the chancellor, Monsignor Stenson, in September 1995.

Yet despite these obvious concerns about Reynolds's behaviour, the Monsignor did not meet him until March 1996. During that meeting Reynolds acknowledged to Stenson that the description of the complaints of child sexual abuse being made about him were correct. He also revealed to Stenson that he had abnormal obsessions with children that probably stemmed from a loneliness that had its roots in his mother's premature death when he was four. In the contemporaneous notes that Stenson took during that meeting, he wrote that Reynolds told him that 'his sexual orientation is towards children. Children would arouse me sexually.'[6]

It should have been glaringly obvious to Stenson that Reynolds was a child predator. He should have been immediately removed from his position and referred to the Gardaí for further investigation. This did not happen.

Instead, Reynolds stayed on as Glendalough's parish priest and it was only in March 1997 that his case was referred to an advisory panel. In April 1997 that panel concluded 'that it did not consider there was any firm evidence that any incidents of child sexual abuse took place although it seemed clear that some inappropriate behaviour did happen.'[7] The panel recommended that Reynolds be assessed by Dr Patrick Walsh of the Granada Institute. During all this time this paedophile was still serving as the parish priest in Glendalough.

In his assessment of Reynolds, Dr Walsh concluded that he showed 'considerable confusion in his relationships with children'.[8] He recommended that his contact with children should be limited but bizarrely he also concluded that Reynolds 'was capable of a positive and appropriate ministry to children but in a limited way'.[9] Walsh suggested that a priest support person be put in place for him. This was not done until July 1998.

In July 1997, despite mounting concerns and complaints about Reynolds, he was appointed by Archbishop Desmond Connell as chaplain to the National Rehabilitation Hospital in Dun Laoghaire. The hospital authorities were not informed of Reynolds's history of abuse despite the fact that they had a children's ward and a school.

It transpired that Noel Reynolds had been abusing children as far back as the 1970s when he was a curate to Kilmore Road Parish. One woman told the Murphy Commission how Reynolds used to spend a lot of time in their family home. He used to ask her for permission to say goodnight to her daughters. What she didn't realise was that he was sexually abusing the girls in their own bedroom.

In November 1998 the mother of the two girls abused by Reynolds in Kilmore met with him and his support priest. During that meeting Reynolds admitted to her that he had indeed abused her daughters. Yet despite this admission, the Church did nothing about the complaints and did not refer the matter to the Gardaí. By then Reynolds was in ill health and living in a nursing home. Eventually the two sisters themselves went to the Gardaí to make complaints against him.

Reynolds had sexually assaulted the girls on a regular basis in Kilmore in the 1970s, but it was only in October 1999 that he was eventually arrested for the offence of raping one of the sisters.

The Murphy Report states that:

... during the course of his interviews with the Gardaí, Fr Reynolds admitted abusing one of the sisters when she was eleven and the other when she was six years old and putting his finger into their vaginas when they were in bed in their own home. He told the Gardaí that he was sexually attracted to young girls and that they were not the only two victims in Kilmore. He could remember about twenty girls in total; there were others in East Wall and on the island in the diocese of Tuam. He admitted inserting a crucifix into

one girl's vagina and back passage. He said he had admitted to their
mother that he had abused her daughters. He said he offered their
mother £30,000 in compensation but that she did not accept it.[10]

Reynolds even offered the crucifix he had used to rape one of the girls
as evidence to the Gardaí. A file was sent to the DPP but, according to
the Murphy Report, the DPP in the end did not initiate a prosecution
because he was swayed by a solicitor representing Reynolds who
pointed to his deteriorating health and the onset of dementia.[11]

According to the Murphy Report, 12 other male and female
complainants contacted the Gardaí with allegations of sexual abuse by
Reynolds. They alleged they were aged between six and 11 when the
abuse took place and that it 'ranged from fondling of genitals to
touching around the leg area, digital penetration, anal rape, attempted
sexual intercourse, oral sex, actual sexual intercourse and inviting the
children to fondle his penis'.[12]

In many cases the abuse continued for between two and seven years.

Fr Noel Reynolds was never brought to book for his sexual abuse of
the children unlucky enough to live near him. Despite the compelling
evidence that he was an abuser, neither Monsignor Stenson nor
Archbishop Connell made any serious steps to go to the Gardaí and
inform them of his paedophile offences. In addition, Bishop O'Mahony,
who was then the liaison bishop responsible for hospital chaplains,
never informed the National Rehabilitation Hospital or the Gardaí after
he became aware that Reynolds may have had a problem with child
sexual abuse.

Fr Noel Reynolds died in April 2002 without ever being brought to
justice.

The Murphy Commission concluded that his case was extremely
badly handled by the Dublin Archdiocese and that numerous
indications of serious abuse and of admissions by Reynolds himself
were ignored. It found that the abuse of children in Dublin was a
scandal and that the failure of Archdiocesan authorities to penalise the
perpetrators was also a scandal.

THE CASE OF MARIE COLLINS

Another paedophile who got away with years of abuse was Fr
Edmondus.[13] He committed a number of sexual assaults on young

patients aged between eight and 11 years in Our Lady's Hospital for Sick Children, Crumlin, in the late 1950s and 1960s. Murphy reported that 16 years later he committed a sexual assault on a nine-year-old girl when he was in Co. Wicklow.[14] In 1997 he was convicted of indecent assault against two girls and he served a nine-month prison sentence.

The Catholic hierarchy's cover-up of Edmondus's paedophile abuses is breathtaking. As far back as 1960 Archbishop John Charles McQuaid[15] was told about a photographic film that Edmondus had sent for development to a lab in England. It contained photos of the genitals of two small girls aged between 10 and 11. Scotland Yard had referred the matter to the Gardaí who in turn informed Archbishop McQuaid. The Garda Commissioner had asked the Archbishop to take over the case. McQuaid met Edmondus shortly after his contact with the Gardaí. During that meeting Edmondus admitted taking inappropriate pictures of the girls. In his record of that meeting, McQuaid outlines Edmondus's account of how he took the photographs of the girls. Edmondus told him that he thought there was 'no grave sin'[16] in the manner in which he lured the girls into innocently posing in sexually explicit postures. In his record McQuaid seemed to excuse Edmondus by referring to the fact that 'he had been reared with brothers' and 'had never moved around socially with girls'.[17] McQuaid's response to Edmondus's confession speaks volumes about the Church's attitude to clerical paedophiles: 'I suggested I could get [a doctor] a good Catholic to instruct him and thus end this wonderment . . . I felt that he clearly understood the nature of the sinful act involved and to send him on retreat would defame him.'[18]

McQuaid did not contact Crumlin hospital nor did he do anything to ensure Edmondus didn't get the opportunity to abuse again. This was all the more egregious given that McQuaid was chairman of the Board of Directors of Crumlin hospital at the time. The Murphy Report reached a devastating conclusion on McQuaid's handling of the Edmondus case.

> The Commission believes that Archbishop McQuaid acted as he did to avoid scandal in both Ireland and Rome and without regard to the protection of children in Crumlin hospital.[19]

Edmondus went on to sexually abuse many more times after that meeting with McQuaid before he was finally convicted in 1997. In 1960, when Marie Collins was 13 years old, she was sexually abused and photographed when she was ill in Crumlin hospital. The abuse affected her enormously over the years and in November 1985 she went to her local curate and told him about Edmondus's abuse of her. Fr Eddie Griffin informed her that he didn't want to know the name of her abuser because he would have to do something about it. In 2004 in a Garda statement he admitted that:

> We as priests had been advised while in college not to seek the name of priests that allegations were being made against. Marie Collins didn't tell me that name of the priest. I told her not to feel any guilt about what had happened and that the priest had done wrong and if she had guilt I could give her absolution.[20]

It would take Marie Collins another 10 years before she felt brave enough to take the matter up with the Archbishop's House. In October 1995, she wrote to Archbishop Connell and told him what had happened to her in Crumlin when she was a child. She also informed Connell about her attempts in 1985 to tell her local curate about Edmondus. This communication finally prompted the Archdiocese to do a trawl of their records and they discovered the 1960 complaints against Edmondus. Archbishop Connell passed Mrs Collins' letter on to Monsignor Alex Stenson, who met her later that month. Although he was very sympathetic towards Mrs Collins, he didn't tell her about the mounting file of complaints that had been made against Edmondus going back to 1960. He waited until March 1996 to do so.

When Monsignor Stenson was interviewed by the Commission he said he was 'constrained by the oath of secrecy which he took when he became chancellor and he could not reveal that information without the consent of Archbishop Connell'.[21] Monsignor Stenson finally informed the Gardaí about the complaints about Edmondus in November 1995.

The Murphy investigations also discovered that other complaints were made about Edmondus over the years. In 1993, when he was a curate in Edenmore in North Dublin, a parishioner complained that Edmondus was driving around with young girls in his car and that girls changed in his house before going swimming. It was also alleged that he spent time with groups of youngsters who were missing school and that he didn't allow adults into his home. Those complaints were brought to the attention of Bishop James Moriarty, who was the auxiliary bishop for that area at the time.

Bishop Moriarty discussed the problem with the local priests and with Archbishop Desmond Connell.[22] He warned Fr Edmondus about his behaviour and advised him to desist from the activities mentioned but he made no attempt to remove Edmondus from the parish nor did he take any sanctions against him with a view to stripping him of his clerical duties. Murphy found that the Archdiocesan authorities made no attempt 'to check the archives or other files relating to Fr Edmondus'.[23] The Archdiocese also didn't act on other information they had received about Edmondus that he was recording children's voices and taking more photographs of children.

In March 1997 Edmondus was arrested and charged with the abuse of a girl in Co. Wicklow when she was nine and the abuse of Marie Collins when she was in Crumlin hospital. In June 1997 he pleaded guilty to two counts of indecent assault on Mrs Collins and a few days later also pleaded guilty to the assault of the girl in Co. Wicklow. He was sentenced to 18 months' imprisonment. This was reduced to nine months on appeal.

The Murphy Report concluded that the Edmondus case was 'very badly handled by Archbishop McQuaid' and that his conclusion 'that Fr Edmondus's actions arose merely from a "wonderment" about the female anatomy is risible'.[24]

FR IVAN PAYNE

The case of the notorious paedophile Fr Ivan Payne is also included in the sample list of 46 priests investigated by the Murphy Inquiry. Payne was ordained in Dublin in 1967 and he went on to serve as chaplain to Our Lady's Hospital for Sick Children in Crumlin. In 1976 he was appointed as parish chaplain in Cabra and subsequently in Sutton in 1983. In 1998 Payne pleaded guilty to charges of indecent assault on 10 victims. He was sentenced in June 1998 to six years' imprisonment. He was released in October 2002 and was also laicised that year. Payne had been accused of abusing boys during his chaplaincy in Crumlin when the children were sick in the hospital and he was also charged with abusing boys in his Cabra community. Allegations were also made that he had abused boys in Sutton parish.

One of Payne's victims was Andrew Madden. In November 1981, when he was 17, Andrew Madden made a complaint to his school guidance counsellor. He told him that he had been sexually abused by Payne since he was 12 years old and that the abuse used to take place in the house in which Payne lived in Cabra. Andrew Madden used to visit Payne's house every Saturday. The abuse, which involved fondling and masturbation, continued until 1981. Andrew also mentioned that there was another boy who seemed to have a relationship with Payne and that he was vulnerable because of his home circumstances.[25]

When the school guidance counsellor heard Andrew's complaints, he contacted Monsignor Alex Stenson and informed him about the allegations. Stenson then informed Archbishop Dermot Ryan, who referred the case to Auxiliary Bishop Dermot O'Mahony. The Bishop met Fr Payne in December 1981 and he admitted that he had indeed assaulted Andrew Madden. Instead of taking immediate action and informing the Gardaí of Payne's paedophile activities, O'Mahony referred Payne to a consultant psychiatrist who was not fully informed about the details of the abuse. He was under the impression that Payne had developed an inappropriate relationship with a 17-year-old. He did not realise that Payne had been abusing Andrew Madden since he was 12 because Bishop O'Mahony had not made that crystal clear to him. The psychiatrist therefore wrongly concluded that Payne had 'successfully overcome the crisis in question'.[26]

Bishop O'Mahony did not pursue any further investigations of Payne and he made no attempt to contact Andrew Madden to find out more information about the abuse. In September 1982 Payne was appointed to Sutton parish as the chaplain there. The clergy in the parish hadn't been informed of his abusive background. In 1989 Andrew Madden met Bishop O'Mahony and expressed his concern about Payne's appointment to Sutton. The Bishop assured him that 'he had no reason to believe Fr Payne was sexually abusing children in Sutton'.[27]

In March 1992 Andrew Madden wrote to Fr Payne looking for compensation for the abuse he had suffered. A settlement was finally reached between the two men in May 1993. It later transpired that the Archdiocese of Dublin had contributed by way of a loan to that fund. In the mid-1990s Mr Madden began to go public with his story about Fr Payne. That opened the floodgates and a series of allegations began to emerge about Payne's abusive behaviour. The complaints included cases of boys who had been abused by Payne when he was chaplain in Crumlin hospital and further allegations were made that Payne had abused boys when he was chaplain in Sutton.

Payne was finally charged in March 1997 with 13 counts of indecent assault on nine victims and he was later charged with 29 counts of indecent assault on Andrew Madden. Some of Payne's victims may have been saved from further abuse had Bishop O'Mahony acted immediately upon the original complaint he received in 1981. The Bishop's atrocious handling of Payne's case illustrated the Dublin Archdiocese's utter failure to properly deal with allegations of clerical sexual abuse and it highlighted their determination to ignore and cover up clerical paedophiles in order to protect the Church's reputation.

The Murphy Report slammed the Archdiocese for its handling of the Payne case.

> The initial complaint against Fr Payne was handled very badly and, as a result of the failure to deal with it properly, many other children were abused or potentially exposed to abuse. Archbishop Ryan and Bishop O'Mahony were particularly culpable. Archbishop Ryan did not properly address the complaint at all. He left it to Bishop O'Mahony but did not specify what was to be done. Bishop O'Mahony sent Fr Payne for psychiatric assessment but did not brief the psychiatrist properly. He then received a report from which it is clear that the psychiatrist was under a misapprehension about the age of the victim when the abuse occurred and he did nothing to rectify that misapprehension. He reported to Archbishop Ryan that there was a favourable assessment. Archbishop Ryan did not even read the report; if he had, he might have discovered its complete uselessness as it was based on erroneous information. Nobody contacted the victim or made any attempt to find out about the other boy mentioned by the victim. When they eventually met, Andrew Madden thought that Bishop O'Mahony was sympathetic and generally a nice man but was very clear that the bishop was not really addressing the issue of the safety of children.[28]

The Report also concluded that Archbishop Connell 'did not inform himself properly when he first became aware of the problem' and that he took a very 'hands off approach' to the case. Murphy also castigated the Archdiocese for using Canon law as an excuse to avoid handing over Payne to the Gardaí for investigation.

CONCLUSION

The above three cases are just a sample of a long list of damning incidents documented in the Murphy Report that expose how the Archdiocese of Dublin ignored and covered up clerical child sexual abuse for decades. The Church's preservation of its own reputation took precedence over everything else, including the safety of boys and girls who were unlucky enough to be living in communities where paedophile priests and chaplains were stalking children.

The fall-out from the Murphy Report shattered the reputation of the Catholic hierarchy in Ireland. After its publication, demands were made for the resignations of bishops implicated in the cover-up and negligence. In December 2009 Limerick Bishop Donal Murray resigned over his failure to handle abuse allegations over Fr Thomas Naughton, who was sentenced that month to three years in prison for abusing a boy in Co. Wicklow in the 1980s. Parents who had complained about Naughton to Bishop Murray when he was auxiliary bishop said he had dismissed their complaints. Naughton had already been convicted in 1998 of abusing boys in the parish of Donnycarney in the 1980s. By the end of January 2010 four of the five bishops implicated in the Murphy Report had offered their resignations.

It may take many more years yet to assess what impact the Ferns, Ryan and Murphy Reports will have on the Catholic Church in Ireland. It certainly seems to be facing a bleak future in the twenty-first century. There is a growing demand for a complete separation of the Church and State in Ireland and calls have been made to remove all Church involvement in the provision of education and hospital services. The Pope's ongoing refusal to allow women to become priests and his insistence on celibacy has drastically stymied the Church's ability to attract new recruits for the new century. These outdated theological policies are dovetailing with a growing secularism in Ireland. Fewer people are attending Mass and the Church's influence over Irish people is waning considerably.

The Ryan and Murphy Reports have weakened Irish people's faith in their Church, their State and their own society. They've made us all question what kind of a country we have been living in and what sort of State we need to shape for the future to ensure such catastrophic abuse of children never happens again.

NOTES

Chapter 1 — Exposing the Abuse: The Ryan Report, May 2009

1. Referred to from now on as the Ryan Report
2. CICA, vol. 1, Ch. 8, p. 390
3. ibid.
4. CICA, vol. 1, Ch.8, p. 391
5. Commission to Inquire into Child Abuse, Executive Summary, p. 19
6. CICA ES, p. 20
7. ibid.
8. ibid.
9. CICA ES, p. 23
10. CICA ES, p. 24
11. CICA ES, p. 25
12. CICA ES, p. 20
13. CICA ES, p. 23
14. ibid.
15. CICA ES, p. 22
16. CICA ES, p. 25
17. CICA, vol. 1, Ch. 13, p. 578
18. ibid.
19. CICA, vol. 2, Ch. 3, p. 97
20. CICA, vol. 2, Ch. 7, p. 272
21. CICA, vol. 1, Ch. 7, p. 120
22. CICA ES, p. 16
23. ibid.
24. Known as the Murphy Report

Chapter 2 — Noel Kelly and Daingean

1. Interview with the author, September 2010 — applicable for all Noel Kelly quotes
2. Commission to Inquire into Child Abuse Report, vol. 1, Ch. 15, p. 609
3. CICA, vol. 1, Ch. 15, p. 616
4. CICA, vol. 1, Ch. 15, p. 620
5. ibid.
6. Pseudonym
7. Pseudonym
8. Pseudonym
9. Pseudonym
10. Pseudonym

11. CICA, vol. 1, Ch. 15, p. 650
12. CICA, vol. 1, Ch. 15, p. 651
13. CICA, vol. 1, Ch. 15, p. 651
14. CICA, vol. 1, Ch. 15, p. 651
15. ibid.
16. CICA, vol. 1, Ch. 15, p. 652
17. ibid.
18. CICA, vol. 1, Ch. 15, p. 653
19. ibid.
20. ibid.
21. CICA, vol. 1, Ch. 15, p. 665
22. CICA, vol. 1, Ch. 15, p. 661
23. ibid.
24. CICA, vol. 1, Ch. 15, p. 663
25. ibid.
26. CICA, vol. 1, Ch. 15, p. 664
27. ibid.
28. ibid.

Chapter 3 — Michael O'Brien and Ferryhouse

1.   Commission to Inquire into Child Abuse Report, vol. 2, Ch. 3, p. 131
2.   ibid.
3.   CICA, vol. 2, Ch. 3, p. 132
4.   ibid.
5.   Interview with Michael O'Brien on 'The Wide Angle' with Karen Coleman, Newstalk 106, 24 May 2009
6.   Interview with Michael O'Brien, August 2010
7.   Pseudonym
8.   Pseudonym
9.   Pseudonym

Chapter 4 — The Girl with the Broken Heart: Teresa Gormley and the Sisters of Mercy

1.   Irish Society for the Prevention of Cruelty to Children
2.   Pseudonym
3.   Pseudonym
4.   Commission to Inquire into Child Abuse Report, vol. 2, Ch. 8, p. 375
5.   ibid.
6.   Pseudonym used in the Ryan Report
7.   ibid.
8.   CICA, vol. 2, Ch. 8, p. 373
9.   ibid.
10. ibid.
11. CICA, vol. 2, Ch. 8. p. 376
12. Pseudonym used in the Ryan Report
13. CICA, vol. 2, Ch. 8, p. 376
14. CICA, vol. 2, Ch. 8, p. 377

15. CICA, vol. 2, Ch. 13, p. 482
16. ibid.

Chapter 5 — The Boy with the Broken Arm: Mickey Flanagan and Artane

1. Interview with Kevin Flanagan, 9 February 2010
2. Interview with James (Jack) Flanagan, 11 February 2010
3. Pseudonym as used in the Commission to Inquire into Child Abuse Report, vol. 1, Ch. 7, p. 124
4. ibid.
5. Peadar Cowan TD — Dáil Éireann — Volume 145 — 23 April 1954 Adjournment Debate — Punishment of Industrial Schoolboy
6. Minister Sean Boylan's response to Peadar Cowan TD — Dáil Éireann — Volume 145 — 23 April 1954 Adjournment Debate — Punishment of Industrial Schoolboy
7. Pseudonym as used in the CICA, vol. 1, Ch. 7, p. 116
8. ibid.
9. CICA, vol. 1, Ch. 7, p. 116
10. ibid.
11. Pseudonym as used in the CICA, vol. 1, Ch. 7, p. 119
12. ibid.
13. Pseudonym as used in the CICA, vol. 1, Ch. 7, p. 110
14. CICA, vol. 1, Ch. 7, p. 119
15. CICA, vol. 1, Ch. 7, p. 120
16. CICA, vol. 1, Ch. 7, p. 121
17. CICA, vol. 1, Ch. 7, p. 191

Chapter 6 — 'John Brown' and Upton and Letterfrack

1. Pseudonym
2. Pseudonym
3. Commission to Inquire into Child Abuse Report, vol. 2, Ch. 2, p. 14
4. ibid.
5. CICA, vol. 1, Ch. 8, p. 285
6. ibid.
7. CICA, vol. 1, Ch. 8, p. 289
8. ibid.
9. *Founded on Fear* by Peter Tyrrell (edited and introduced by Diarmuid Whelan)
10. CICA, vol. 1, Ch. 8, p. 290
11. CICA, vol. 1, Ch. 8, p. 325
12. ibid.
13. Pseudonym given in CICA, vol. 1, Ch. 8, p .301
14. CICA, vol. 1, Ch. 8, p. 301
15. Pseudonym given in CICA, vol. 1, Ch. 8, p. 317
16. CICA, vol. 1, Ch. 8, p. 317
17. ibid.
18. CICA, vol. 1, Ch. 8, p. 356
19. CICA, vol. 1, Ch. 8, p. 344
20. CICA, vol. 1, Ch. 8, p. 345

Chapter 7 — Marie Therese O'Loughlin and Goldenbridge

1. Commission to Inquire into Child Abuse Report, vol. 2, Ch. 7, p. 265
2. CICA, vol. 2, Ch. 7, p. 263
3. CICA, vol. 2, Ch. 7, p. 266
4. CICA, vol. 2, Ch. 7, p. 273
5. ibid.
6. Pseudonym
7. CICA, vol. 2, Ch. 7, p. 274
8. ibid.
9. Interview on 'The Wide Angle' with Karen Coleman, Newstalk 106, 24 May 2009
10. ibid.
11. CICA, vol. 2, Ch. 7, p. 271
12. ibid.
13. CICA, vol. 2, Ch. 7, p. 272
14. CICA, vol. 2, Ch. 7, p. 268
15. CICA, vol. 2, Ch. 7, p. 269
16. CICA, vol. 2, Ch. 7, p. 276
17. CICA, vol. 2, Ch. 7, p. 273
18. Pseudonym
19. Pseudonym
20. Pseudonym
21. CICA, vol. 2, Ch. 7, p. 283
22. ibid.
23. Pseudonym in CICA, vol. 2, Ch. 7 for Sr Xeveria
24. CICA, vol. 2, Ch. 7, p. 291
25. CICA, vol. 2, Ch. 7, p. 292
26. ibid.
27. CICA, vol. 2, Ch. 7, pp. 292–3
28. CICA, vol. 2, Ch. 7, p. 293

Chapter 8 — Tommy Millar and Lenaboy and Salthill

1. Irish Society for the Prevention of Cruelty to Children
2. Also known as Lenaboy
3. Bread and milk
4. Pseudonym
5. Pseudonym
6. Pseudonym
7. Pseudonym
8. Pseudonym
9. Pseudonym
10. Pseudonym
11. Pseudonym

Chapter 9 — Martina Keogh and Clifden and the Magdalene Laundries

1. Pseudonym
2. Pseudonym

3. Pseudonym
4. Also known as Sean MacDermott Street

Chapter 10 — Still Looking for Justice: John Kelly
1. Commission to Inquire into Child Abuse Report, vol. 1, Ch. 15, p. 690
2. ibid.
3. ibid.
4. Pseudonym
5. Pseudonym
6. Pseudonym
7. CICA, vol. 1, Ch. 15, p. 690
8. Pseudonym
9. Pseudonym

Chapter 11 — Maureen Sullivan and the Magdalene Laundries
1. Pseudonym
2. *The Irish Times*, 18 September 2009
3. ibid.

Chapter 12 — From Homelessness to Hope: Gerry Carey
1. Pseudonym
2. Pseudonym

Chapter 13 — The Abusers: How and Why?
1. Commission to Inquire into Child Abuse Report, vol. 1, Ch. 7, p. 155
2. ibid.
3. CICA, vol. 1, Ch. 7, pp. 155–6
4. CICA, vol. 1, Ch. 7, p. 156
5. CICA, vol. 1, Ch. 6, p. 81
6. ibid.
7. CICA, vol. 1, Ch. 6, p. 82
8. ibid.
9. ibid.
10. CICA, vol. 1, Ch. 6, p. 83
11. ibid.
12. CICA, vol. 1, Ch. 6, p. 84
13. Interview with Dr Eoin O'Sullivan, 6 September 2009
14. ibid.
15. CICA, vol. 1, Ch. 8, p. 340
16. ibid.
17. ibid.
18. CICA, vol. 2, Ch. 7, p. 308
19. CICA, vol. 2, Ch. 6, p. 242
20. ibid.
21. ibid.
22. CICA, vol. 2, Ch. 6, p. 243

23. ibid.
24. *Responding to the Ryan Report* (Columba Press, 2009), edited by Tony Flannery
25. *Responding to the Ryan Report*, Ch. 3, p. 44
26. *Responding to the Ryan Report*, Ch. 3, p. 48
27. ibid.
28. *Responding to the Ryan Report*, Ch. 3, p. 49
29. *Responding to the Ryan Report*, Ch. 3, p. 51
30. CICA, Executive Summary, p. 19
31. ibid.
32. ibid.
33. CICA, ES, p. 20
34. ibid.
35. CICA, ES, p. 23
36. Pseudonym
37. National Society for the Prevention of Cruelty to Children

Chapter 14 — Rough Justice: The Residential Institutions Redress Board

1. Residential Institutions Redress Board website *www.rirb.ie*
2. ibid.
3. Dr Michael Corry's letter to *The Irish Times*, 19 May 2005
4. Auditor and Comptroller General 2002 Annual Report, Ch. 7, p. 86
5. Auditor and Comptroller General 2002 Annual Report, Ch. 7, p. 82
6. Auditor and Comptroller General 2002 Annual Report, Ch. 7, p. 92
7. Interview of Dr Michael Woods on RTÉ, 'Prime Time', 30 September 2003
8. Auditor and Comptroller General 2002 Annual Report, Ch. 7, p. 92
9. Auditor and Comptroller General 2002 Annual Report, Ch. 7, p. 93
10. ibid.
11. Pat Rabbitte speaking during a Dáil Debate on the Ryan Report, 12 June 2009
12. ibid.
13. Dr Michael Woods speaking during the above Dáil Debate on the Ryan Report, 12 June 2009
14. Auditor and Comptroller General 2002 Annual Report, Ch. 7, p. 83

Chapter 15 — A Reputation in Tatters: The Catholic Church in Ireland

1. Ferns Report 2005, Executive Summary, p. 1
2. ibid.
3. Ferns Report 2005, ES, p. 2
4. Ferns Report 2005, ES, p. 3
5. Commission to Inquire into the Catholic Archdiocese of Dublin Report, vol. 1, p. 4
6. Report into the Catholic Archdiocese of Dublin, 2009, otherwise known as the Murphy Report, vol. 2, p. 518
7. The Murphy Report, vol. 2, p. 520
8. ibid.
9. ibid.
10. Murphy Report, vol. 2, Ch. 35, p. 525
11. ibid.

12. Murphy Report, vol. 2, Ch. 35, p. 526
13. Pseudonym as used in the Murphy Report
14. Murphy Report, vol. 2, Ch. 13, p. 188
15. Catholic Archbishop of Dublin and Primate of Ireland from 1940 to 1972
16. Murphy Report, vol. 2, Ch. 13, p. 189
17. Murphy Report, vol. 2, Ch. 13, pp. 189–190
18. Murphy Report, vol. 2, Ch. 13, p. 190
19. Murphy Report, vol. 2, Ch. 13, p. 191
20. ibid.
21. Murphy Report, vol. 2, Ch. 13, p. 194
22. Cardinal Desmond Connell, Archbishop of Dublin 1988–2004
23. Murphy Report, vol. 2, Ch. 13, p. 192
24. Murphy Report, vol. 2, Ch. 13, p. 205
25. Murphy Report, vol. 2, Ch. 24, pp. 364–5
26. Murphy Report, vol. 2, Ch. 24, p. 366
27. Murphy Report, vol. 2, Ch. 24, p. 370
28. Murphy Report, vol. 2, Ch. 24, p. 383